THE
CUBAN EXILE MOVEMENT

Thanks for your support and affection:

Nabor Calvo, Elvia Ospina, Tijl Declercq, Paula Andrea Calvo, Sara, Menno and Jana Steel, Koen Steel, Karine Alvarez, Annemie Verbruggen, Pedro and Odile, Manuel and Alina, Antonio and Ana, Lourdes Castro.

To Rosita, the most beautiful grandmother in Havana.

To Alfi, for his affection in Miami.

THE CUBAN EXILE MOVEMENT

Dissidents or Mercenaries?

Hernando Calvo
Katlijn Declercq

Translated by Mary Todd

OCEAN PRESS

Melbourne • New York

Cover design by David Spratt

ISBN 1-876175-15-X

First printed 2000

Printed in Australia

Published by Ocean Press
Australia: GPO Box 3279, Melbourne, Victoria 3001, Australia
   • Fax: (61-3) 9329 5040 • E-mail: edit@oceanpress.com.au
USA: PO Box 834, Hoboken, NJ 07030 • Fax: 201-617 0203

www.oceanpress.com.au

Library of Congress Card No: 99-070349

OCEAN PRESS DISTRIBUTORS
United States: LPC/InBook,
    1436 West Randolph St, Chicago, IL 60607, USA
Canada: Login Brothers,
    324 Salteaux Cres, Winnipeg, Manitoba R3J 3T2, Canada
Britain and Europe: Global Book Marketing,
    38 King Street, London, WC2E 8JT, UK
Australia and New Zealand: Astam Books,
    57-61 John Street, Leichhardt, NSW 2040, Australia
Cuba and Latin America: Ocean Press,
    Calle 21 #406, Vedado, Havana, Cuba
Southern Africa: Phambili Agencies,
    PO Box 28680, Kensington 2101, Johannesburg, South Africa

Table of contents

A Little History: 1959-79

"It is dangerous to be our enemy. It is fatal to be our ally."
Henry Kissinger, Former U.S. Secretary of State
and winner of the Nobel Peace Prize

I

Dictator Fulgencio Batista fled from Cuba just before dawn on January 1, 1959. Nobody wanted him any more: not the capitalist class, not the Mafia, not the United States. The news caught many Cubans by surprise. In Havana, the people began pulling up parking meters, symbols of the dictatorship's tax system, and attacked cabarets and luxury properties. The guerrillas, "the bearded ones," began to restore order. Cuba went back to having a good time, though the privileged minority of the wealthy looked askance at the delirious excitement. And with reason: the young Fidel Castro, whom the people acknowledged as their leader, had promised to change many things. With the support and participation of the majority, the core of society quickly began to be transformed.

It is undeniable that, at the time of the 1959 revolution, the statistics showed a very high per capita income. But income was one thing, and whether or not each Cuban received their share was another. As had been promised to the people, the first laws that were issued stated that per capita income should become a reality, not just something on paper. The fact that the new government began to provide food, education and health care on an equal basis was considered manipulation, because, as many enemies of the revolution claimed, "It played on the sentiments of the masses."[1]

The revolutionaries had warned early on that the distribution of wealth and the meaning of sovereignty were going to change. The

---

[1] Enrique Encinosa, *Cuba en guerra: Historia de la oposición anti-castrista, 1959-1993* (Cuba at War: History of the Anti-Castro Opposition, 1959-93), (Miami: The Endowment for Cuban American Studies of the Cuban American National Foundation, 1995).

Cuban aristocrats, both in the cities and in the countryside, didn't believe it. In Washington, it was barely suspected. Then what should happen, actually did. "By June 1959, the National Institute of the Agrarian Reform (INRA) had taken over 400 private farms, and by December of the same year 400 'people's stores' and 485 cooperatives had been established."[2] One year later, 380 corporations and industries belonging to U.S. and Cuban capitalists had been nationalized.

An underdeveloped country didn't have the right to do that, especially if it was in America's[3] backyard. Moreover, the United States had always viewed Cuba as a natural extension of its territory. Doing what Cuba was doing was an attack on sacred interests — such as those of William Pawley, owner of Havana's Compañía de Gas and President Eisenhower's adviser on Cuban affairs, and of Colonel J.C. King, head of the Central Intelligence Agency's Western Hemisphere Division, an associate of Pawley's with his own substantial investments in Cuba. Then there were the immense businesses in Cuba owned by the Italian-U.S. Mafia, known as Cosa Nostra and headed by Meyer Lansky and Santos Trafficante.

Immediate action had to be — and was — taken. On March 10, 1959, one of the main points on the U.S. National Security Council's secret agenda was to put another government in power in Cuba. *Time* magazine of April 6, 1959, expressed outrage over the independent attitude taken by the rulers of that bit of Caribbean territory, describing Castro's neutrality as a challenge to the United States. It was understandable; "No" didn't sound good when, in the past, it had always been "Yes, sir."

Cuba would have to be put back on its normal course, no matter what the means required. It was a desire shared by those Cubans who had always dreamed of seeing what they called their "homeland" as another star in the U.S. flag.

II

The plotting against the revolutionary government began even before it had been fully installed. From the neighboring Dominican Republic, the "Anti-Communist Legion of the Caribbean" was organized under the auspices of dictator Leónidas Trujillo and with the blessing of

---

[2] Ibid.
[3] America is the name of two continents, not a country. It is a mistake to call the citizens of a nation whose name is the United States "Americans." Therefore, we will use the term "U.S." for everything pertaining or related to that country and its inhabitants. However, we will respect the terms used by those we interviewed and those found in sources that have been cited.

Washington. Its 800 Cuban, French, Spanish, Belgian and other mercenaries prepared to invade Cuba. Unfortunately for the "Trujillo conspiracy," the first advance unit (which, logically, consisted of Cubans) was captured. That was in late 1959, and the plot collapsed. But Operation 40, the first integral plan that the CIA orchestrated to put an end to the fledgling revolution, was already in the works — "integral" because military and terrorist operations were combined with ideological and psychological warfare as well as diplomatic and economic pressure.

Although it had all imaginable resources and more, it, too, failed — mainly because the United States never managed to organize counter-revolutionary groups inside Cuba that could maintain a presence on the island. Out of arrogance, it underrated the essential thing: the majority of the people wanted the revolution and supported its leaders. Moreover, the new government knew whom it was confronting and quickly created a shield. Thus, in 1960, the Committees for the Defense of the Revolution (Comités de Defensa de la Revolución, CDRs) were established. They were neighborhood vigilance associations: "They supported [Cuban] State Security, supplying it with constant information about any suspicious activities at the block level."[4]

Little by little, but decisively, Operation 40 was isolated and crushed for lack of the resources it needed to survive. One after another, its ringleaders fell. All those setbacks were explained in various ways. The saddest explanation goes like this: "Right from the beginning, the conspirators were unlucky."[5]

In view of the impossibility of obtaining even minimal social support, the counterrevolution decided to step up its terrorist attacks. On March 4, 1960, the French ship *La Coubre*, carrying weapons from Belgium, was blown up in the Bay of Havana. Seventy-five people were killed and 200 wounded. Small planes from Florida dropped incendiary bombs on sugar mills, fields and factories. Attackers in fast combat support ships machine-gunned coastal towns, sank boats and kidnapped fishermen, showing no respect for the civilian population.

III

All reports told President Eisenhower that he was steadily losing strategic control over the island. As a first measure, Eisenhower ordered that support for the counterrevolutionary groups be increased. In March 1960, he also gave the CIA the go-ahead for preparing a large-scale military attack — an order that was ratified by his successor, John F.

---

[4] Encinosa, *Cuba en guerra.*
[5] Ibid.

Kennedy. The United States didn't want to appear as an invader again. Although it had been "forced" to send Marines to Nicaragua, the Dominican Republic, Guatemala and other places to ensure that its interests were protected, it didn't think it necessary in this case, because it had thousands of Cuban mercenaries.

The only thing needed, as a formality, was that the mercenaries create some kind of unified political structure in exile that, when the time came, would be recognized internationally as a transition government. But, what with all the personal and group ambitions involved, the CIA found it wasn't easy to do this. Even though the Revolutionary Cuban Council (Consejo Cubano Revolucionario, CCR) consisted of only five groups, Allen Dulles, Director of the CIA, told President Kennedy that it would be a very difficult task to establish a Cuban government in exile that would unite 184 anti-Castro organizations.[6] Moreover, the fact that a lot of money was up for grabs led every three or four people to create their own group, both in Cuba and abroad. Like ghosts, they kept appearing and disappearing.

At last, the ill-prepared unity plan came to fruition. From its first public appearance, the Council was given prominent press coverage. The mass media couldn't do otherwise, since it was being set up as an alternative to the insolent Havana government.

What did it matter if some of those groups had almost no social base inside Cuba — just a couple of people and some initials? In the end, the Council was just window dressing to sell abroad. What did it matter if none of the leaders of the Council had anything to say about the U.S. preparations against their homeland? When power was seized, Washington would give them their slice of the governmental pie. What did it matter if the leaders of the Council couldn't stand one another? "We didn't trust each other, but we had great confidence in the Americans."[7] Naturally. It was a case not just of military or political dependence but of moral and psychological subservience, as well.

One of the largest offices of the CIA was opened in Miami with the main mission of recruiting — and, naturally, paying — Cubans who wanted to invade their own country. As later investigations showed, George Bush, a young CIA officer and future president of the United States, was one of those drumming up business for the recruiting office.[8] Every mercenary was given an enlistment number. The numbers began

---

[6] Ibid.

[7] Haynes Johnson, *La Baie des Cochons: L'invasion manquée de Cuba* (The Bay of Pigs: The Unsuccessful Invasion of Cuba), (Paris: Ed. Robert Laffont, 1965).

[8] Because of investigations into the illegal financing of the Nicaraguan contras, the FBI had to make these documents public in 1988.

at 2500, to give the idea that it was a very large force. Training camps were set up in Florida and Central America. The Brigade's first casualty was number 2506 — he was killed during training — and it became Brigade 2506 in honor of his memory. At first, $13 million was appropriated for financing the operation, part of that sum coming from the traffic in opium that the CIA had established from the Golden Triangle.[9]

When Washington unilaterally broke off diplomatic relations with Cuba on January 3, 1961, and prohibited its citizens from visiting the island on January 17, the enemies of the revolution were in seventh heaven. However, it must have been difficult for those in Washington, Miami, Europe and who knows where else to swallow on April 16. While giving a last farewell to several Cubans killed in bombings by U.S. planes, Fidel Castro proclaimed the socialist character of the Cuban revolution.

Within a few hours, ships and planes transporting around 1,500 mercenaries were on their way to the Bay of Pigs.

All of the U.S. leaders, from Kennedy down, were sure that most of the Cuban people would support the invaders. Through the Revolutionary Cuban Council, they had contributed many dollars for buying souls on the island that they just couldn't fail.

The goal was for the mercenary brigade to establish a beachhead and wage a war of attrition. When a general uprising began, the provisional government would be proclaimed and would be easily and readily recognized internationally. What they found, however, was an army supported by the militia which, within a few hours, had the invading force at the gates of hell. The invaders had been so confident that they hadn't even drawn up an evacuation plan for use in case they were defeated.

The first man ashore wasn't a Cuban mercenary but a U.S. officer, William "Rip" Robertson. "The die is cast. At dawn on April 19, the last units of the Brigade collapsed in the face of the enemy's superiority... Nearly a hundred Brigade members had died in the invasion, another 100 were wounded, and more than 1,000 were captured."[10] The invaders could do nothing to break the courage of a nation that was defending its recently won sovereignty for love, not money.

When the Cuban mercenaries realized that the United States was no

---

[9] Martin Lee and Bruce Shlain, *LSD et CIA: Quand l'Amérique était sous acide* (LSD and the CIA: When America Was on Acid), (Paris: Les Editions du Lézard, 1994). The Golden Triangle is an immense territory including large parts of what was Laos, Burma and Thailand.

[10] Encinosa, *Cuba en guerra.*

longer going to stick its neck out, they forgot that they had come to "free" their homeland and "lost their will to fight."[11] But that was just part of the worst military humiliation dealt the United States in the Americas up until then.

Meanwhile, Fidel Castro and his *barbudos* [bearded ones] were likened to Davids defeating Goliath, portrayed as "bold, rebellious, super he-men who could defeat an empire on its own doorstep."[12]

A few days later, on April 24, Kennedy accepted the responsibility for the mercenary aggression. The next day, however, he began the real aggression, which continues to this day: the total blockade on trade. It had begun, in a small way, in October 1960. On September 7, the U.S. Congress passed a bill stating that any country that helped Cuba would not be eligible for receiving aid from the United States, unless the U.S. president decided that such aid would serve U.S. interests. Thus, the U.S. Government began to involve other nations in "its war" against Cuba, and it encountered little resistance.

What about the mercenaries? Just when they believed they were on the way to a firing squad for being "part of a military invasion organized and supported by a foreign power,"[13] they were freed — or, rather, exchanged for medicine, food and agricultural equipment. They were back home in Miami by Christmas 1962. On December 29, a ceremony was held in their honor, which President Kennedy and his wife, Jacqueline, attended. Kennedy described the mercenaries as "the bravest men in the world." Later, when the Brigade leaders presented the president with the Brigade's flag, he promised to give it back to them in Havana "when it's free." The counterrevolutionaries gave the president an ovation. Fifteen years later, the association of former Brigade members asked the Kennedy Library to return their flag, as Kennedy hadn't kept his word.

It was mailed to them.

IV

After analyzing the report on the failure of the counterrevolutionary mercenary invasion, President Kennedy created a special committee in the National Security Council. The pride of the nation had been hurt, and the top levels of the administration had to save it. Attorney General Robert Kennedy was on the committee. According to declassified documents, the president's brother noted during the November 4, 1961, meeting that his idea was to solve matters by means of espionage, acts of

---

[11] Ibid.
[12] Ibid.
[13] Luis Báez, *Los que se fueron* (Those Who Left), (Havana: Editora Política, 1994).

sabotage and general disorder carried out and headed by Cubans from all groups except Batista's followers. Batista's followers were excepted because of their bad international image. But the counterrevolutionaries would have to be the public face, even though everybody knew that they were only a part of the U.S. global strategy.

That committee approved Operation Mongoose — which, according to the president's November 30 announcement, was aimed at using the available means to "help the people of Cuba overthrow the communist regime from within Cuba and institute a new government with which the United States can live at peace."[14] It may have been the first time, in its incipient war against the Cuban Government, that the United States emphasized using means within the country; it would become — and still is — a constant.

The most important thing was to bring about "general disorder" that would lead to a people's insurrection. When that happened, the anti-Castro groups would request international assistance on the pretext of protecting the Cuban people from being massacred by the communist government. When the hue and cry was raised, the United States and other American nations would help, under the flag of the Organization of American States. What is now known as "humanitarian intervention" was being invented.

The unexpected challenge thrown down by Cuba, combined with outbreaks of insurgency in several other Latin American countries, meant that the U.S. military strategists had to revise their ideological war. John Foster Dulles, Kennedy's Secretary of State, complained that the United States had spent millions of dollars preparing for a hot war, but very little on a war of ideas. The director of the United States Information Agency, one of the most powerful of the U.S. propaganda apparatus,[15] was developing a solution, saying that simply planting doubt in people's minds would be a great success.[16]

That aspect of the conflict was kept very much in mind in Operation

---

[14] Jon Elliston, *Psywar on Cuba* (Melbourne: Ocean Press, 1999), 75.

[15] Claude Julien, *L'empire Americain* (The American Empire), (Paris: Ed. Le Livre de Poche, 1972).

[16] *Alleged Assassination Plots Involving Foreign Leaders* (Washington, D.C.: November 1975), a report of the U.S. Senate's Special Committee on Conspiracies for Assassinating the Leaders of Other Countries. On Monday, November 17, 1997, the Pentagon declassified another 1,500 pages on Cuba. They contain a great many suggestions — which the Spanish daily *El País* described as "surrealistic" — which the various U.S. espionage and security agencies had proposed to President Kennedy for overthrowing or discrediting the revolutionary government. For example, if the spaceship *Mercury* hadn't been able to return to earth on February 20, 1962, after its first space flight, Kennedy would have accused "the Cuban communists" of having caused "electronic interference."

Mongoose. Documents that have been made public included the following: "To set the deeply moving tone and motivating force for the liberation of Cuba. To demonstrate concern for plight of refugees, particularly parentless children. To demonstrate Cuban regime's failure to live up to promises of the July 26 Movement. To illuminate intolerable conditions in Cuba and the plight of the Cubans who remain inside. To publicize that ordinary citizens, not just the rich, have fled tyranny... All media. This means maximum use of spiritual appeal... recapturing the ideal of Martí... and popularizing songs by commercial recordings."[17] With only a few words changed, this could be a description of the present plan.

Operation Mongoose also included chemical warfare against sugarcane and other agricultural products and plots against Fidel Castro which ran from assassination attempts to trying to make his beard fall out — which was supposed to make him lose his popularity. For these and other terrorist actions, the CIA sought support in the world of crime, including such powerful Mafia figures as John Rosselli, Santos Trafficante and Momo Salvatore Giancana.[18]

In late January 1962, Cuba was expelled from the Organization of American States (OAS). The United States immediately asked the North Atlantic Treaty Organization to keep the OAS decision in mind, so its members would bring pressure to bear against the Cuban Government. It also asked its allies to voluntarily ban sales of strategic materials to Cuba and to cut back their trade with Cuba. Nearly all of the governments in the world agreed to do so.

Meanwhile, the CIA infiltrated several teams of agents into Cuba to unite counterrevolutionaries and train them in tactics of sabotage and communications systems.

V

The last redoubts of the 1961 mercenary force had just been defeated when Kennedy replied to a note from the Soviets which warned that another military attack on Cuba could endanger world peace. The U.S. president once again denied that the United States had any intention of invading Cuba, but he made it clear that, even though they would abstain from direct military intervention, the people of the United States wouldn't hide their admiration for the Cuban patriots.

In early 1962, as part of Operation Mongoose, massive recruiting began to form "Cuban units" of the U.S. Army. Acknowledging the

---

[17] *Alleged Assassination Plots.*
[18] Ibid.

favor, the members of the defeated Brigade 2506 joined as officers.

The Cuban Government realized that a new invasion attempt was in the offing. If the United States really used its military clout, it would be hard to maintain Cuba's sovereignty, but at least the invading forces would be dealt heavy blows before they took over the island. Cuba had to get some heavy weapons, and the Soviet Union provided them.

On October 16, 1962, President Kennedy learned that missiles with nuclear warheads were being installed in Cuba, so he approved a naval blockade of the island to halt the Soviet ships that were transporting weapons. At the same time, he ordered thousands of men, planes and ships to be placed on maximum alert. A part of that military force had been ready since April, as the bastion of Operation Mongoose. The Cuban Missile Crisis began, which took the world to the brink of an apocalyptic conflagration. Naturally, the counterrevolutionaries who hadn't already joined the U.S. Army rushed to do so at that time. The U.S. naval blockade, with air support, didn't let anything through — except that "it proved no obstacle to the continuation of commando attacks on the coasts of Cuba."[19]

Negotiation began. The Soviet Union withdrew the missiles, and the United States pledged not to invade Cuba and not to allow the exiles to carry out offensive actions from its territory. This seriously wounded the counterrevolutionaries' pride, for they felt betrayed, pushed aside and abandoned. On November 22, 1963, President Kennedy was assassinated. Investigations didn't rule out the possibility that Cuban exiles may have taken part in the crime as a means of retaliation. The same suspicions arose when Robert Kennedy and Momo Salvatore Giancana, of the Mafia, died as a result of violence. They, too, had failed to keep their word of "freeing" Cuba.

When Lyndon Johnson became president, one of the first statements he made was to the effect that the first task of the United States should be to isolate Cuba from the inter-American system, and that's what it did. All Latin American countries except Mexico turned their backs on the Cuban Government, and the isolation wasn't to be at the government level only. Following CIA instructions, Cuban exiles were sent to live in several Latin American countries. Their job was to set up units that would engage in counterrevolutionary propaganda. However, "[w]e were plowing in the sea. The false image of Fidel Castro as a romantic rebel was very powerful... The anti-American feeling in Latin America was very strong, and we were financed by the United

---

[19] Miguel Talleda, *Alpha 66 y su histórica tarea* (Alpha 66 and its Historic Task), (Miami: Ediciones Universal, 1995).

States…"[20]

It was bad luck for the Cuban counterrevolutionaries that Washington gradually turned its attention to the conflict in Vietnam and Southeast Asia. Many U.S. citizens of Cuban origin went to fight there, just as the CIA had sent dozens of former members of the Brigade to the Congo to hunt Che Guevara. That "Cuban Voluntary Group" would remain active until 1966, fighting against the rebel forces led by Pierre Mulele and Laurent-Désiré Kabila, as members of a huge mercenary force which included English, Belgian, South African, French and German combatants. The survivors of that group still boast of having provided air cover for the evacuation of Leopoldville and about having halted Mulele's offensive with their brutal bombing of the Kwilo Valley.

In Vietnam, their main military activity was to collaborate with the Hmong tribe of Laos. "This tribe was known to traffic in opium, an activity which the CIA didn't try to halt. To the contrary, the borderline between weapons and drugs was quite flexible in this secret operation. In this aspect, the Cubans who had gained experience in the Havana Mafia prior to the revolution were good collaborators."[21] CIA officer Félix Rodríguez, a specialist in commando operations who had just "won glory for himself" by advising the Bolivian Army in the capture and murder of Che Guevara in October 1967, was the most famous of them.

The fact that military and economic resources were focused on Vietnam seriously damaged anti-Cuba actions. "Toward the end of the 1960s, the [Cuban] exiles were worn out. Many movements had gradually disappeared. The situation was sad, and collective exhaustion prevailed among the fighters. The Americans didn't provide any economic financing for buying fast combat support ships and other war materiel. A few, the most stubborn, remained active, forming groups, splitting up and coming together again…"[22]

VI

On April 4, 1972, a powerful bomb exploded on the roof of Cuba's trade office in Montreal, Canada. The bomb, which was made of plastic explosives of the kind used frequently by the CIA, killed one diplomat and wounded seven others. The National Liberation Front of Cuba (Frente de Liberación Nacional de Cuba, FLNC) — a terrorist

---

[20] Encinosa, *Cuba en guerra.*
[21] Vegard Bye, *La paz prohibida: El laberinto centroamericano en la década de los ochenta* (The Banned Peace: The Central American Labyrinth in the Decade of the 1980s), (Costa Rica: Ed. Departamento Ecuménico de Investigaciones, 1991).
[22] Encinosa, *Cuba en guerra.*

organization with a legal branch, Abdala,[23] in charge of recruitment and logistics — claimed "credit" for the attack. It wasn't the first time that this kind of terrorist action had been carried out against officials or property of the Cuban Government, but it marked the beginning of a period in which such actions ceased to be sporadic but turned into a worldwide war on Cuba. The number of bombs multiplied, and they were used not only against Cuban targets but also against government and privately owned offices that had relations with the Cuban Government.

In New York, a bomb was thrown at the car of Cuban diplomat Ricardo Alarcón, but nobody was killed. Bombs went off in Mexico, Argentina, Jamaica, Venezuela, Colombia, Puerto Rico and other places. The FLNC claimed "credit" for most of them. Even though splits caused by personal and group interests weren't lacking, two other exile groups shared the bloody strategy of the FLNC. One was Alpha 66, and the other, the Cuban Delegation in Exile (Representación Cubana en el Exilio, RECE), one of whose leaders at the time was Jorge Mas Canosa, a former Brigade member. According to the FBI, this last group was created and financed by the CIA, though the participation and million-dollar contributions by the owners of the Bacardi Rum Company have always been acknowledged.

Juan Felipe de la Cruz went to Spain and then to France, helped by Carlos Alberto Montaner, a CIA contact in Madrid, according to Cuban State Security. His mission was to place a bomb in the Cuban Embassy in Paris. The plan went astray when the bomb exploded while he was assembling it in a hotel in Avrainville, close to Paris, on August 3, 1973. Huge crowds attended his burial in Miami, and both the FLNC and RECE claimed "credit" for the bomb attempt.

Terrorism was stepped up in the mid-1970s. Two CIA specialists in sabotage — Orlando Bosch and Guillermo Novo — were released after spending a short time in prison for having committed acts of terrorism. By 1976, they were the main supporters of the Coordinator of Unified Revolutionary Organizations (Coordinadora de Organizaciones Revolucionarias Unitarias, CORU). Later, the Federal Bureau of Investigation stated that they had carried out over 70 acts of terrorism — not counting their participation in the drug trade, along with other counterrevolutionaries, an activity which both financed their terrorist

---

[23] Ibid. Enrique Encinosa, the author of this book, admits that he was a member of Abdala. Therefore, he had reason to be authoritative when he wrote that the FLNC was organized by "several veterans of the CIA's operations in the 1960s, some members of Brigade 2506 and leaders of the Abdala group." The Abdala group, "with its hundreds of young members, gave the FLNC a broader support base than other groups, in terms of both money raising and its operational level."

actions and lined their pockets.[24]

But the U.S. authorities began to get worried. They were losing control of the situation. They knew what kind of elements had been created and how far they could go if allowed to. In addition, there was the pressure which many governments, particularly those of France and Spain, began to exert. In Paris, terrorists managed to attack the Cuban Embassy; meanwhile, the French Consulate in Miami was shaken by another explosion. In Madrid, a bomb destroyed the floor occupied by the Cuban diplomatic mission.

There was no alternative to going after and imprisoning some of the more recalcitrant exiles, and that hurt them. "The Americans had taught us how to use explosives, had trained us in navigation and had prepared us militarily, and then one day they decided that they didn't need us any more... What we had done with the CIA's permission in 1963 was a criminal act 10 years later..."[25] Their cup ran over when, in the mid-1970s, a peace agreement was signed in Vietnam and the CIA discharged thousands of its agents, most of them of Cuban origin. In view of all this, it is hardly surprising that nine bombs were placed in FBI offices and the airport in Miami in 1975.

According to members of the Cuban exile community, they took to the path of blind, almost crazy violence when they were left without U.S. political and financial support. "Whereas a commando mission might cost $50,000 and involve two dozen fighters, two men could dynamite an embassy in another country at a cost of less than $10,000 per action."[26]

In August 1976, Orlando Letelier, who had been a minister in Salvador Allende's Cabinet, and Ronni Moffit, his U.S. secretary, died when a bomb blew up his car. This unleashed one of the largest federal investigations ever held. Over the next four years, several hundred counterrevolutionaries were arrested, until Michael Townley, a U.S. citizen who worked as an explosives expert for the intelligence service of Chilean dictator Augusto Pinochet, accused the brothers Ignacio and Guillermo Novo. They had blown up the car in return for payment and because, according to them, Letelier was working for Cuban Security. At almost the same time, a commando kidnapped two Cuban diplomats in

---

[24] During that period, according to federal investigations, CORU and Abdala-FLNC, among others, were partly financed by the traffic in drugs in which some of their members engaged. Frank Castro (a former Brigade member) and René Corvo were among those who contributed the most illegal money to those organizations. Both were implicated in Iran-Contragate. See Peter Dale Scott and Jonathan Marshall, *Cocaine Politics: Drugs, Armies, and the CIA in Central America* (Los Angeles: University of California Press, 1991).

[25] Encinosa, *Cuba en guerra*.

[26] Ibid.

Buenos Aires; they were never seen again. The most reactionary sectors in the exile community called the action "a daring operation."

Bombs weren't the only weapons that the counterrevolutionaries used to threaten the Cuban people and their government, trading partners and political allies. A UPI dispatch dated January 9, 1977, stated that the CIA refused to comment on a report saying that it might have been implicated in a deliberately caused epidemic of African swine fever which broke out in Cuba in 1971. It went on to say that the disease had been introduced in Cuba by anti-Castro Cuban agents. In September 1984, several press agencies published the statements of Eduardo Arocena, a Cuban-U.S. citizen, who admitted to a U.S. court that, following orders of the CIA, he had taken biological substances into Cuba in the 1970s to spread diseases among the population. These are only two examples. There are a great many such cases, all of which occurred after the 1959 revolution, that have been proved before international courts.

The worst act of terrorism which formed part of that strategy was the blowing up of a Cubana de Aviación plane off the coast of Barbados on October 6, 1976. Orlando Bosch and Luis Posada Carriles, both CIA operatives who had been trained at Fort Benning, were arrested in Venezuela and accused of having planned the attack. Seventy-three people were killed in the explosion, including all the members of Cuba's junior fencing team. "The impact of the action was brutal, both for Cuba and for the exile community."[27] It was the prelude to the end of the worldwide campaign against Cuba.

Attacks continued, however. In the 1980s, the U.S. strategy for crushing Cuba's socialist system was revamped, and the counter-revolutionaries had to adjust; that's what collaborators have to do.

---

[27] Ibid.

1

Monsignor Agustín Román
Auxiliary Bishop of Miami

"In Poland, Marxism was forced on the people. It seems that, in Cuba, the revolution was more intelligent and got the people involved."

The Hermitage of La Caridad is small, not very high, with simple architecture. Some of the few meters which separate it from the sea are reserved for meditation; several signs make this clear. Its interior decoration is sober. When you go in, there's a table on the right with two medium-sized boxes containing small plastic bottles which, we imagine, have a capacity of no more than 150 milliliters. A sign says you may take as many as you wish to the curia, to be filled with consecrated water. Each bottle has a label stating how the liquid should be used. The price is low: three for a dollar.

A few minutes after the time agreed upon, Monsignor Agustín Román arrived, dressed all in black — in spite of the hot sun — which contrasted with his extremely white hair. After four or five questions about where we were from and the purpose of the interview, he invited us into his office. It was 4:00 p.m., and we were very thirsty, but Monsignor Román was able to offer us only hot coffee. We had to go out. Luckily, two meters from the door, in the shade, we found three Pepsi Cola machines.

Monsignor Agustín Román was ordained a priest in 1959 and was forced to leave Cuba for Spain, along with 130 other priests and a bishop, in September 1961. In May of that year, the revolutionary government had announced that it would not allow counter-revolutionary religious figures to remain in the country, no matter what their nationality. Even though we insisted in several ways and mentioned some sources, the bishop always denied that any clergymen had participated in any seditious groups. It may be that he is one of the few people in Miami who doesn't know that they did. "At the beginning of the underground struggle, the churches and religious sects played an important role... Many priests, including Father Ismael Testé, took an active part in the underground."[1] Nor did he know, for example, that the November 30 Movement (Movimiento 30 de Noviembre, M30N), a Catholic terrorist group, had hidden more than a ton of explosives contributed by the CIA "in the basement of a church in the capital."[2]

Monsignor Román denied many things that are as real as the palm trees of his country. As a result, every minute that he spoke in his deliberate, punctilious way annoyed us. Wasn't it true that, soon after the *barbudos* took power, plotting for the Trujillo conspiracy began? Many texts state that Father Ricardo Velasco was the contact for sending in the weapons. Velasco was arrested in August 1959, when he arrived in Cuba clandestinely to finalize the last details. It is also known that two priests landed and were captured along with the mercenaries who took part in the Bay of Pigs invasion and that, also in 1961, three Spanish prelates and a Cuban prelate were arrested "for serving as chaplains of armed groups."[3]

Not even counterrevolutionary chief Manuel Artime denied that the Jesuits had helped him get into the U.S. Embassy disguised as a Jesuit. In addition, those clergymen, along with CIA agents, helped to sneak him out of Cuba and to the United States in December 1959.[4] Apparently, Monsignor Román is one of the few who are unaware of what a blow it was for the counterrevolution when that number of religious figures had to leave in the 1960s, although according to Enrique Encinosa, this meant that "the resistance began to lose one of its main points of support."[5]

In March 1966, the Franciscan Miguel Angel Loredo provided one of its last "supports." He allowed a counterrevolutionary who had tried to hijack a plane — who on failing to do so, had murdered the pilot and another member of the crew — to hide in the monastery.

And, since Monsignor Román didn't know anything about it, we decided not to ask him about Operation Peter Pan. Later, however, we learned from a pamphlet he gave us that he had known about it. For Monsignor Román and other ecclesiastical authorities serving the exiles, Operation Peter Pan was "a notable example of the fruits obtained thanks to the willingness and organization of civil society on the island and to human and ecclesiastical solidarity abroad."[6] Some lines later, however, it was more precise, acknowledging that "it was done through

---

[1] Encinosa, *Cuba en guerra*.
[2] Ibid.
[3] *El Nuevo Herald*, Miami, December 21, 1997.
[4] Testimony of Manuel Artime Buesa in *La Baie des Cochons*.
[5] Encinosa, *Cuba en guerra*.
[6] *Creced: Documento final* (Creced: Final Document), (Miami: Ed. Creced, 1993), conclusions of the International Meeting of Communities of Cuban Ecclesiastical Reflection in Dispersion.

a network of people on the island, the Catholic Church and the U.S. Government."[7]

Operation Peter Pan was one of the dirtiest acts of ideological and psychological warfare that the U.S. Government has carried out against the Cuban revolution. The participation of various churches, especially the Catholic Church, was of prime importance. In January 1961, an enormous propaganda campaign was launched, claiming that "communism" would take children away from their parents and send them to socialist countries for indoctrination. Broad powers were given to Miami-based Father Bryan Walsh to give visas to Cuban children between six and 16 years old. Terrified parents opted for separation.

The Catholic Welfare Bureau was particularly active in the dirty work. It not only sent representatives to meet the children in Miami but also set up a clandestine network in Cuba to help thousands of them to leave. The main member of that network was Revolutionary Rescue (Rescate Revolucionario, RR), a terrorist movement headed in Miami by former Senator (under Batista) Antonio "Tony" Varona, a member of the CIA and an associate of the powerful Mafia chief Santos Trafficante.[8] The aristocratic family of former Cuban President Ramón Grau was in charge of most of those departures, mainly using the British and Spanish embassies. The Grau family was joined by "dozens of Catholic priests and Protestant ministers..."[9] The network included Pan American Airways and KLM of Holland.

Hundreds of visas were sent to Cuba. When they were not sufficient to meet the demand, "the movement decided to print its own visas in Cuba."[10] Between January 1961 and October 1962, some 14,156 visas were issued. When the children and adolescents reached Miami, they were put in special centers as part of a program called "Unaccompanied Children," run by the Diocese of Miami. First Lady Jacqueline Kennedy gave the operation worldwide publicity by visiting the camps.[11] In mid-1961, Operation Peter Pan was made a part of Operation Mongoose, directed by the United States Information Agency. The last of the camps wasn't closed until 1981.

Contra viento y marea (Against All Odds), written by some of the young people who went through that experience, includes the following: "The children's departure had mainly been used as a propaganda

---

[7] Ibid.

[8] The relationship between Varona and Trafficante was brought out in *Alleged Assassination Plots*.

[9] Mignon Medrano, *Todo lo dieron por Cuba* (They Gave Everything for Cuba), (Miami: El Fondo de Estudios Cubanos of the Cuban American National Foundation, 1995).

[10] Encinosa, *Cuba en guerra* and Mignon Medrano, *Todo lo dieron*.

[11] *Alleged Assassination Plots*.

campaign. Those who came out of the camps were a wounded generation."

We would have liked to ask Monsignor Román many things, but what for? He claimed not to have any information about the essentials, even going so far as to deny that a large part of the exile community has been characterized by violence and intransigence. Murders and other acts of terrorism weren't restricted to the worldwide campaign against Cuba. According to the FBI, Miami had more anonymous assassination attempts and attacks than any other city in the United States in the 1986-90 period, mainly against individuals and institutions that proposed rapprochement and dialogue between the Cuban and U.S. governments.

We have regretted not having asked Monsignor Román why he was one of those who supported and prayed for the freeing of terrorist Orlando Bosch and why he joined the board of the organization Of Human Rights, an entity created by the former terrorist organization Abdala.

What Monsignor Román did make obvious was that he shared the pessimism that many had about the results of Pope John Paul II's visit to Cuba in 1998. Few people thought that the Pontiff would try to help destabilize the regime. They knew that other high-ranking religious figures, such as the Great Rabbi of Israel, had visited Cuba without their visits causing any repercussions in the political system. But the Pope was, undoubtedly, the spiritual guide with the greatest influence in the world.

Politically dispassionate studies have shown that freedom of belief has always been permitted in Cuba. How else could there be 54 officially registered religions, including some which are described as sects in Europe and the United States? It is no secret that Father Guillermo Sardiñas (now deceased), who had the rank of Major of the revolution, never stopped giving Mass, wearing an olive green cassock. That is, there is a spiritual belief that seems not to have been incompatible with the socialist revolution of Cuba.

Even though we called several times, we didn't manage to find Monsignor Román in again. We wanted to ask him what he thought about being one of the four religious figures in the world whom the Cuban Government refused to allow in the country during the Pope's visit.[12]

---

[12] Monsignor Agustín Román and Francisco Santana, another priest at the Hermitage of la Caridad, were denied permission to enter Cuba because of their close relations with the extreme right wing in the Cuban exile community. Prelate Miguel Loredo and Miguel Obando y Bravo, Cardinal of Nicaragua, are the other two religious figures who will not be able to enter Cuban territory — Loredo for having been the accomplice of a murderer, and the cardinal because of his ultrareactionary positions

* * *

"Monsignor Román, several books written by people who say they are against Castro led us to conclude that a large number of the Catholic priests participated in and/or supported counterrevolutionary actions in the 1960s and that they hid weapons and explosives — which were subsequently used in terrorist attacks — in the churches."

"My children, that is not true. I don't know where the authors got that information, but it is not true. It is enough for a priest to show the way to the Kingdom of God. And, in my own case, I never had political contacts with anybody."

"But it is said that, when around 130 priests — yourself among them — were forced to leave Cuba, the counterrevolution lost one of its main supports."

"I repeat, that isn't true. Even before the [1959 revolution], we saw that it had a Marxist ideology, against the principles of the Church. Moreover, we had so much pastoral work that there wasn't any time to support those who weren't with the revolution.

"As for me, I still don't know why they forced me to leave. I think the government wanted only a few priests to remain, especially those who were mixed up with the ideal of the revolution. The revolution wanted to have a national Church and looked for a bishop for that purpose, but none of them lent himself to that. Then, with a few priests and a group of young laymen, they created what was called 'With the Cross and with the Homeland.' But I didn't know that any of those who were forced to leave had ever helped those who were setting bombs. That was made up."

"Monsignor Román, you were forced to go to Spain. Why, then, did you decide to come to Miami?"

"I decided to come to this city to help the exiles, hoping that the Cuban system would fall. But here we still are."

"The intransigence and violence of this exile community has been widely commented on, both in the United States and in many other countries. Moreover, this exile community is split into many groups. As their spiritual

and the support he gave the mercenary contras. Concerning the Pope's visit to Cuba, we believe that it is important to quote from an article by Giulio Girardi in the daily *El País* of Spain (February 16, 1998). Girardi — who, along with three other theologians, had a long dialogue with Fidel Castro about the pastoral visit — wrote the following: "[Fidel] was convinced that most of the people had become involved in the activities by the mass organizations and because of his own comments over television. It seemed to us [theologians] that the Pope hadn't been told of that effort of persuasion and organization carried out by the revolution; therefore, he frequently addressed those who were present in the various squares as if all of them were Catholics — when, in fact, the majority weren't. It is also probable that the local Church had tried to make the Pope think that it was mainly responsible for the people's mobilization."

guide, what do you think of this?"

"My children, the exile community is united in the search for freedom. Now, I think that its intransigence is the consequence of Marxism. In Cuba, the people have to ask permission for everything, even to dance. When they get here, to a free country, they realize that they can say whatever they want. Then they give vent to their feelings and argue in loud voices. But nothing more. I think that the exile community has a poor image because the Europeans and Americans don't realize that this fieriness is part of the Caribbean sun."

"But, Monsignor, is the intransigence due to the influence of Marxism or to the fiery nature of the Caribbean sun?"

"To both. My children, it is a mixture. Here, they argue about anything and everything, as if the world were about to end. But this is a part of the culture of the Caribbean, of Latins. Now, I think that the fact that there are many groups is a part of democracy. Democracy is freedom of thought. Because everyone can decide how to make Cuba free. Here, there aren't any divisions; there are simply different ways of thinking — sometimes very excitable ones, I insist, in the Caribbean style."

"Excuse us for repeating our question more directly. People have insulted you, tried to attack you physically in the street and given you death threats over the telephone, and the police have had to protect this Hermitage because of bomb threats after you launched a campaign to send food and medicine to Cuba when Hurricane Lily went through in 1996. Is all that due to the Caribbean sun?"

"I don't think it's so serious. No, no. They were simply threats and a little shouting. You know that there are always some crazy people. But I think that this is how some groups express themselves. It's simply a lot of noise that frightens the Europeans. My children, we are Latins, and we always exaggerate. If they threatened me, it was an emotional thing, nothing more."

"Monsignor, you can't tell us that they are simply exaggerations, when many people have been murdered here, shot down or killed by bombs. The FBI offices were even attacked because they opened investigations against some of the leaders of the exile community."

"Some bombs have gone off, but not many. There have been very few assassinations for political reasons or out of intransigence... You should look for another source of information, because I know very little about these things. But, look, when those crimes were committed, the people protested. I don't know the names of any groups that have attacked anyone. I don't think there are any groups in this exile community that have it in them to hurt any other."

"Monsignor Román, some sectors think, both in the United States and in Europe, that the Pope's visit to Cuba will prove destabilizing. Some people have

even gone so far as to say that the Pope played an important role in Poland's moving toward capitalism and that the same thing might happen in Cuba. What do you think?"

"My children, the Holy Father is going to Cuba because the people have been awaiting him for several years. Now, I don't believe that the Pope is going to question the Cuban system. But, if he should do so, it would be to reaffirm what the human rights groups have already said and done. But Cuba isn't Poland. In Latin America, evangelization put down roots only 500 years ago; in Poland, its roots date from a millennium ago. Evangelization in Poland had already reached maturity. That is why the Pope's message in Poland was so valuable, like a history class, in which he reminded them of many things."

"But it is easier to convince a child than an adult."

"Don't believe it. Moreover, the Cuban people received more Marxist ideology than the Poles. From what I have understood about communism — I'm not a specialist in it — in Poland, Marxism was forced on the people. It seems that, in Cuba, the revolution was more intelligent and got the people involved. Now, unfortunately, the Holy Father's visit to Cuba won't have the same effect, the impact, to help destabilize the government. We'll be able to see that in the coming years.

"The Holy Father's message won't be new for the Cubans, because they have already heard many messages from the Church, over the radio in the exile community, and that has undoubtedly made them think. As always, the Pope's message will be one of love, reconciliation, hope and charity. Another kind of message has been reaching the Cuban people to help them open their eyes. Even the European press has done this when its reporters go to Cuba: those reporters talk with the people, urging them not to keep on letting themselves be fooled by that Marxist system."

"Let's go on to another subject, Monsignor Román. It seems to us that the Catholic Church supports the dissident movements in Cuba."

"The Church considers that those groups deserve respect, especially those which are concerned with human rights, because that is a very important topic for the Church. But the Church as such doesn't support any of them."

"But, as far as we know, you and other religious figures make broadcasts to Cuba over Radio Martí and La Voz del CID, supporting the groups which have proclaimed themselves to be Christian."

"But those are unimportant things. Our main task is to spread the message of the Kingdom of God to everyone."

"Monsignor Román, tell us about the present situation of the Catholic Church in Cuba."

"The Church has gone through several processes. First, it was persecuted, losing colleges, hospitals, old people's homes, all those institutions, remaining only with the churches and the faith, because the government took everything. That caused tremendous terror, because the illusion of the revolution was to create a new man — Marxists and scientists, as they said — ignoring the spiritual. For many years, the Church remained weak. But, at the end of the 1980s, there was an awakening, and small steps have been taken; I believe that there are many of the faithful now. That is because there has been no repression for several years. But the Church has nothing more than the churches, though it can print pamphlets to be distributed."

"Lastly, Monsignor Román, what do you think Cuba's future will be like?"

"It may be... My children, the surveys we have made among believers and theological-pastoral reflections have brought out analogies between the Cuban exile community and the Exodus and the Diaspora narrated in the Bible. This has reaffirmed the belief that many Cubans have, that what has happened in Cuba hasn't come about by chance, but there is a Divine plan behind it all and God expects something special of the Cuban people.

"But, my children, it isn't so easy. The future may have been viewed as easier some years ago. I only believe that the system should fall — either suddenly, from one moment to the next, or slowly. But it isn't easy to reconstruct a society after it has been subjected to Marxism."

"But few people, even in the Miami exile community, deny that the present Cuban political system has given the people very positive things."

"But, for example, family values have been lost. The number of divorces shows this. In Cuba, my children, people get married, get divorced and get married again, all very easily. Or they don't get married, but simply live together. That cannot be. But they aren't to blame: it's Marxism."

"Monsignor Román, the same thing happens in the United States and Europe."

"But not so easily, though that's not why the Church accepts it.

"Another thing that Marxism has made the Cuban people lose is creativity. God has given man great creativity, which cannot be developed with Marxism. You see this in the Cubans who come here. For a while, they have problems getting used to this country; they think the government should keep on giving them everything. They are dependent. They have the government complex. And, for there to be a change in Cuba, that dependent way of thinking must be changed; the government shouldn't continue to give them jobs, food, education and health care.

"My children, when I was a boy, I wanted to study. But, of course, I had a lot of trouble doing it, because I had to go from the countryside to a small town, where I caught the bus to go to Havana. I made sacrifices, because I also had to work at home; nobody gave me anything for free.

"But that's not the way it is in Cuba: the revolution gives you everything. Poor children don't realize that you have to deserve it. And those technicians, scientists and athletes — Cuba has gotten everything very easily, so they become dependent on that system."

2

Andrés Nazario Sargén
General Secretary of the
Alpha 66 paramilitary group

"We act within U.S. law. In the camps, the most we have are semi-automatic weapons. Of course, they shoot well."

It was 11:00 a.m. when we arrived at the headquarters of Alpha 66, in the area known as Little Havana. The Cuban friend who had taken us there apologized for leaving us three blocks away. Even though he was against Fidel Castro, he didn't hesitate to admit that the counter-revolutionary organizations — which he considered bunches of crazy people — scared him. Three months earlier, a Molotov cocktail had been thrown at a neighbor's house simply because the owner had sent a letter to a newspaper criticizing some of the leaders of the exile community. As a result, our friend didn't want to leave us in front of Alpha 66, where they could write down the number of his license plate and take reprisals if they didn't like our interview. His concern seemed exaggerated to us, but we respected his decision.

Two men were talking at the door. We asked for Mr. Nazario Sargén. Very courteously, they told us he was waiting for us. It was a very modest place. Most of the walls were covered with photos of meetings, military training and the pictures of members "fallen in combat" or imprisoned in Cuba. The person at the reception desk wrote down our names and the time of our arrival in a notebook.

A few minutes later, a short man wearing glasses, with an inoffensive air, appeared and smilingly introduced himself as Andrés Nazario Sargén. Without more ado, he took us to a narrow room filled with papers, where he gave us cups of delicious coffee. But he never stopped talking, and, finally, we had to ask him to wait while we set up the tape recorder. After greeting us, he tried to convince us of his group's "victories" in the "war" against Fidel Castro's government. Sitting in front of us, this 75-year-old man looked like somebody's grandfather, incapable of hurting anybody. He smiled constantly, and it was difficult to think that he was the head of the most popular paramilitary group in Miami. Following the triumph of the revolution and after participating in the

Escambray Second Front, Nazario Sargén decided to flee to the United States. Shortly afterwards, he was part of the founding nucleus of Alpha 66. Nazario lost no opportunities to remind us that his group had never had anything to do with the CIA, and he even denied things which documents of the CIA itself have certified as true. Former members of the group say that Nazario and other Alpha leaders received money from the CIA so they would dedicate themselves to preparing terrorist attacks on Cuba.[1]

Alpha 66's neofascist principles led its members into confrontation with groups which opposed the war in Vietnam. In Los Angeles, New York, Washington and other cities, they violently attacked demonstrators, whom they described as part of "the international communist movement." They claimed that Americans — and Cubans — were fighting in Vietnam "for something as sacred as freedom."[2] One *Los Angeles Times* headline read, "Nazis and Cubans Attack Pacifists."

In the 1970s, the fascist World Anti-Communist League accepted Alpha 66 as a member. In an excess of delirium, during its Sixth Congress, held in Mexico in 1972, it resolved "unanimously to ask the OAS to have Alpha 66 take the seat of communist Cuba."[3] Nazario wasn't able to attend that congress or the regional one that was held in Brazil in 1974, because there was "an order from Washington which said that, for REASONS OF NATIONAL SECURITY [all caps in the original], the U.S. Government refused to give that permission."[4] Later, however, he attended other meetings of the Anti-Communist League.

The investigation that a U.S. Senate special committee made in 1975 concluded that Alpha 66 was one of the exile groups which had "the motives, the capacity and the resources" to assassinate President Kennedy. Even so, the Miami City Commission gave it $100,000 in 1982. The same investigation showed that the group had participated, along with the CIA, in at least two assassination attempts against Fidel Castro.

Journalists Manuel Abadía, of *Excelsior* of Mexico, and Jack Anderson, of the United States, have described Alpha 66 as a tool of the CIA. Abadía was murdered in 1984 when he denounced Alpha 66's "heartless thugs" and their relations with the Mexican extreme right wing. In the late 1980s, it was rumored in Miami that Alpha 66 was planning to assassinate Jorge Mas Canosa because the head of CANF wanted to impose his leadership on the other counterrevolutionary

---

[1] Testimony of Enoel Salas in Roberto Orihuela's *Nunca fui un traido: Retrato de un farsante* (I Never Was a Traitor: Portrait of a Hypocrite), (Havana: Ed. Capitán San Luis, 1991).

[2] Miguel Talleda, *Alpha 66.*

[3] Ibid.

[4] Ibid.

groups. The impasse was quickly solved, however. Nazario went on criticizing the members of the Foundation, but the relations between the two groups are those of collaboration.

Nazario's eyes shone, and he expressed his pride over his group's "constant actions" against Fidel Castro's regime. This means that, every so often, fast combat support ships machine-gun defenseless fishing vessels. Later, those criminal actions are presented as tremendous military feats, whipping up the warlike sentiments that the leaders of the exile community have inculcated in most of their compatriots, mainly in Miami. They know that naive workers will send them financial contributions, which will enable them to continue to live well without lifting a finger.

Taking advantage of the facilities which all the U.S. administrations have offered them since 1959, Alpha 66 and other paramilitary groups set up training camps in several parts of the country, but mainly in Florida. Mexican, Vietnamese, South Korean and Nicaraguan contra and fascist groups are trained there in military techniques. The camps most visited by members of the press in the last 10 years were set up just outside Miami. Nazario offered to take us to one of them.

The next Sunday, he drove us to a place 45 minutes from Miami. At the entrance to the camp, three armed men paced back and forth under flagstaffs flying the U.S. and Cuban flags. Inside, around 20 men came to attention, and Nazario inspected them. Immediately after that, headed by a former instructor of the U.S. Special Forces, they did exercises for around 30 minutes. At first sight, it didn't seem possible that a commando capable of frightening the Cuban Security forces could be trained there. Most of the men were over 40, and many found it difficult to trot 100 meters, throw themselves to the ground, shoot, get up and run again with the dexterity needed for an attack.

The sound of the semi-automatic weapons hammered on our eardrums, but it seemed to us to be more of a good pretext for spending a weekend with buddies and, at the same time, trying to impress us. At the end of the demonstration, they offered us huge, delicious sandwiches. While eating, we kept looking at a 10-year-old boy whose father was teaching him how to shoot with a pistol. His brother, who was a little older, was practicing with a rifle. Both wore camouflage outfits.

On our way to and from the camp, we finished interviewing Sargén.

* * *

"Let's start with a simple question. How was Alpha 66 created?"

"When a group of 12 officers and I realized that Castro was turning the country over to the Soviet Union, we decided to leave for the United

States clandestinely. We were kept at a military installation, because they didn't trust us. The Bay of Pigs disaster came a few months later, and that's when they let us go free."

"Excuse us for interrupting, but how did the exiles feel about the Bay of Pigs defeat?"

"They didn't believe in anything; everybody was depressed. The Cubans, most of whom were Batista followers, said that we were the ones who had been wiped out, because Castro hadn't been overthrown in spite of all the resources the Americans had.

"So we decided to create a new movement. That's why we called it 'Alpha,' which means 'the beginning.' We added '66' because that's how many of us there were at first — in Puerto Rico at the end of 1961. We set ourselves the task of organizing — not an invasion, since that had been shown to be inefficient, but something with a new way of thinking and strategy. We can say that, during the course of all these years, even though we've lost some battles, we have never been defeated."

"You haven't been defeated, but Fidel Castro, who is your bogeyman, is still there. What did you plan at that time?"

"Castro hasn't gone, but we haven't, either. At that time, we proposed waging an irregular — Cuban — war without asking permission from the Americans, using our own human and economic resources. We were also sure that an organization should be created in Cuba so that the Cuban people, not us, would overthrow Castro from within. We would be support factors. To achieve that, we would have to engage in military actions that would create a mystique, a legend, because, without that, there wouldn't be any uprising."

"Mr. Nazario, the revolution has been in power for nearly 40 years now, and the people haven't staged any uprisings. Isn't that a defeat?"

"No. We know that the Cuban people believe in Alpha. They continue to engage in small acts of sabotage, following our slogans, paving the way for the uprising."

"We imagine that the U.S. Government has offered you all kinds of support over the years."

"Yes, but not on the terms you're thinking of. We began with commando type actions. During the first two years, we made 14 attacks. The U.S. Government began to intervene, obviously because it considered us very independent. It began to arrest people, but it didn't sentence them or take their weapons away. But Kennedy was killed, and the situation got worse. We kept on, though, and several of us went to jail. Moreover, it wasn't easy to get the resources we needed."

"That is, you didn't have good relations with the CIA, which was in charge of all the counterrevolutionary actions."

"We haven't had bad relations with the CIA, but sometimes they come around sticking their noses into things and even trying to frighten us. They have made us several offers over the years, proposing that we work together, but we told them we didn't want to have links with any government. We've asked them not to harass us and not to take away our weapons, ships and radio installations. We've always proposed that, if they really wanted to help us, they should drop some weapons there, and we'd go get them. They told us there wasn't any problem about that and asked how much money we wanted. They knew that, if they paid us anything, we'd be committed to them. There wasn't any argument about that."

"The Cuban Government has protested about the actions that exiles have carried out from U.S. territory. Did that have any repercussions for you?"

"When Fidel has protested, the FBI, the CIA and even the Customs Service have come to go through everything. They tell us we can't use U.S. territory to attack a country with which the United States isn't at war. Listen: they aren't waging war on Castro, but we are."

"According to our information, you beam radio broadcasts at Cuba. Do they keep bothering you about that?"

"No, that's been fixed. They came here and told us they'd put us in jail if we went back on the air clandestinely. So, now, we have to pay them several thousand dollars, and they let us broadcast for a few hours to Cuba. Got that? Now, we broadcast as a commercial station."

"Moreover, you train men near Miami with real weapons, real bullets and campaign uniforms. That is, you have Washington's complicity."

"But that's legal! We act within U.S. law. In the camps, the most we have are semi-automatic weapons. Of course, they shoot well."

"In addition to commando operations, have you engaged in any other kinds of military actions — assassination attempts against Fidel Castro, for example?"

"We've made several attempts to kill him, even inside Cuba. I myself took part in an assassination attempt against Castro in New York, but the FBI discovered it."

"Mr. Nazario, the head of the FBI in charge of Fidel Castro's security on that occasion told a Congressional committee that the CIA had organized that attack."

"That isn't true. It was us: all of us were Cubans.

"The closest we came was in Chile in 1972. We put a pistol in a camera and got one of our men accredited as a journalist. But, when push came to shove, he didn't shoot; he chose to escape, instead. The thing is, anybody who kills Castro will die, too; too much courage is required."

"According to declassified CIA documents, the CIA organized that assassination attempt, too."

"I repeat: that isn't true. That was the Alpha people. But the CIA may have wanted to claim credit for it."

"You were part of the World Anti-Communist League, in which..."

"Yes, that's right. We used to belong to the World Anti-Communist League, because we could use it as a platform for making denunciations. It always seemed very reactionary to me, but they talked a lot and didn't give much real support. That's why we broke with them. Did you know that even high-ranking leaders of the Catholic Church and world-renowned politicians were members of it?"

"Yes, we knew, though not with as much precision as you. Now, let's go on to another topic. Mr. Nazario, what should Fidel Castro do to initiate the changes you want?"

"First of all, and most important, he should set up a provisional government and leave Cuba. There isn't any other solution. He and his henchmen — about 80 or 100 of them — have to leave the island... We have only one goal: to put an end to Castro. If we have to kill him, that's OK, but he has to disappear. You shouldn't think that I'm a criminal."

"Are you carrying out military actions against the Cuban regime right now?"

"We've gone into Cuba, although we've always been detected, which is why many of our members have been imprisoned and we have a lot of martyrs. But we've managed to create a spontaneous movement inside the country, because 95 percent of the people are against Castro. We know that many underground cells of Alpha 66 have been created, consisting of just one person each — when there are more than three members, they are quickly destroyed. Castro's repressive apparatus is very effective..."

"We would think that, if they detect them so easily, it's because there is close cooperation between the people and State Security..."

"Yes, that may be so, too. We've tried to destroy the economy through acts of sabotage — not to make the people hungry, but to put an end to Fidel's economic base. That's being done. Now, Fidel can't depend on his military apparatus, can't confront anybody, because he doesn't have spare parts for his armaments."

"If you know that's so, that Cuba's military defense is so limited, why don't you step up your actions? Why doesn't the White House order an invasion?"

"I've already told you that the Americans keep a close eye on us, and the Americans don't invade. Ever since the Bay of Pigs, they've been seeking political solutions."

"If Fidel Castro leaves, dies or is overthrown, what will happen?"

"Everything depends on who takes power. If a group that is bloodstained takes it, there will be war. If communism continues, there will be war. But, if neither of those possibilities occurs, we hope that they will take steps to form a transitional government that will call an election."

"We have three final, more precise questions. Fidel Castro's enemies keep saying that he was the one who, because of a power struggle, caused the disappearance of Major Camilo Cienfuegos. What do you think of this — as someone who was close to Cienfuegos and consider Fidel Castro your worst enemy?"

"I'm going to be frank with you. Castro is my enemy, but I'm sure that he didn't have anything to do with Major Camilo Cienfuegos's death. Camilo, whom I admired enormously, disappeared at sea. I helped look for his small plane for several days. And nothing. What happened? The weather was bad that day, and nearly all of the pilots the revolution had were novices. I think that the bad weather and the pilot's inexperience were responsible."

"Our next-to-the-last question. We imagine that you know of the statements that Che's daughter Aleida made in August 1996. She said that the French writer Régis Debray talked too much when he was captured in Bolivia and that that was how they found out where her father was… "

"That's the only thing on which I could agree with Che's daughter. I never agreed with Che, because he was just like Castro, but that's no reason for ignoring the fact that Debray was an evil, dangerous person. It is known that Debray was so scared that he spilled his guts even though he wasn't really tortured. He squealed because he didn't believe in that revolution. He said he was a communist, but he was nothing but an adventurer, an opportunist. I didn't know Debray personally, but I knew he had a tremendous ego and thought he was powerful enough to solve all our problems… I repeat: I never agreed with Che, but informers like Debray are worthless; they are the scum of the earth… "

"Now, our last question. Mr. Nazario, we would like you to clear something up for us — if you can, of course. Is it true that the U.S. Government has paid or pays every organization which says it is fighting against the Cuban Government?"

"Look, I repeat: Alpha 66 has never received any money from the Americans. But here, in the 1960s, all the other groups were paid. The Americans gave money to any organization so it could keep on functioning. Now, that isn't the case so much, because it seems that some things are being done through Europe. Up to the 1980s, the Americans supported nearly all the organizations."

"What things are being done through Europe?"

"Ah, what a shame! You said you didn't have any more time."

3

José Basulto
Former member of Brigade 2506 and
Director of Brothers to the Rescue (HAR)

"The Americans and we in the exile community should seek the support of the Europeans, because they have a better image in Cuba."

The day after arriving in Miami, we came across a man selling newspapers in the street. We didn't have to ask him for identification to know that he was a young Cuban. We were amazed that, in a country which boasted of giving those who arrived from Cuba everything they needed, he should be engaged in that activity, which was the domain of the poorest sectors in U.S. society. We then set out to see which of us could find the most Cuban street vendors of flowers, peanuts, cigarettes, bread, cracklings and gooey snacks. Before 12 days had passed, we called off our competition, because both of us had lost count.

It wasn't necessary to walk far in the city: the popular Calle Ocho (8th Street, S.W.) is enough to show that Miami has stopped being the promised land for those who leave Cuba. We aren't going to say that there are thousands of them. Many thousands work in sweatshops for $4.50 an hour, barely enough money to keep them alive. As Luis Ortega, a Cuban-U.S. journalist, noted in *La Prensa* of New York, "The image of the exile community as one of rich Batista supporters who escaped from Castro doesn't correspond to reality any more. Now, most are working class, living in modest houses in Hialeah."

In Miami, the vast majority of the immigrants feel frustrated because Fidel Castro, whom they blame for all their ills, remains in power. But they don't want to go back. Even though they miss the island, they are more concerned about their future in a country that is steadily closing the door to them, denying them opportunities. The area called Little Havana, in the center of the city, is a portrait of their present situation. Up until 10 years ago, it was a wonderful place in which to live and relax. Now, the businesses have grates and security systems; delinquency has grown enormously, because of economic difficulties. A large part of the middle class has no alternative to moving far out if they want to live and relax in peace.

In 1961, a few minutes after leaving Havana airport, those who had fled could hear President Kennedy's voice welcoming and encouraging them, urging them to take up their opportunity of beginning new lives in the United States with faith and enthusiasm.[1] They were considered freedom fighters. Automatically, they were given authorization to stay, and, without any great difficulty, U.S. citizenship. For many years, they had privileges that no other Latin American immigrants had. That was only to be expected; the empire should support those who offered to be the enemies of its enemy.

While the revolutionary government emphasized pride in Cuba's sovereignty, the United States began a psychological campaign of defamation, disinformation and acts of provocation. One of its purposes was to get Cubans to leave their country, to show that the system was incompatible with the population. To achieve this, it used the mass media, mainly the radio. The many stations dedicated to that task interviewed somebody called "Pepito Pérez," who was supposed to have arrived two days earlier and was already working in a company with a salary of several thousand dollars a month. "In the United States," the announcers trumpeted, "all you have to do is make 'a little effort,' and you'll easily be the manager of a large industry or set up in business for yourself." "What a shame," one of the announcers lamented, "that the women in Cuba don't have access to the fancy dresses we'll be wearing this season."

The result was that, in 1980, at least 200,000 Cubans left through the port of Mariel — the "Marielitos." When they reached the United States, Panama and Peru, many of them were kept in veritable concentration camps, which led to revolts — that were put down with guns, leaving a toll of several dead. It was claimed that the Cuban Government had taken advantage of the exodus to get rid of a large number of criminals, but, "in fact, the proportion of criminals was minimal, compared to the total number."[2]

In Miami, "Hundreds of people who had left Cuba through Mariel died in the first few years of their exile, stabbed to death in fights, killed in squabbles or shot down by the police or by other criminals. Hundreds were imprisoned for a variety of criminal acts, including robbery, rape, trafficking in drugs and assault."[3] The United States had offered them so much that, when those who left through Mariel arrived and found a few handouts rather than El Dorado, they just exploded. The explanation put forward was a little simplistic, however: "They had serious problems in adapting to a new society in a strange country, cultural clashes after

---

[1] Ibid.
[2] Encinosa, *Cuba en guerra*.
[3] Ibid.

having lived for decades under a dictatorship."[4] It makes you wonder if it was due to the "dictatorship" or whether, as Monsignor Román said, the Cubans in Cuba are accustomed to having the government give them everything.

In spite of all the social problems caused by the massive flight, the ideological and psychological incitements didn't stop — rather, they increased. When the Cuban Government declared the "special period" in 1990, announcers in Miami bellowed that, in the United States, there was plenty of water, electric power, meat, chicken, milk and clothing. What they didn't say was that you needed to make more than "a little effort" to buy those things.

That was how they created the crisis of the "rafters," who got onto anything that would float so as to get the privileges offered in the U.S. "paradise" — privileges which, at the time, existed only in the lies of the people instigating departures from Cuba. The first "rafters" were welcomed as heroes, but when their numbers rose to 400 in just a few months, Washington began to get worried. Moreover, they began to rub the Miami Cubans the wrong way — to such an extent that the formula for wishing someone ill changed from "May lightning strike you dead" to "May a rafter come to live in your house."

José Basulto knew how to cut himself a good piece of the pie created by the desperation of those who fled. He went to Cuba in 1960 as part of the infiltration units that were to pave the way for the Bay of Pigs invasion. In the Brigade, he was number 2522. That is, he was the 22nd Cuban to be recruited by the CIA. Starting a few weeks before and continuing until after the Bay of Pigs invasion, the mercenaries in those units were detected and captured. Basulto managed to escape and fled to the Guantánamo Naval Base.

He continued his counterrevolutionary activities, making raids along Cuba's coasts to attack civilian objectives. Although he denies this vehemently, it seems that he never broke with the CIA, as proved by his participation in the contras, a mercenary force directed by the upper echelons of the Pentagon against the Sandinistas. Andrés Nazario, of Alpha 66, told us that Basulto was "a volunteer mercenary run by the Americans."

When the "rafters crisis" began, Basulto joined Billy Schuss, another CIA veteran who was a specialist in infiltration and commando attacks, and dreamed up Brothers to the Rescue (Hermanos al Rescate, HAR).[5] Brothers to the Rescue, whose members are of several nationalities, all united "by their love of adventure and by their deep anti-communist

---

[4] Ibid.
[5] Ibid.

convictions,"[6] was apparently created to save rafters from the dangerous water of the Straits of Florida. In fact, it did rescue several of them — and, as a result, was described as a "humanitarian" organization by the world press and human rights institutions. But that was simply a facade hiding its true purposes, which were far from altruistic.

In late 1994, the U.S. Government, which was worried by the dimensions of what it had helped to provoke, proposed to the Cuban Government that they sign an agreement on immigration. They did so, and in May 1995 the illegal entry of Cubans into the United States was banned. In practice, however, anybody who represented a political and propaganda interest against the Cuban Government would still be welcomed.

In any case, from then on, those for whom the U.S. Government did not make an exception would no longer be considered "heroes of freedom fleeing from communism" — but would be given the same treatment as "mere Haitians." They would be immediately turned over to the Cuban authorities or kept provisionally at the Guantánamo Naval Base in subhuman conditions. This shook the exile leaders in Miami, who felt that Clinton was making a gesture of rapprochement toward Cuba and that this marked the beginning of the end of their privileges.

The leaders of some 20 organizations, all of the extreme right, held an emergency meeting. They included representatives of the Cuban American National Foundation, the Valladares Foundation (Fundación Valladares), Alpha 66, Independent and Democratic Cuba (Cuba Independiente y Democrática, CID) and Brothers to the Rescue. The meeting was held at the headquarters of Brigade 2506, the paramilitary group whose leaders included José Basulto. Congressman Lincoln Díaz-Balart, who had collaborated in the drafting of the Helms-Burton Bill, and terrorist Orlando Bosch were among the special guests.[7] At first, the main purpose was to draw up a line of action for pressuring the U.S. administration into going back on the migratory agreement. Once again, however, the reason for the meeting was "to plan how to overthrow Fidel Castro."[8]

When the flow of rafters was halted, Brothers to the Rescue saw its existence threatened, so it came up with a new purpose: "to be the eyes of the exile community over the Straits of Florida, so the United States and Cuba won't violate the human rights of Cubans."[9]

In fact, however, Basulto and Brothers to the Rescue kept on with

---

[6] *El País*, Madrid, March 1, 1996.

[7] *El País*, Madrid, May 1995.

[8] Ibid.

[9] *El País*, Madrid, March 3, 1996.

what they had been doing all along: inciting the Cuban people to plot against their government. But not only that: according to Juan Pablo Roque, a Cuban counterintelligence agent infiltrated in that organization, Brothers to the Rescue worked on terrorist attacks on civilian and military objectives in Cuba. All this information, plus what he gathered on other organizations, such as the Cuban American National Foundation, was turned over to the FBI — for which he also worked and from which he received $7,000, as stated by the FBI itself.[10] Thus, small planes continued to violate Cuban airspace in acts of provocation until two of them were shot down on February 24, 1996. Roque had returned to Cuba the day before.

In mid-1996, Brothers to the Rescue launched another fundraising campaign so it could continue its illegal activities. Basulto's Miami residence cost more than half a million dollars, and, as is the case with many exile leaders, he doesn't have a job with a big enough salary to pay for such a luxury.

The headquarters of Brothers to the Rescue is in one of the most exclusive sections of Miami. José Basulto's office features pictures of Christ and Gandhi and clippings from the international press with banner headlines on the shooting down of the planes. A meek old woman, the mother of one of the downed pilots, was with him. Basulto insisted that we interview her, so we did, but she had very little to say, apart from expressing her grief. Then we spoke with Basulto, who gave his answers energetically and with great confidence, as if he were wearing a uniform.

Basulto invited us to accompany his group the following Sunday, when they would fly close to the 24th parallel, but we had another commitment and couldn't accept. Naturally, we would have liked to go — if Basulto went with us in the same small plane.

* * *

"Mr. Basulto, tell us how Brothers to the Rescue's activities began."

"First of all, I would like to state that, even though some people say we are political, Brothers to the Rescue has been a humanitarian organization.

"We made our first flight to rescue rafters in 1991, in my own plane. We asked the exile community for help, but nobody responded. However, the number of rafters kept increasing. In 1994, we flew 32 missions a week, at a cost of nearly $1.3 million a year. By then, it had become an operation entirely financed by the exile community and by contributions from wealthy individuals, such as the singer Gloria

---

[10] *Le Point*, Paris, July 27, 1996.

Estefan, who donated a plane in which I crashed. American Airlines also made contributions."

"What is your version of the shooting down of the light planes on February 24, 1996?"

"The Americans and the Cuban Government knew that we were going to fly that day and pass the 24th parallel, because Juan Pablo Roque, a Cuban pilot who was welcomed here as a dissident and a hero, saw them. He had infiltrated our group, working for the FBI and Castro's intelligence services."

"But, Mr. Basulto, several news media have stated that the FBI had warned you that, on that occasion, the planes would be shot down, because the Cuban Government wouldn't allow any more violations of its territory. Moreover, several media have pointed out that that was why you remained five miles behind the other two, outside Cuban jurisdictional limits, so you wouldn't be shot down. The pilot-spy Roque said that you had gained four martyrs..."

"That's a lie! A lie! I can see that a lot of people are working for the communists!"

"Excuse us, but it is what we have read. Other reports say that Brothers to the Rescue's planes have violated Cuban airspace at least 20 times and, on nearly all those occasions, dropped propaganda against the Cuban Government. Is that true?"

"Affirmative. We made one of those flights on August 13, 1995, when we flew over Havana. But it was to [act as a decoy] in order to draw off the military surveillance the Cuban Government had mounted over several exile vessels. We also flew on January 9 and 13, 1996, and, taking advantage of the meteorological conditions and our height, dropped half a million leaflets with simple messages..."

"Just a minute, Mr. Basulto. Those vessels were violating Cuban jurisdictional waters. Their crews consisted of Cuban exiles, they had U.S. registration, and they flew U.S. flags. You know very well that they were seeking to provoke the Cuban Government. They were trying to see just how far they could go..."

"Affirmative. But we wanted to hold a celebration and show our support for the Cuban people."

"Going back to our question. Why didn't they shoot down your planes or force them to land on any of the earlier occasions? That would have been done in any other country."

"I don't know! I don't know why they didn't shoot us down. And, almost every time, we dropped pamphlets over Havana, saying the same things as the one we dropped on the Cuban warships. The message was simple, inoffensive — such as, for example, 'Brothers, not comrades,' meaning that we weren't communists. We also dropped some which called for civil disobedience...

"Later, people who opposed the Cuban Government — dissidents of the Cuban Council and independent journalists whom we were supporting — called Miami radio stations to say that several people had picked up leaflets and distributed them."

"*Mr. Basulto, even though repeatedly violating a country's airspace to incite the population to act against its government is very serious, do you think there was another reason for the downing of the planes?*"

"Affirmative. I am sure it was also because of our support for and financing of the Cuban Council and other resistance organizations inside Cuba. We wanted and want to help create a political alternative to Castro's government. That's why we decided to give Sebastián Arcos several thousand dollars in a ceremony here in Miami, as support for the Cuban Council. Yes, the most important thing for the Castro government is that Brothers to the Rescue had become a destabilizing factor. That must have been the main reason why they shot down the two planes."

"*Mr. Basulto, let's go on to another topic. Pardon the question, but it is said that Brothers to the Rescue is financed by the CIA.*"

"Just let them show us their proof! We have proof of how we are financed!"

"*Not only that, but it is also said that you yourself work for the CIA.*"

"That's another accusation that the Cuban Government makes against me and against the other leaders of the exile community to discredit us! It has thrown all of its international public relations machinery into that effort."

"*So you broke off your relations with the CIA after the Bay of Pigs?*"

"In 1961, I, like the other members of Brigade 2506, worked *with* — not *for* — the CIA. We Cubans who represented the interests of Cuba have never worked for the CIA or for the U.S. Government. That would have been a vile thing to do. Yes, I was with them until November 1961. At that time, I told them that they were deceiving the Cuban people, that they weren't really helping to overthrow the regime, and that they were causing my fellow countrymen to be killed and imprisoned."

"*Forgive us for insisting, but there are documents saying that you were in Brazil and Central America for the CIA.*"

"Negative; that's a lie. I haven't taken part in any kind of activity with the Americans, apart from my serving in their army for 13 months."

"*Mr. Basulto, you can't deny that you were in Honduras with the Nicaraguan contras. And it has been proved that the contras were entirely controlled by the CIA...*"

"I, José Basulto, helped the contras in Honduras for a while as an individual, without any U.S. financing. I went as part of an operation of the Cuban exile community. Several organizations sent representatives there; I was with Brigade 2506, of which I was military director."

"Excuse me, did you say 'military director'?"

"Affirmative. I stayed in Honduras only for humanitarian reasons, helping to set up campaign hospitals on the border with Nicaragua. I was there under the orders of Nicaraguan Colonel Enrique Bermúdez."

"Let's go on to another subject. How do you explain the fact that the United States, the biggest world power, hasn't been able to overthrow Fidel Castro's government?"

"The United States has a great responsibility for the Cuban political system's continued existence. In 1961, when, for the first and only time, the Castro regime was attacked militarily, in the Bay of Pigs invasion, the United States abandoned the Cuban people in their search for freedom. The conditions began to be created for that regime to be consolidated in power. The next year, there was the October Missile Crisis, over the missiles that the Soviets wanted to install in Cuba. And a new possibility of direct confrontation arose. But, fearful of what the Soviet Union might do, the Americans negotiated about something that was none of their business: our freedom. The Americans pledged not to militarily intervene in Cuba, and they didn't allow us Cubans to do it on our own. As a result, the Castro system was finally consolidated.

"The United States knows that a large-scale action against Castro could prove costly, triggering massive immigration or some crazy action of Castro's. Castro has enough military materiel to bomb Florida's nuclear power plant and other U.S. strategic objectives. Now, an invasion of Cuba would take thousands of lives."

"What alternative do you see for Cuba, Mr. Basulto?"

"We are trying to overthrow that regime. The Cuban people should use nonviolent confrontation without ruling out the use of violence. We know that it would be suicidal to attack Castro militarily, but the regime must be changed, somehow eliminating Castro and his clique.

"It may be possible to effect change if the internal resistance manages to establish the required space for working in the political sphere and becomes an alternative to Castro. That's why we should keep on supporting and fomenting human rights groups: they are our best weapon against that regime. To do so, the Americans and we in the exile community should seek the support of the Europeans, because they have a better image in Cuba. That's what we're doing, although very slowly."

"Mr. Basulto..."

"I suggest that we continue another time. Now, I have to see the lawyer who is handling the case of the planes that were shot down."

4

Ninoska Pérez Castellón
Journalist, announcer on Radio La Cubanísima, and Director of La Voz de la Fundación, the radio station of the Cuban American National Foundation

"I am amazed by European hypocrisy! There, the politicians make decisions about other countries on the basis of what is advantageous to them."

Roberto Martín Pérez
Member of the governing body of the Cuban American National Foundation

"We're considering the possibility that Castro's already dead."

At last, when we called for the sixth time, Ms. Ninoska Pérez Castellón agreed to see us. She told us to be sure to be punctual, because she had to tape a radio broadcast afterwards, so we arrived early at the address she had given us.

We asked the taxi driver if it was the headquarters of La Cubanísima or of La Voz de la Fundación. He looked at us in the rearview mirror and told us dryly that it was the Cuban American National Foundation (CANF). Was it possible? We had spent more than a week urging two secretaries to let us have an interview with one of the top leaders of CANF and had gotten nowhere. They wouldn't even allow us to go by to pick up some of its publications. They always asked us to tell them where to send them to us in Miami. And that wasn't possible, because none of the people we knew — people who kept a distance from hysterical, sterile arguments — wanted their addresses in those hands.

While one camera was trained on the large parking area, another followed anyone approaching from the front. We walked up to the large glass door. Inside, a beefy guard opened it. He informed us impassively that Ms. Pérez hadn't yet arrived, but we could write our names in the registration book and take a seat to wait. We did, seeing out of the corners of our eyes that a third camera was observing us.

Ms. Pérez arrived 10 long minutes late. She greeted the guard, and he announced us. She turned to look at us, attempted a smile, said hello and invited us to accompany her. When the door and the grille closed behind us, we found ourselves in a long — very long — hall which we thought would swallow us. She escorted us along it to the last door on the left — that of the office of the director of La Voz de la Fundación — a distance of only about 30 meters. There, Ms. Pérez, a large, robust woman with well-cared-for hands, served us fragrant instant coffee.

Our original plan hadn't called for interviewing her. But, when we heard La Cubanísima early one afternoon, we decided to do it. She surprised us. Every word concerning the Cuban Government — and especially Fidel Castro — was filled with hatred, and she used a vocabulary which left us wondering why she wasn't censored. To the contrary, she won the 1996 Journalist of the Year Award presented by the "National College of Journalists of Cuba," whose headquarters is in Miami. When you know who pulls the strings in Miami, you don't question anything. What authority would dare oppose her? We wouldn't, even if she and those like her allowed us to become mayor of the city.

We became even more eager to interview her when we heard the second part of her program, "Here, with Ninoska." This was because she broadcasts calls from people who are described as dissidents in Cuba. In the 13 or so broadcasts we heard, all of those people, who claimed to be champions of human rights or independent journalists, expressed identical, negative views: there wasn't any soap, meat or milk in Cuba; electric power and gas were rationed; blah, blah, blah about the government and about the Security services. They all wound up thanking and praising Ms. Pérez, Mas Canosa and other counter-revolutionary leaders in Miami "for everything you have done for Cuba's freedom" and saying that the exile community could count on their organizations for whatever they thought was necessary. By then, they had repeated their names and those of their groups several times, so they wouldn't be forgotten. Later, those broadcasts are sent to Cuba over La Voz de la Fundación.

Since Cubans are passionate and unrestrained in their way of speaking, you can imagine how this came out. And Ms. Pérez always adds an incendiary melodramatic touch. Now, it can't be pleasant to have meat and soap rationed — much less, to believe yourself persecuted by the police and by your neighbors — but the announcer turns those protests into a show that deliberately whips up hatred against the Cuban Government every day, both in Cuba and abroad.

Before hanging up, Ms. Pérez advises her callers to get their neighbors involved in the crusade and to practice civil disobedience. She urges them to carry out acts of sabotage and to paint slogans against the government whenever they can. And all that is over the radio, openly! But that isn't all. The journalist has called Havana — the Ministry of the Interior, the Ministry of Foreign Relations and the Central Committee of the Communist Party — in acts of provocation to interview and criticize officials for many minutes. And they listen to and answer her. The only thing they ask her is that she limit herself to decent language, or they will hang up.

We had been talking with her for several minutes — and she was doing her utmost to change her style from the one she uses over the radio — when Roberto Martín Pérez, her husband, came in. Without any by your leave, after greeting us, he jumped into the conversation.

His father, like his wife's, had been an officer under Batista. He was captured in 1959 while trying to enter Cuba clandestinely as an advance man for the Trujillo conspiracy. That same year, Pérez had taken part in an assassination attempt against the Cuban ambassador in Santo Domingo. After spending 18 years in prison, he was freed in 1978 as the result of a dialogue and rapprochement between a sector of the exile community and the Cuban Government.

In Miami, even counterrevolutionary circles are afraid of him. It is said that he has no scruples in dealing with those who oppose the Foundation's plans. The U.S. authorities presume that he is a power behind the Foundation's paramilitary apparatus. Some newspaper reports (which have not been disproved) state that Pérez was an important link between the Foundation's leaders — especially Mas Canosa — and the mercenary force of the Nicaraguan contras.

While we were saying goodbye to Ms. Pérez, her assistant told her that a Cuban dissident was on the phone. She took the call, beginning to tape it. Then she told us it would be important for us to talk with him. We didn't have any choice. The man told us that, the day before, State Security had picked up a neighbor of his and held him for three hours; that two men had come to ask him questions about the neighbor; and that there were two policemen at the corner of his house. We asked if they had hurt him, if they had searched his house or if they had beaten his neighbor. No, nothing like that. We asked if he knew why his neighbor had been arrested. He said he imagined it was because he and some friends of his phoned Ms. Pérez and Radio Martí frequently. "Sir, can you tell us where you're calling from so calmly?" "From my neighbor's house."

* * *

"Ms. Pérez, we have listened to your radio program. The extremely aggressive, almost virulent, way you attack the Cuban Government surprised us."

"No dictator has the right to keep me from living in my country, and I'm not about to accept it. Moreover, when I pick up the telephone and somebody in Cuba tells me about a tragedy committed by that dictator — well, I can't just sit there and do nothing or use a cordial tone. Even though we live comfortably and with freedom here in this country, we don't forget what's going on in Cuba. Nor have the Cuban American Congressmen forgotten it, even though they have achieved the great dream of this nation. Nor have others who have amassed great fortunes and could live in peace; they keep on working for Cuba."

"Documents we have read and things that other Cubans in Miami have told us, suggest that the Cuban American National Foundation shares and encourages the U.S. policy on Cuba."

"Well, we aren't anti-American, and we work with the possibilities offered us by this system. One example of this is the Helms-Burton Act, which stiffens the embargo against Castro's government, prohibiting all European and Canadian investors from trafficking with the property which that dictatorship stole from its original owners, both Cuban and American. The support of American politicians in Congress was required to pass that bill. At the same time, they needed the Cubans' votes, and we were able to provide that. That's how political power is used in this country. That's how this system works.

"But then, what happened? When President Bill Clinton was undecided about signing the bill into law, the Castro regime shot down two Brothers to the Rescue planes in February 1996. And, well, the planes had U.S. registration, and there were four people on board. Then the Foundation put the pressure on, and President Clinton was forced to sign the bill."

"It was that simple?"

"Don't forget that the election was coming up, and Clinton couldn't stay in office without Cuban votes. I repeat, this is the way the Foundation works: with the possibilities provided by this system. Moreover — we don't deny it — the Foundation has been very close to such presidents as Reagan and Bush. Before making a decision on Cuba, Clinton himself has called Mas Canosa or another director of the Foundation. Why? Because they know about our work and because the directors of the Cuban American National Foundation have helped finance their campaigns."

"You have promoted the laws of the embargo against Cuba — such as the Torricelli and Helms-Burton Acts — confident that with this legislation the government of Fidel Castro would fall. But the Europeans say that you will change that political system more easily by investing in Cuba."

"How can the Europeans and Canadians think that they can change that dictatorship by taking capital to Cuba? I don't understand them!

That murderer has always said that there would never be any political changes! I am amazed by European hypocrisy! There, the politicians make decisions regarding other countries on the basis of what is advantageous to them. And the same thing goes for Canada. All of those countries have been bitten by an anti-American bug. But what are the facts? The Helms-Burton Act has already frightened several companies into pulling out of Cuba, because they know that the law will be used against those who support that murderous dictatorship."

"Every day, on your program, you take calls from people who are supposedly putting up resistance against the government in Cuba. What, really, does that opposition amount to?"

"The resistance is very difficult, but it exists. Every day, I talk with people in Cuba who oppose that regime and who have organized groups, a thing it was impossible to do before, because for many years all opponents were put in prison so they wouldn't bother Castro…"

At this point Roberto Martín Pérez came in. He intervened, taking the floor from his wife, in a way that made us think he had been listening behind the door.

MR. PÉREZ: "It may be that, like other European journalists, you won't understand what I'm going to tell you, because you don't live in a police state such as Cuba. That's why they make a thousand mistakes when they write their stories. In Cuba, there have been many forms of peaceful resistance. For example, Cuban men and women haven't worked, because they haven't been interested in the communist process."

"But, Mr. Pérez, according to what we've been told here in Miami, the resistance in Cuba is very minimal and has no real support among the population."

"You don't even imagine what's happening in Cuba. For example, if you have a daughter studying, they send her to the countryside, supposedly to help production. There, they subject her to all kinds of abuse to make you and your daughter afraid. If your son goes to jail, he will be raped. I don't need to tell you any more… Just imagine, there are some prisoners called 'lions' that they have there just to rape the others. They are given better food for doing that. They are always kept drugged, like dead people."

"Can anybody who is drugged rape somebody else?"

"Just wait. I'll tell you another anecdote of how that criminal regime terrifies people so there won't be any resistance. If you are in a military unit, you have to work in the countryside, always near a girls' school. During the day, the girls are working in the same place. The contact between men and women, of course, results in certain actions. At night, the boys run away to meet the girls who've also gotten out. The officials of the regime set this up to give the girls and boys incentives for producing more. They have to give the [Communist] Party five million hours of forced labor each year."

"Mr. Pérez, what was imprisonment like for you?"

"I spent 18 years in solitary, in a tiny cell, in nothing but my underwear. I survived because I believed in a cause and in God. We were all badly fed, getting no milk or fruit. We weren't beaten, but they kept us there, vegetating. The result: we all came out with tremendous physical and psychological traumas. I think that I was an exception because I didn't lose any teeth and didn't get hemorrhoids (which are frequently caused by malnutrition), ulcers or insomnia..."

"What had you done against the Cuban Government that led to your imprisonment?"

"I believed in God and fought for freedom..."

MS. PÉREZ: "That prison-related terror shows why there isn't any great opposition. Everything is manipulated. That dictatorship is a system of dreadful repression..."

MR. PÉREZ: "You should know that the machinery..."

MS. PÉREZ: "Roberto, just a minute. They want to know about the present opposition..."

MR. PÉREZ: "Just wait, and I'll tell you. I have known Castro since we were children, and I know that he's a violent man. I don't think you know that Castro was a gangster. He was a criminal who joined other Cubans and foreigners. Those foreigners had fought with the Allies in World War II or in the Spanish Civil War, fighting against Franco. All of them wanted to live as gunmen in Cuba. And capitalists, who earned their millions honorably through their work, couldn't defend their values and gave them a few pesos rather than see themselves in the hands of those bandits..."

"But if, as you have told us, Fidel was practically a criminal, why did the majority of the people give him their support?"

"Castro came to power because, as always, the communists began brainwashing people, saying that Cuban society was full of defects. In Cuba, as in the rest of the world, there were frustrated, marginalized classes, but Castro and communism manipulated them to get them on their side."

"Mr. Pérez, what do you think Cuba's future will be like?"

"Castro is a man worn out by power. Castro, who used to be able to promise the people a pound of rice, can't even give them a bit of bread now. He's worse than the slave owners, because even the slave owners gave the blacks a balanced diet. That's why Castro is going to fall. I say this with confidence; this isn't a utopian dream. We in the Foundation are working for this; we are organizing, and we know what we want; that's why the Helms-Burton Act is so important.

"I'll tell you something else, too: we're considering the possibility that Castro's already dead. I don't think he's still alive. We know that he has three doubles. And, if you don't know Castro and somebody tells you that that tall, bearded man is Castro, you believe it. But he's dead..."

"Mr. Pérez, you say that Fidel Castro is dead? Really, that..."

MS. PÉREZ: "But, Roberto, you shouldn't exaggerate. They may use doubles, and I believe they do, for security reasons, but the images you see on television — that's him... And, Roberto, pardon me, but they are interviewing me to talk about other things..."

At last, Pérez left...

"Ms. Pérez, we know that you are opposed to any dialogue with the Cuban Government. Why?"

"Well, it seems to me that those in favor of dialogue are naïve fools dreaming about nonsense. They may propose a dialogue to Fidel Castro, but why bother, if Castro's reaction is that no political changes will be made?"

"The meetings that have been held in Cuba haven't led and will not lead to anything positive, then?"

"That dictator held a conference in Cuba with a few exiles who believed his idiocies. During that conference, unfortunately, a woman lawyer from Miami — poor woman! — threw her arms around Castro, kissed him and told him he was her teacher. What melodrama! That's why, when she got back, the people threw eggs at her and even the people who worked for her denounced her. And then another exile, a former political prisoner..."

"Mr. Menoyo?"

"Everybody knows who he is... That man started saying good things about the dictator, because he'd had a drink with him. What crap! And what is the result of that foolishness? Have human rights been respected? Have they been allowed to express themselves? No. They've only been allowed to go where they like on the island, nothing more."

"Permit us to ask one last question. All over the world, Miami is synonymous with sunshine and beaches, but also with the Cuban exile community's violence. What is your opinion?"

"Look, I know that the European press and many politicians from there say that Miami's exile community is violent, but I don't have any respect for those statements. You can't deny that violent things have happened. They say that the exile community is reactionary because a bomb went off here in a museum or a radio announcer who proposed a dialogue with Castro had his legs blown off. But where's the person who set the bomb? Has any Cuban exile group been found guilty?

"One day the English-language papers here said it was intolerable that the exile community had put a bomb in a place from which packages are sent to Cuba. They also blamed it for an attack on the Centro Vasco, where that old hag Rosita Fornés was going to sing. She still dresses like an ingenue and looks so ridiculous that it makes no difference whether you hear her or not. She came here looking for trouble, because she still supports Castro's tyrannical regime."

"This is the other image of the exile community: aggressive intolerance. Look what happened to the world-renowned pianist Rubalcaba."

"Look, as a matter of principle, nobody should have anything against a pianist, but he's a Cuban who lives in the Dominican Republic and engages in propaganda, saying marvelous things about Cuba. And that is political work, which serves Castro's interests. Mr. Rubalcaba came to perform here in Miami, and around four people went by shouting, insulting him and trying to spit on him; they were going to fight with some members of the audience. But all they were doing was protesting against his being here, and it's legal to do that in a real democracy, such as in America. Then the English-language and European press said that the exiles were provocateurs and terrorists. Why didn't it occur to anybody that Castro's people had staged those actions? They benefited the tyrant more than anybody else."

"Excuse me, but pro-Cuban Government provocateurs or terrorists in the middle of Miami?! Moreover, it wasn't just one or two actions of this kind; it seems that there were a lot of them..."

"Well, anything is possible. Castro is very astute... "

5

Hubert Matos Benítez
President of
Independent and Democratic Cuba (CID)

"The French Ambassador in Washington told me that they wanted to have a foothold there, to get in on the ground floor, and that, for the time being, the investments would be small; later, after the Castro government had fallen, they would be large."

We rang the bell. We were going to ring again when we heard the sound of a lock being opened from inside. In a few steps, we crossed the front yard. We stopped in front of the door to the house. While we waited for it to be opened, we noted that there was a closed-circuit camera over our heads. It was as old as the first one we had noted at the other side of the house. A man opened the door. After we answered three or four questions, he led us to a large, modestly furnished meeting room. There were heavy iron bars on the windows to the street, which were high enough to make it difficult for anyone to look in.

We had been told to be there at 11:00 a.m. Time passed, and the man we were supposed to interview didn't come. The receptionist tried to entertain us, telling us everything he knew about the goodness of the capitalist system in Latin America. We had been waiting around 20 minutes when the President of Independent and Democratic Cuba (Cuba Independiente y Democrática, CID), a thin, gray-haired man wearing glasses and a suit and tie, appeared.

Hubert Matos Benítez spent 20 years in a Cuban jail after a revolutionary court sentenced him for conspiracy in 1959. He denies that he engaged in any attacks on the principles of the revolution, but he states categorically that he opposed the course taken by most of the leaders — which was only to be expected, as it went against his own interests. In the first half of 1958, Matos, a teacher and small landowner, joined the struggle against Batista — which was supported by the large landowners, bourgeoisie and reactionary clergy. Matos was promoted as a political leader in Oriente Province. He finally attained the rank of major, the highest in the revolutionary army.

On October 19, 1959, Matos — who headed the Rebel Army in

Camagüey Province at the time — staged an uprising with his men, claiming that there were communists in the government. Major Camilo Cienfuegos got him to surrender. A few days earlier, when the Trujillo conspiracy had been crushed, a letter had been found among the documents taken from the mercenaries which recommended that they contact Matos.

He was freed in 1979 and left for Costa Rica. Journalist Luis Manuel Martínez, a former supporter of Batista's, reported that, from that moment on, Matos "was in the CIA's hands."[1]

The next year, he moved to Venezuela, to found CID, for which purpose the U.S. Government gave him $200,000.[2] One of the organization's main purposes was to spread propaganda among the Latin American and European governments and political parties. That was nothing new; the CIA had already tried this, using other counterrevolutionaries, in the 1970s. Now, because the head of CID had been a Cuban major and a political prisoner, it might just work. At least, when he toured the Old Continent, the major media gave him good coverage.

One of his tasks that acquired tremendous importance was that of setting up La Voz del CID, a short-wave radio broadcasting station aimed at Cuba. In late 1997, nobody knew where its transmitters were, though they had been in the Dominican Republic and Costa Rica up until shortly before then.

Matos says that CID's activities are financed by contributions from its members, but this is hard to believe, both because there aren't very many of them and because they aren't very rich. The contributions which U.S. Government agencies have given to the organization publicly and legally aren't enough to cover its expenses. Among others, Jeff White — owner of Radio Miami International, a commercial station over which several counterrevolutionary groups broadcast to Cuba — has said that a large part of CID's money comes from the CIA.

Broadcasts to Cuba aren't anything new, however. Even though they violate all international agreements, the various U.S. administrations have produced, motivated or turned a blind eye to these broadcasts ever since the triumph of the revolution. Washington started using the mass media for political propaganda purposes and to complement its foreign policy as far back as the 1920s. Its strategy on Cuba was adapted to ideological and psychological warfare, and now those broadcasts are aimed at overthrowing the government.

In 1960, Radio Swan was set up as part of Operation 40, broadcasting

---

[1] Interview with Luis Manuel Martínez in Luis Báez, *Los que se fueron*.
[2] Ibid.

24 hours a day from an island off the Atlantic coast of Honduras. Its function was to slander the new Cuban Government and its nationalizations and expropriations. At the time of the Cuban Missile Crisis, broadcasts were stepped up from both legal and illegal stations controlled or financed by the CIA. After that perilous episode, with the United States ever more committed in wars in Southeast Asia, the pressure against the Cuban revolution eased.

That stage lasted until 1979, when the Carter Administration renewed the offensive. Radio broadcasts were increased again in 1981, when Ronald Reagan became president, reaching an average of 200 hours a day, broadcast over some 15 stations. That was when La Voz del CID was created, and it quickly took the lead (though only for a short while, because of the competition) in that seditious work.

In May 1980, a group of neoconservatives in the Republican Party gave candidate Ronald Reagan the Santa Fe Document, which contained the bases of what would be the U.S. Government's policy toward Latin America. In the chapter on Cuba, it said that Cuba had been a problem for the drafters of U.S. policy for more than two decades and that the problem was no closer to a solution than it had been in 1961 — to the contrary, it had increased, taking on truly dangerous proportions... One of the schemes proposed for solving the "problem" was to create a powerful radio station that would provide the Cuban people with "objective information." The station should have all possible resources so it could carry out its task, because, if propaganda failed, it would be necessary to wage "a war of liberation against Castro."

Once installed in the White House, Reagan created a committee in charge of doing what had been advised. Its members included Charles Wick, director of the United States Information Agency, and Cuban American Jorge Mas Canosa.[3] In late 1983, Reagan signed the Radio Broadcasts to Cuba Bill,[4] creating Radio Martí, which began its broadcasts on May 20, 1985. Paradoxically, the test broadcast was made from the antennas which the CIA had used in the 1960s to communicate with the special mission groups and agents it had infiltrated in Cuba. Radio Martí was an insult to the Cuban Government and people, not only because it invaded their territory but also because it used the name of a figure who had fought against Spain for Cuba's independence and sovereignty.

Jorge Mas Canosa was named Chairman of the Presidential Advisory

---

[3] Jean-Marc Pillas, *Nos agents à La Havane: Comment les Cubains ont ridiculisé la CIA* (Our Men in Havana: How the Cubans Have Made Fun of the CIA), (Paris: Ed. Albin Michel, 1995).

[4] Translated from the Spanish.

Board on Radio Martí. Ramón Mestre, one of the first directors of the radio's news service, had been militarily active in the Abdala group[5] and an official in the U.S. intelligence services. Now, he is a member of the Editorial Board of *El Nuevo Herald*.[6] But Mestre wasn't the only former member of Abdala in Radio Martí; "So were several department heads, reporters and advisers."[7]

Enrique Encinosa gives an idea of the role which that station was to play: "Hilda Inclán, of the news department, left Radio Martí accusing its directors of having violated federal laws and of having engaged in irresponsible journalism. Inclán complained that the radio company's news department was an Intelligence apparatus.

"Precisely, the Radio Martí news department had become the station's backbone. The 23 news employees interviewed 400 recent arrivals from Cuba every month, analyzing the information received to constantly update the broadcasts..."[8]

Radio Martí's competition was too much for La Voz del CID, especially since it had no way of getting $16 million a year, which was the government's station's approximate annual budget. La Voz del CID had pioneered with its programming and language. Now, warlike, vengeful messages were controlled.

Even though it left a lot to be desired in terms of professionalism, it did handle current issues of general interest, using a popular vocabulary that reached its listeners. Unquestionably, CID had been given good advice by experts on the pros and cons of radio subversion toward Cuba. But the official U.S. station copied and outdid it, and it also included "soaps," horoscopes and even advice to the lovelorn. The two stations had the same strategy: to sow doubt about the benefits of the revolution, what its leaders were doing and socialism's ability to solve economic and social problems and to undermine Fidel Castro's moral authority.

As part of that, the message in the programs over La Voz del CID and Radio Martí was readjusted, since it became absolutely necessary to motivate counterrevolutionary — or, as they began to be called, "dissident" or "independent" — groups in Cuba. The strategists of the Reagan Administration could see how much such groups were doing in

---

[5] Encinosa, *Cuba en guerra*.

[6] In June 1991, Cuban counterintelligence agent José Fernández Brenes returned to Cuba. Since 1988, he had been infiltrated in the TV Martí project. From there, he and others obtained detailed knowledge of the seditious activities that were promoted in Radio Martí. Ramón Mestre was his boss. Neither the U.S. Government nor any of the defendants were able to disprove Fernández Brenes's statements.

[7] Encinosa, *Cuba en guerra*.

[8] Ibid.

destabilizing the Eastern European countries, and they thought they might achieve similar results in Cuba.

This was implied in Santa Fe II, a Strategy for Latin America in the Decade of the 1990s,[9] which was made public in August 1988. In its ninth proposal, the document said that the United States should broaden its broadcasts to Cuba over the mass media as a means of civic education to create a democratic regime. A little farther along, it stated that, encouraged by Radio Martí, which had successfully broken "Castro's monopoly over information and propaganda," the internal opposition was growing.

Starting in 1992, La Voz de la Fundación, the radio station of CANF, joined in that seditious task. According to its Board of Directors, its first year's budget was $1.5 million — but it didn't say where the money had come from. The three stations had the same purpose. "For dissidents in Cuba and the small human rights groups which tried to catch public attention, Radio Martí was an umbilical cord, their direct line of information which might give those movements legitimacy."

Shortly after Bill Clinton took up residence in the White House, he implemented the provocatively named Cuban Democracy Act, which had been introduced by Democrat Representative Robert Torricelli, thus increasing the U.S. ideological influence and tightening its blockade of Cuba. In 1997, at least 20 broadcasting stations and radio ham operators beamed over 70,000 hours of illegal programs to Cuba, setting a record in the world's history of declared and undeclared wars.

CID has managed to get close to some high-ranking individuals in the U.S. political apparatus, such as Elliot Abrams, former Assistant Secretary of State for Inter-American Affairs. Up until recently, CID said it was working actively in some cities in the United States and Venezuela and had contacts in several other South American and European countries. Matos kept mentioning that CID was the first counterrevolutionary organization to have an office in Poland, which it opened when the Eastern bloc was on the verge of collapse. Like other sectors of the reactionary exile community that adhere to the policy drawn up in Washington, it has tried to destroy trade relations with Cuba.

At the same time, several people have dropped out of CID, claiming that it is inflexible and suffers from nepotism. It may be that the most serious problem CID has confronted arose when the Canadian police arrested several of its members, accusing them of trafficking in drugs.

In addition to being late, Hubert Matos told us he couldn't give us more than an hour for our interview, and then spent an hour and a half

---

[9] Translated from the Spanish.

giving us his version of why he had been arrested and tried in 1959. It was very difficult to pry him away from that subject, and we weren't there to hear about that. He answered our questions in three quarters of an hour while every so often — whether intentionally or involuntarily — letting us catch glimpses of the revolver he had stuck in his belt.

* * *

"Mr. Matos, what are the proposals that CID makes over its radio station to Cubans on the island? In addition, do you know if they are welcomed or not?"

"I can assure you that they are warmly welcomed. The Cubans who come from there or who call us have commented on that..."

"Excuse me, but the people at La Voz de la Fundación also told us that their programs are welcomed."

"But the Cubans from there have told us that there is a great difference, and they identify with us. They feel that Radio Martí is somewhat distant. Nor do they identify very much with La Voz de la Fundación. That's because we say what the people want to hear. Our purpose, which is very clear, is to broadcast a sincere message without hatred or vengeance. We tell the Cuban people that, logically, since Fidel will never allow change or leave power, he must be removed. And not only him — his brother and around 12 other people, too, because they're Cuba's main problem. How can it be done? Look, we use a slogan that sums up our goal: Power to the people in alliance with the military.

"We use La Voz del CID to tell the Cubans over there that the communist model of society has failed. And, since it doesn't work, it should be destroyed. Understand? That system denies freedom of expression and of religion, so it has smothered the Cuban people. The other thing they should do is undermine the present economic system, because the government shouldn't continue to have complete control over the economy."

"But it cannot be denied that..."

"Yes, I know what you're going to say. Yes, the system has provided education, medicine, housing and something to eat for many years, but the economic crisis has already ended that. This is why it must be removed. Now, multi-party freedom must be sought. And, as I told you, the alliance between the military and the people should take charge of those first steps toward the transition. That alliance will set up a Council of National Salvation. But, of course, the civilians will have more say on the Council than the military, beginning with those who have been in the resistance, both there and in exile."

"Do you think you will have a place on that transitional council you propose?"

"People have started saying that I may have aspirations within a new Cuban Government, but I've never wanted to take such a place. Of course, if CID — not necessarily Hubert Matos — is called upon to participate in that first stage, it should be there."

"You spoke of seeking 'multi-party freedom.' Following the current trend in world politics, that has become a synonym for elections. Don't you think, Mr. Matos, that, when it comes to elections of that kind, either now or in a post-revolutionary Cuba, the pro-U.S. organizations will have all the advantages for winning? Is this the kind of future you want for Cuba? Look what happened to Nicaragua."

"We and other organizations say that post-Castro Cuba won't be an American Cuba. Yes, you're right, some people here want Cuba to be like Puerto Rico — they're annexationists. We reject that. They may have many millions of dollars, but we can get them, too. We're working on that.

"CID knows that there will be great struggles in the post-Castro period, because some people will try to place their personal or group interests ahead of the public interest. But what's going to happen? No organization is going to go there and impose its will because it has more economic and political clout or closer relations with the United States. We aren't annexationists."

"We weren't talking about annexation."

"Naturally, we aren't against the United States — or Europe, either. Saying that we're very interested in political and economic support from the United States is something else. That's why we applauded the proposal that President Clinton made in early 1997 of giving from $4 billion to $8 billion in what he called the plan of assistance for transition in Cuba, which is included in the Helms-Burton Act. It's a contribution to the transition that, logically, will come when Castro and communism disappear. That's why it's so important that they do so. Moreover, we applauded that proposal because it should fall like a bomb on the head of the Revolutionary Armed Forces (Fuerzas Armadas Revolucionarias, FAR). For the first time, a U.S. administration has emphasized the positive role which Cuban military men can play in that transition."

"Don't you think that, if there were generalized discontent in the Revolutionary Armed Forces, there would have been a coup long ago, especially since it is known that the United States and Europe would support it immediately?"

"The thing is, the Castro brothers and the dozen others have manipulated, imprisoned and shot the military officers who oppose them. But, the time will come; it isn't far off..."

"We still have doubts, but let's go back to the earlier topic. Your statement about your need for U.S. economic and political backing, mainly..."

"No. Let me explain. In that first stage, we will need U.S. support, and that of Europe, too. One of my great worries is about what money we'll have for reactivating the economy. And, even though we're sure that the United States will support us, I've also gone to several Latin American and European countries to talk with bankers and government figures. I know the money will come from somewhere."

"*But you should know that loans or economic contributions inevitably mean political commitments.*"

"Yes, I know that that money, those contributions, may mean political commitments. Naturally, they won't be given to a new dictator. But the United States and Europe will support us, because the system that will be installed in post-Castro Cuba will be similar to those governments. If we're fighting for the same kind of free society as that in the United States, they will help us. There won't be any political commitment that infringes on our sovereignty."

"*Mr. Matos, we respect your point of view, but, in view of the economic, political and military dependence which nearly all of the Latin American, African and Asian countries and even those of the former Eastern European bloc have on the United States and Western Europe, we think you are too optimistic.*"

"But it won't be like that with us. Tell me: how many years was Cuba controlled by the Soviet Union?"

"*Analyzing things objectively, we would say that you can't compare what you suggest with the kind of relationship that existed between the Soviet Union, Cuba and the other countries of the Eastern European bloc. Those countries had more or less fair economic exchange.*"

"We can discuss what happened between the Soviet Union and Cuba later on. But you can be sure that, with us, Cuba won't lose its sovereignty. The Americans know that they'll come up against the resistance of the Cuban people, because they are very nationalistic..."

"*Mr. Matos, you can't deny that that high degree of nationalism, that great sense of sovereignty, which the Cuban people now have is the product of the revolution...*"

"Well, a part of the population was nationalistic before, too...

"But you shouldn't be afraid of strong economic commitments with the United States. If it proposes something that clashes with my concept of my nation's sovereignty, I won't accept it. No. We're going to treat the United States on a nation-to-nation basis. The new Cuba cannot allow the Americans to decide every two to five years if Cuba is democratic or not, because our sovereignty would be lost."

"*Mr. Matos, Mexico, Iran, Iraq and other countries that have more strategic resources than Cuba, have to let the United States make such shameful decisions about them every year and bow to its pretext of waging war on the traffic in drugs. How, then, could Cuba... ? But, anyway, do you think that the Cubans on the island will accept your statements, knowing that that nation has always wanted to annex their country?"*

"I've already told you that we won't accept any violation of our sovereignty, much less be another Puerto Rico.

"But I am sure that the people in Cuba and in the exile community are convinced that the United States is the best country in the world and that its institutions are the best ones on earth. All of them know that it is a successful society which gives opportunities to all. Here, all you have to do is make an effort, and you advance. Of course, not everything is good, and there are some unacceptable things... That's why we should achieve something basic: a trade alliance with this country. We should enter into a free trade agreement."

"Mr. Matos, let's continue. After the present Cuban Government has fallen, the Council of Salvation will be established, with CID as part of it. What are the first measures you would propose?"

"We've had a programmatic plan for that stage for several years. There, we will establish that no one can be evicted from his house, but we'll also guarantee that compensation is given to the former owners. The companies should be returned to their former owners. This is important, because it may facilitate the entry of hard currency and reinforce the economy.

"Moreover, whether or not they are there, Fidel Castro, his brother and a dozen other people should be tried for crimes committed against the Cuban nation.

"The foreign companies associated with the present Cuban Government should be taken over, because they are in virtual complicity with that tyranny. And those companies would be subject to the process of decentralization and privatization of the national economy which we propose."

"What role should the European Union play in that transition?"

"We would like Europe to play a very important role in the solution of Cuba's problems. I have always said that Europe lets Cuba do what it wants. The European countries forget that Cuba was their colony. That's why they — especially Spain — don't play the role which history has assigned to them. We are pleased by the concern that President Aznar of Spain has shown in seeking a solution for the Cuban problem.

"Before becoming President, Aznar came here and talked with the Foundation, with us and with other groups. He told us that, if he won the election, he would promote a new policy toward Cuba in the European Union. I also talked with José Salafranca, the deputy of Spain's People's Party to the European Union, who was interested in helping us. Moreover, I was received by Abel Matutes, Minister of Foreign Relations of that government. I told all of them that overthrowing the Castro tyranny would be in the interests of the Europeans, the Americans and ourselves. We can see from the way they have acted that they understood this."

"We know that you, other exile organizations and various agencies of the U.S. administration have held meetings with the boards of companies that want to invest in Cuba."

"That is so. We've told all of those gentlemen that we oppose their investing in Cuba in association with Fidel Castro. We told them that we couldn't offer them any security concerning those investments when the regime fell and that they would cause friction. Now, if they propose to give us economic assistance, we can negotiate. We have made it clear to all of them that the purpose of our visit was to warn them, not discuss investments.

"I have visited several governments or talked with their Ambassadors. For example, the French Ambassador in Washington told me that they wanted to have a foothold there, to get in on the ground floor, and that, for the time being, the investments would be small; later, when the Castro government had fallen, they would be large."

"And now for a final topic, Mr. Matos. What relations do you have with the groups of so-called internal dissidents? Is CID one of them?"

"Look, we support the dissidents. We do so independently if we coincide with their statements. We gave them our support when they were grouped in the Cuban Council. Moreover, this time they asked that a CID leader in Cuba take part publicly, but we told them that, if he appeared as a member of CID, he would be imprisoned. However, we agreed to participate under the name our movement has there, which is the Democratic Solidarity Party (Partido Solidaridad Democrática, PSD)."[10]

"How does CID function inside Cuba?"

"Our movement functions as a human rights organization. Many members of CID also belong to human rights groups which are very well known outside Cuba... I can't give you many details... They form underground CID cells..."

"Lastly, Mr. Matos, according to you, there is nothing good about the Cuban revolution, right?"

"The Cuban revolution has done something, but not so much —

---

[10] Héctor Palacio Ruiz, president of the group called the Democratic Solidarity Party, was one of the four national deputy delegates in the "structure" of the Cuban Council. Likewise, according to the List of Dissident, Opposition and Human Rights Organizations which counterrevolutionary organizations in Miami put out and distribute over Internet, Raúl Rivero and Héctor Peraza, who are described as "independent journalists," are also members of that tiny group.

naturally, except for education, health and its success in sports. But it hasn't done anything important for families. We must make use of all the technicians, professionals, scientists and skilled workers there are in Cuba..."

6

Francisco José ("Pepe") Hernández
President of the
Cuban American National Foundation

"The United States cannot allow the Europeans to give credits to the Cuban Government or to invest there easily. How could the Americans and we allow that to happen?"

Six months after having interviewed Ninoska Pérez and her husband, Roberto, we found ourselves again in the headquarters of CANF. Even though we had been given kind treatment, we once again felt the atmosphere to be rarefied and indescribable. It must be because, politically and in human terms, we couldn't accept the activities which that organization, the most powerful one in the reactionary exile community, has maintained against the Cuban Government and people. But we were determined to continue with our work, so there we were again. We felt the same with most of the people we interviewed, and not just in Miami.

We reached the large, cool office of Francisco José "Pepe" Hernández, President of CANF. We were interviewing him because we hadn't been able to get an interview with Jorge Mas Canosa, the Foundation's number-one man and Chairman of the Board. Some years back, Mas Canosa had decided to give almost no interviews to those who weren't in his circle of friends. This was because, according to him, interviewers always wound up twisting his words. He maintained that stand up to the day of his death.

OK. Right from the moment we asked Hernández our first question and he denied that the Reagan Administration had been the parent of CANF, we knew that he wouldn't tell us the truth, either.

When Ronald Reagan moved into the White House in January 1981, he restored to the CIA the international role that Congress had taken away from it in the mid-1970s because it had exceeded its powers. He also adopted the Santa Fe Document as the strategic design of his policy toward Latin America — which went down just fine with George Bush, his Vice-President and former head of the CIA, and with William Casey, the new director of the CIA, both of whom were obsessed with regaining power in Cuba and Nicaragua.

In the logic of the Reagan Administration, in order to overthrow the recently installed and popular Sandinista government, they would have to neutralize the Cuban Government — which they accused of being the basic prop of the former. Therefore, they felt that they should go ahead vigorously. But, in spite of its warlike mentality, the Reagan Administration was worried by the activities of the Cuban counterrevolutionaries. The bombs and deaths caused by the worldwide campaign against Cuba were still fresh in the people's memories.

According to several documents,[1] Roger Fontaine, one of the ideologues of the Santa Fe Document and the man in charge of Latin America on the National Security Council, suggested the possibility of creating a lobby in the U.S. Congress to justify the implementation of a

---

[1] In order not to overwhelm readers with the large number of references and so as to facilitate reading this report, we have combined the main information sources used in writing this introduction. Several directives of the National Security Council state that the Cuban American National Foundation (CANF) was a project of the Reagan Administration. Most of them have been declassified since the Iran-Contragate scandal. The declassified document Executive Directive 77, of 1983, treats with Project Democracy. Other research works on the topic include the following: Reinaldo Taladrid and Lázaro Barredo, *El chairman soy yo: La "verdadera" historia de Jorge Mas Canosa* (I Am the Chairman: The "True" History of Jorge Mas Canosa), (Ed. Trébol, 1994); Gaeton Fonzi published extensive articles on Mas Canosa and the Cuban American National Foundation in several U.S. publications. Fonzi worked as an investigator for special commissions of the U.S. Congress. Ann Louise Bardach published a long, well-documented report entitled "Who is Jorge Mas Canosa?" in *The New Republic*, October 1994, of Washington, DC. Journalist José Luis Morales published several articles on CANF and Mas Canosa, its leader, in *Interviú* magazine, of Madrid. Alvaro Vargas Llosa, *El exilio indomable: Historia de la disidencia cubana en el destierro* (Indomitable Exile: History of Cuban Dissidence in Exile), (Spain: Ed. Espasa-Hoy, 1998). The key document showing that part of the Nicaraguan contras' funding came from the traffic in drugs and what role many Cuban-U.S. citizens played in it, both in maintaining the clandestine network and for their own personal benefit, was *Drugs, Law Enforcement and Foreign Policy*, a report by the Subcommittee on Terrorism, Narcotics and International Operations of the U.S. Senate Foreign Relations Committee (the Kerry Commission), (Washington, DC: U.S. Government Printing Office, 1989). Other reports on the same topic include the following: Scott and Marshall, *Cocaine Politics*; Marshall, Scott and Hunter, *The Iran-Contra Connection: Secret Themes and Covert Operations in the Reagan Era* (Boston: Ed. South End, 1985); Leslie Cockburn, *Out of Control: The Story of the Reagan Administration's Secret War in Nicaragua. The Illegal Arms Pipeline, and the Contra Drug Connection* (New York: Atlantic City Monthly Press, 1987); Vegard Bye, *La Paz Prohibida*; La Contragate Connection (The Contragate Connection), Christie Institute, European information campaign on drugs, mimeographed, Paris, 1989. Gary Webb wrote a report for *The Mercury News* in August 1996 in which he stated that, in the 1980s, poor neighborhoods in Los Angeles and other cities in the United States were flooded with crack made from cocaine, which helped to finance the contras illegally.

more aggressive policy against Cuba. When the idea caught on, Casey presented a project in which he proposed creating a public relations structure that would convince the members of Congress to support the strategy that Reagan's advisers had drawn up. As had been the case since the Kennedy era, it wasn't to be related to the administration but would be an initiative and interest of the Cuban counterrevolution.

Carrying out a directive of the National Security Council, Richard Allen — a veteran of the CIA and Reagan's National Security Adviser — chose a small group of millionaires of Cuban origin to put the plan into effect. Coincidentally, all of the first 14 who were selected had been or were in the CIA. They included Raúl Masvidal, a banker and former member of Brigade 2506, and Carlos Salmán, who was linked to the Republican Party and was a close friend of the Bush family. Frank Calzón, a former leader of Abdala and the National Liberation Front of Cuba, both terrorist organizations, was its first Executive President. Even though he was under investigation for laundering money, Luis Botifoll, President of the Republic National Bank, was a member of the board. José Sorzano, a former member of the National Security Council, was another important figure in those first years.

Almost immediately, at Allen's request, Jorge Mas Canosa was made Chairman of the Board. He was chosen because of his ceaseless political activism and friendship — which Mas Canosa himself acknowledged — with Casey and Theodore Shackley, Deputy Director of Special Operations of the CIA.

That's how CANF began. Now, it is an "educational" monster that doesn't pay taxes, even though it has more than 100 rich directors, all on the extreme right, each of whom contributes between $5,000 and $50,000 a year.

Secret Executive Directive 77, known internationally as Project Democracy, which Reagan signed in January 1983, catapulted the Foundation's objectives. When the Iran-Contragate scandal was aired at the end of 1986, it was learned that the Project had two branches: one legal and the other underground. The former, which had Congressional approval, was called the National Endowment for Democracy and was supervised by an official of the CIA's Special Operations Department. Even though it was described as a private, nonprofit corporation, its funds were approved in the federal budget and channeled through structures of the Republican and Democratic Parties and such nongovernmental organizations as Freedom House, the Puebla Catholic Institute and the American Institute for Free Labor Development. The Agency for International Development, the United States Information Agency and other mechanisms of U.S. public diplomacy complemented its work.

The National Endowment for Democracy was institutionalized as a program for funneling money to organizations that promoted democracy abroad. It channeled large amounts of money that, in the past, had been supplied through the CIA or in other clandestine ways to political forces, human rights and "humanitarian" organizations, and the media. According to the law, NED isn't allowed to hand over funds for lobbying or propaganda aimed at influencing the public policy decisions of the U.S. Government, but it has always done precisely that. In 1988, it was discovered — without any legal consequences for those responsible — that it had donated $390,000 to CANF. As an interesting coincidence, the Foundation had "donated" an identical amount to politicians who supported attacks on the Cuban Government.

NED turned over several million dollars for the Foundation's many projects. Moreover, as a privileged partner, the Foundation has frequently served as intermediary in passing large sums on to other counterrevolutionary organizations, not only in Miami but also in Europe and Cuba. And, in almost all of those cases, it was to finance "human rights" campaigns.

With that support, the Foundation quickly became a monster that devoured everything that went counter to its interests and took over nearly everything that was proposed inside the United States. Several analysts say that its success is due to three aspects.

First, it is an apparatus at the service of Washington's policy, which in many cases goes beyond the Cuban sphere, as happened in the cases of Angola and Nicaragua.

Second, it has become a past master at lobbying — which, in the United States, is the art of greasing the palms of key politicians in Congress. Republican Congressmen have been its favorites, but no expense has been spared when it needed the Democrats, too, as happened with those who voted for the Torricelli Bill. Bill Clinton was given close to $400,000 for his war chest the first time he ran for president, when he pledged he would support that bill. In later declarations, Mas Canosa stated that the president had received at least $2 million during his reelection campaign, even though the official figures note only $400,000.

And the third aspect of the Foundation's success is that, when money, political and personal contacts don't do the trick, it doesn't jib at engaging in blackmail, threats and paramilitary actions.

Let's take a look at some typical cases, which show how the Foundation works.

In October 1976, a Cubana de Aviación plane was dynamited off the coast of Barbados. Orlando Bosch and Luis Posada Carriles were arrested in Venezuela, accused of being responsible for the crime. Both had had key roles in the worldwide war against Cuba. In February 1988, Orlando Bosch was freed and went to Miami, even though the FBI had a standing order for his arrest. After two years' imprisonment, he was released on parole. An editorial in *The New York Times* stated that, though the United States had sent planes to bomb Libya and the army to invade Panama in the name of the war on terrorism, now the Bush Administration had freed one of the most notorious terrorists in the Americas. It went on to ask rhetorically why Bush had done this and said that the only possible reason was that he wanted to get in good with southern Florida.

According to reports of the FBI, which didn't want him to be freed, Bosch wasn't just any old criminal, but the worst one of all. While he was in prison, the U.S. authorities put out feelers to see if he could be deported, but Cuba was the only country that was willing to take him — to put him on trial.

Several mass media pointed out that the Attorney General had issued the order to free him due to "political pressures." Where had they come from? Individuals such as Monsignor Román, Congressman Lincoln Díaz-Balart and the directors of the Foundation used their political contacts on the terrorist's behalf. His main champion was Ileana Ros-Lethinen, a Republican Cuban American Congresswoman who even included his release as part of her electoral campaign. The Foundation poured a lot of money into her campaign, and Jeb Bush, son of the U.S. President at the time, was her campaign manager. Jeb not only has headed work teams in CANF but also has business relations with its members.

Now, let's look at what happened with Posada Carriles. He escaped mysteriously in 1985. In 1994, while he was still wanted by the Venezuelan, Cuban and U.S. authorities, *Los caminos del guerrero* (The Paths of the Warrior) was published in Miami. In that biography, he acknowledged the immense "financial and moral" support that the leaders of the Foundation had given him in prison, for his flight and for his subsequent transfer to El Salvador. In that Central American country, he joined in the clandestine work of supporting the Nicaraguan contras.

In one section of the book, he said that, two days after arriving there, "Dr. Alberto Hernández visited me... A group of very important people from Miami, who included Jorge Mas, Feliciano Foyo and Pepe Hernández, created a 'pool' to meet my economic needs... They sent me enough money to keep me going; it came in monthly installments..." It should be noted that Alberto Hernández has been Deputy Chairman; Foyo, Treasurer; and "Pepe" Hernández, Executive President of the Foundation.

What Posada didn't say is that, according to the records of the

Venezuelan police, Mas Canosa, Gaspar Jiménez and Rolando Mendoza were negotiating his release. Later, the last two had to leave the Foundation (when their involvement in the traffic in drugs became too public); they next surfaced as Alberto Hernández's bodyguards.

In November 1996, Channel 23 interviewed Posada Carriles while he was in hiding and broadcast the results in two sections. Over that station, whose relations with the Foundation and other extremely reactionary circles are well known, he called for new terrorist actions to be carried out against Cuba.

At the time, he was working on precisely that. He played a key role in setting off a series of bombs in Cuba between April and September 1997. As Cuban authorities announced and was confirmed by an extensive investigation that was published in the November 16 edition of *El Nuevo Herald*, Posada Carriles was "the key link" in the series of attacks on tourist centers. He recruited both Raúl Ernesto Cruz León (the man who actually set the bombs) and his accomplices in El Salvador and saw to it that $15,000 was raised in Miami for their expenses. The Salvadoran terrorist, who was captured by the Cuban police, stated that the Foundation had put up the most money for him and that its top leaders were in direct contact with Posada Carriles.

But, going back a little, to follow events chronologically, it was no coincidence that, when Posada Carriles escaped from prison in Venezuela, he headed straight for El Salvador. The Foundation and other counterrevolutionary organizations were active there in the second, clandestine branch of Project Democracy, which Colonel Oliver North — following the instructions of the National Security Council — was coordinating from Washington, DC. That branch would support the dirty war against Nicaragua's Sandinista government both logistically and financially. Félix Rodríguez was one of the powers in Central America, working out of the Ilopango Military Base, in El Salvador. From there, the CIA coordinated its supplies of weapons and other materiel for the mercenary contras.

This base was also used by planes taking loads of cocaine and marijuana to the United States — drugs that were purchased from the Colombian Mafia cartels. However hard to imagine, since nearly all the mass media in the world kept repeating that the administration was waging total war on the traffic in drugs, those were the facts.

The investigation by the U.S. Senate's Kerry Commission showed that Reagan and Bush were fully aware of the drug traffic that began in Bolivia and Colombia, passed through Central America and arrived in Miami, where the drugs were distributed to other cities to be sold. It was the most serious aspect of the Iran-Contragate scandal, but, since Richard Nixon's head had just rolled, it wasn't the moment for any other president or vice-president of the world's "first great democracy" to fall; that was simply unthinkable.

Ramón Milián Rodríguez, a Cuban-U.S. citizen who laundered money for the Colombian Mafia, admitted to the Senate commission that, carrying out the orders given him by Félix Rodríguez, he had turned over around $10 million to the contras between 1983 and 1985. Members of CANF had served as contacts between the two men. Félix Rodríguez, to whom Bush had presented the CIA's highest award in 1976, denied it and was believed, even though Milián Rodríguez was far from a nobody — he had donated $180,000 (which "friends" in Colombia had provided) to Reagan's first presidential campaign and had been invited to attend his inauguration.

Jorge Mas Canosa was also called to appear before the Kerry Commission. His personal telephone numbers, dates of meetings and notes on his movements through Central America had been found in Colonel North's pocket diary. In that investigation, as in others made by journalists, it was shown that Mas Canosa had been to the Ilopango Base several times. The number-one man at the Foundation declared that he had simply given "humanitarian assistance to the contras."

The Executive President of the Foundation — the person we were interviewing — was also involved in the mercenary war to "free" Nicaragua, accompanied by friends who were far from exemplary citizens. As reported by Enrique Encinosa in *Cuba en Guerra*, "the Cuban exile community, which supported the opposition forces, gave considerable assistance to the Nicaraguan contras... Francisco José 'Pepe' Hernández and René Corvo... fought actively on the guerrilla front." It should be recalled that the FBI and the Kerry Commission accused Corvo, a former member of Abdala, of having taken part in the traffic in weapons and drugs for the contras, and he had admitted to having done the former.

All of the investigations brought out the fact that the CIA had sent many Cuban-U.S. citizens to El Salvador as advisers to the nascent apparatus, starting as soon as Reagan took office. Others were sent to Honduras, apparently to provide medical assistance to the mercenaries. Alberto Hernández, Deputy Chairman of the Foundation, had a lot of responsibility in that area and in the military aspect. He was experienced in that kind of support, for he had served in UNITA's reactionary force in Angola in the mid-1970s.

In any case, the criminal acts of the clandestine branch of Project Democracy were nothing new. They were simply adaptations of the undercover operations that the CIA had carried out in Southeast Asia.

In January 1990, the members of the Board of Directors of CANF were given copies of a confidential document signed by Jorge Mas

Canosa which outlined "the tactics to follow so that the Foundation will receive full credit from the entire exile community, our captive brothers and sisters on the island, the U.S. Government and the rest of the governments and peoples in the free world, which will enable us to play the important protagonist role which should be ours in the new Cuba." Since word of its contents got out, it has been shown that a large part of its directives have been implemented. For example:

> Organize tours of the member countries of the European Economic Community, of Eastern Europe and of Latin America and the Caribbean, to present ourselves as a belligerent force in the Cuban conflict...
>
> Form a task force that will maintain systematic contacts with the National Security Council, the Central Intelligence Agency and the Federal Bureau of Investigation, so as to guarantee, now more than ever before, a sense of identification with the policy and actions to be carried out against the Stalinist government of Cuba, a greater exchange of intelligence information and the necessary economic support for implementing our plans...
>
> Set up a task force that will systematize and deepen our working relations with the State Department, so that, together, we will draw up and develop new international policy plans that correspond to the current situation... José Sorzano and Armando Valladares will be the chairman and deputy chairman of the task force, respectively, and Ambassador Jeanne Kirkpatrick will be its special adviser...[2]
>
> Create a task force whose main responsibility will be to get our Martí television on the air. At the same time, it will carry out joint plans and studies with the United States Information Agency and the Voice of America so that, in the immediate future, the programming of Radio Martí and TV Martí may be integrated with the radio and television stations already under our control, together with others that we will acquire in the near future... It will carry out studies and make proposals to neutralize or modify the positions of journalists and newspapers which, over the years, have been important opponents of the Foundation's line...[3]
>
> Create another task force that will be responsible for neutralizing those individuals and/or organizations that claim for themselves or try to prevent the Foundation from assuming the leadership it has won...

[2] Author's note: It may well be that these people are no longer serving in those posts.
[3] Author's note: The names given in the document include those of Spanish mass media and Spanish citizens.

Our watchword will be to buy those who can be bought and, in the case of those who don't understand anything but the language of violence, to speak to them in their own language.

Nothing and nobody can make us hesitate; we don't seek it, but, if blood must flow, it will flow.[4]

Jorge Mas Canosa died on November 23, 1997. All of the leaders of the exile community, both in the United States and in Europe, who had been confronted with his arrogance and political intransigence, then acknowledged his merit for having piloted them safely through the shoals of U.S. political life and for having turned the Cuban American community into "a powerful pressure group in Washington." President Clinton — who, only a few days earlier, had admitted in Argentina that CANF was his guide on Cuba — said that Mas Canosa had been a powerful voice calling for Cuba's freedom.

There was talk of the exile community's being orphaned, since no "moral and political" successor to Mas Canosa could be clearly seen. Some believed that the hard-fought, violent struggles for top leadership would be resumed. Others, more optimistic, bet that the moderate positions, including those of the "dialoguers," could gain a lot of ground. The majority, who didn't know the ins and outs of the policy which Washington was implementing against Cuba, believed that the Foundation had been created and grown to prominence because of Mas Canosa's activism. Unquestionably, he had imbued it with his authoritarian dynamism, wrapped up in wisdom, but the main thing, as we have already pointed out, is that CANF, like the other organizations of the recalcitrant exile community, has been a project of the U.S. political leadership, which still dreams of annexing Cuba.

As Carlos Alberto Montaner told the Spanish press, "Mas Canosa's death won't mean any change in U.S. policy, because it is irreducible against the Castro regime."

But let's get back to our subject. "Pepe" Hernández left Cuba in 1960, fleeing from the revolution. He immediately got involved with the Student Revolutionary Directorate (Directorio Revolucionario Estudiantil, DRE), an influential Catholic organization that the CIA used to carry out propaganda tasks — and, on occasion, acts of terrorism. As is reported in *Indomitable Exile*, he was given "a two-week crash course" in sabotage techniques and even in "how to kill a man with a piece of wire" before the CIA infiltrated him in Cuba.

He recalled that, in Cuba, "We carried out several attacks and other actions against the regime, including kidnapping a university professor

---

[4] Author's note: Boldface in the original.

and doing things related to assassination attempts." On his return, he was sent to Guatemala, to one of the camps where the CIA was training the mercenaries who would go on the Bay of Pigs invasion. He landed in Cuba as a member of Brigade 2506 and was captured by Cuba's Rebel Army a few hours later. After being freed, he joined the U.S. Navy, in which he rose to the rank of captain. At Fort Benning, he met Mas Canosa again. After completing that first course, he was sent to the Marine intelligence school at Quantico, Virginia. Because of his abilities and dedication, he was assigned to intelligence work at the Pentagon, under Alexander Haig, who was a lieutenant colonel at the time.

During the war that France and especially the United States waged against the Indo-Chinese peoples, he was sent to Cambodia, where he was put in charge of a unit that interrogated prisoners. Back in the United States, still as a military man, he renewed his collaboration with the groups of Cuban counterrevolutionaries who were carrying out acts of terrorism against Cuba. As he reported, he was particularly helpful to them by giving them training. In 1965, he also took part in the U.S. invasion of Santo Domingo. As usual, he worked mainly in intelligence.

Later, still as a Marine, he went to university. On the conclusion of his studies, in or around 1973, he set up Agrotec Internacional, a company for processing agricultural products, and settled permanently in Miami. The company began working in "a lot of countries, including some in Africa." Hernández didn't say where the money for all this had come from, though he did note that he had two partners: a veterinarian and a nutritionist.

The current president of CANF says that he never let his activities as a businessman interfere with certain special contacts he maintained in Washington:

> Throughout that phase of the expansion of my business, I also had some relations with the American intelligence services. There are services that independent U.S. businesses, private companies, carry out voluntarily for the intelligence agencies of the United States... The system works this way: if you're going to go to Africa and have business in Egypt, Kenya or Nigeria — and I had business in all those countries — and you can help, you do them a good turn by doing so. I gave them what, in intelligence terms, is called 'cover.' I provided cover for some people who worked on their own [for the intelligence services], but they're linked to the companies in one way or another... There are hundreds of companies that can do that all over the world, and they do it quite frequently.

At the beginning of the 1980s, large numbers of Cubans left through the port of Mariel, and businessman Hernández took an active part in welcoming them. "I personally once more put my training in intelligence matters into practice and interrogated them... I had a group of specialists who questioned them in depth. During the interrogations, we decided just who those people were... We did that work in coordination with the FBI. It lasted for around two or three months..."

Almost right from the beginning, as soon as it was a project, Hernández took part in CANF. In *Indomitable Exile*, he named names, stating how people at high levels in the State Department and CIA and even important members of Congress during the Reagan Administration were involved in the Foundation's creation and later development. But then Hernández clammed up, claiming he didn't know who was behind the project and responsible for it: "I don't know exactly who had the original idea, because everything was very hazy at the beginning and there's been a lot of wild talk." Undoubtedly, he could contribute an enormous amount of information, based on his contacts: "Some of my best friends throughout this process have been people who have risen to very high positions in the CIA."

In 1991, he was elected president of CANF. Hernández isn't as good at talking as you would expect from someone in his position. He gave very short answers, and getting him to say anything was like pulling teeth. As we said, after his first answer, we decided not to go deeply into any more burning issues. For example, we had to bite our tongues to keep from asking him why the brothers Ignacio and Guillermo Novo had become connected with the Foundation's public relations and information commission, as *The New York Times* of November 27, 1990, had reported. Wasn't he aware of their background as terrorists and traffickers in drugs? We didn't dare. Rather, we contented ourselves with his version of more general topics.

"Pepe" Hernández has a very delicate court case — brought by the FBI — hanging over him in Puerto Rico. He is accused of having been involved in the preparations for an assassination attempt against President Fidel Castro that was supposed to have been carried out during the Ibero-American Summit that was held in Venezuela in late 1997. Even though Hernández hasn't been arrested, six other Cuban counterrevolutionaries have, including José Antonio Llama, another member of the boards of CANF and of the Hispanic Cuban Foundation, of Spain.

Ever since the death of Jorge Mas Canosa, Hernández has been the big chief of CANF. As such, he tried to bring "international lawsuits against Fidel Castro and his accomplices, charging them with genocide," in the Spanish courts in November 1998.

A few months before Mas Canosa's death, "Pepe" Hernández

commented, "Without a doubt, Jorge is a man with a very authoritarian character; that is, he likes to impose his will." A little farther on in *Indomitable Exile*, he acknowledged, "I'm probably more authoritarian than he is."

* * *

"Mr. Hernández, why was the Cuban American National Foundation created?"

"People say that the Foundation was an initiative of the Reagan Administration, but that isn't so. Look, starting in 1978, interest was expressed by a series of elements, mainly inside the United States, for there to be a rapprochement between the two countries. That is, they wanted the embargo to be lifted. And a group of us in the exile community decided to oppose that situation, because it wouldn't be right to give legitimacy to that regime. That's how the Foundation was created, without anything to do with Reagan or the State Department."

"It can be said that the Cuban American National Foundation came into the world with immense power — so much that it has shouldered the other organizations in the exile community aside. How do you explain this?"

"Nobody knows why one organization develops and prevails over the others. It may be because of its founders' intelligence or its economic resources or because of the clarity of its principles. But the fact is that the Foundation was born with a very effective understanding of how the U.S. political system works. In general, we have been people who, for various reasons, have been in direct contact with politics in this country, and we know how flexible and malleable it is. After the Jewish community, the Cuban exile community has been the minority that has been most successful in penetrating that system. Therefore, we wanted to learn from the Jewish community. And, therefore, we don't deny that we were — not trained, but encouraged and directed by Jewish-American activists in the first few years.

"The other Cuban exile groups have never made much effort to take their concerns and interests to Washington. They all believed they would have repercussions in Congress or the White House if they shouted and held demonstrations in Miami. We decided to set about influencing U.S. politics, and Washington was the ideal place for doing that.

"Of course, we didn't limit ourselves to that city. That's why we went to Moscow before the Soviet Union collapsed and brought in Russians. We invited Boris Yeltsin in 1989, when he was still Mr. Nobody. And Mas Canosa went to Poland with Armando Valladares to meet with Lech Walesa. The result was that the Soviet Union's and the socialist bloc's economic and military assistance to the Castro regime was cut off.

"The Foundation's influence can be attributed to a modus operandi that hadn't been used before. But, above all, it is due to the fact that we struggle with the truth. Even Rev. Jesse Jackson, a Congressman who used to be totally opposed to us, wound up supporting us. When Mas Canosa testified in the U.S. Congress in March 1994 about human rights violations in Cuba, Jackson went up to him and said he wanted to be his friend and the friend of the free Cubans."

"But it is said that CANF has influenced both Congress and the White House because it is a 'millionaires' club' that hands out money to politicians."

"I'm not going to waste my time defending the Foundation against that bullshit. This isn't a millionaires' club. Of course — and we haven't tried to hide this — the men on the Board of Directors have been very successful in economic terms and, therefore, make extremely large contributions. It's difficult to find — in any Latin American country and in the historic process of the Cuban exile community — others who have been so successful who have dedicated their time and money to trying to restore their country's freedom. I believe that, in the not too distant future, the Cuban people will feel proud of them."

"Mr. Hernández, one of the comments you hear most frequently about the directors of the Foundation is that their most cherished ambition is to head a post-revolutionary government."

"That's just more crap. First of all, we aren't a political party; we want to free our people. Of course, if, after driving communism out of Cuba, some of us are elected to important posts in the new government, that will be because we deserve it, as anybody else may..."

"Excuse me for interrupting, but it seems that the Cuban American National Foundation hasn't ruled out the possibility of entering Cuba with U.S. support."

"How ridiculous! How time is wasted! Right from the beginning, we've shown that we listen to the Cuban people, not the U.S. Government. We are sure that, if it hadn't been for the Foundation, the U.S. Government would already have negotiated with Castro. If you look at our transition plan, which was drawn up for when we can go back, you'll see that we don't proclaim that Cuba should be another Puerto Rico. But it is true that Cuba is a nation privileged to be 90 miles from the United States — and, therefore, there may be cordial, friendly economic relations leading to the opening of our markets. What we say is that the relations between Cuba and the United States cannot be normalized until there is democracy."

"Mr. Hernández, you used the term 'transition'..."

"The transition in Cuba began mentally some time ago, when those in the spheres of power, within the regime, realized that Castro's intransigence was an obstacle to coming to an agreement with the

United States. Castro wants to come to an understanding with the Americans without losing any power or freedoms. We know that there is a circle, even in the armed forces, that knows that Castro isn't going to save Cuba. And we're ready to come to an understanding with those who are in power and who agree to giving the Cuban people freedoms again."

"Mr. Hernández, what have been CANF's greatest achievements over the years?"

"Basically, we've publicized what is really happening in Cuba and to Cubans all over the world. We have had a great many successes in this, which it would take me too long to list, but one of the main ones is Radio Martí and TV Martí. This gave a great boost to the Foundation. We've also moved in other spheres, such as that of humanitarian assistance, helping needy Cubans, which has given us a lot of influence in the exile community. We have also had a series of projects, such as the Martí Mission, whose members are being trained as a peace corps for when the country is liberated. We've trained more than 2,000 young Cubans in the Martí Mission, preparing them to go and help reconstruct the country for a year or two. We have the Human Rights in Cuba Foundation (Fundación para los Derechos Humanos en Cuba, FDHC), with which we've gone to the Human Rights Commission in Geneva seven times.

"As you can see, the Foundation has moved in various spheres, but the only thing you hear about is its political work, such as the Torricelli and Helms-Burton Acts, in which — we aren't going to deny it — we've had substantial participation."

"Now that you mention it, because of the possibility that the United States will apply the Helms-Burton Act decisively and that it may adversely affect its relations with the countries of the European Union, Cuba has once more become a topic of discussion..."

"Yes, we know that interest in the Cuban problem has increased in Europe. That was one of our goals; that's why the Helms-Burton Act was passed. If the European investors didn't understand when it was explained to them nicely, they had to be taught in another way. The Europeans can't go on sending their investors to reap the benefits of and steal what doesn't belong to them. If they go on doing that, they'll have to take the consequences — now, from the Americans, and later, in freed Cuba, from us."

"But it seems that President Clinton wants to negotiate with the European governments on the thorniest points."

"It may be that the Clinton Administration and the Europeans will negotiate, but don't forget that that would have to be approved by the U.S. Congress. And it isn't going to repeal that law. We've managed to take U.S. policy on Cuba out of the hands of the administrations, which change every four years. Now, the only ones who can lift the embargo are the true representatives of the U.S. people, not the president, and that triumph was achieved by the Cuban exile community.

"The fact is that Europe must choose between the United States and Castro. The Europeans aren't about to fight with the Americans, and they know perfectly well that they can't be good friends of both. The English have told us this. The United States cannot allow the Europeans to give credits to the Cuban Government or to invest there easily. How could the Americans and we allow that to happen?"

"Mr. Hernández, does the Foundation have representatives in any European countries?"

"We have representatives in Prague, Moscow and Spain. We are in those countries to prevent the establishment of governmental relations that favor the Castro regime. Moreover, the Board of Directors has also decided to open another office, in Brussels. We are in that process. We know that work in Europe is different, but we're learning. And, as the Foundation, we will do it well. Right now, it's very important to be in the European Union to guide the Europeans to opposing the Cuban regime."

"In any case, you've already managed to get a firm foothold in Spain, both because of your closeness to the People's Party and through the Hispanic Cuban Foundation."

"Yes, we have very good relations with the PP [People's Party]. We don't deny it. But we don't have anything to do with the Hispanic Cuban Foundation. Naturally, acting as individuals, some other directors of CANF and I are on its board, which they call the *patronato*. But it's headed by Spaniards. Moreover, there are people in the Hispanic Foundation — such as Elizardo Sánchez — with whom we disagree regarding methods of struggle. But, in general, we all agree that we want freedom for the Cuban people."

"It seems to us that you support the work that President Clinton's Special Ambassador for Cuban Affairs is doing..."

"We respect and support his work. He's done a very good job with the Canadian and European nongovernmental organizations. He keeps insisting that they not accept the conditions that the Cuban Government lays down for their being there. Also, we know that he has been welcomed by some NGOs in Spain, France and Holland. We will complement his work; we're already approaching a dialogue with those organizations, seeking mutual support."

"Mr. Hernández, one final question. What relations does CANF have with the so-called internal Cuban dissident movement?"

"Over the years, we have supported and encouraged the dissident movement. Above all, through human rights work. The Foundation was one of the first organizations to begin that work there, and we convinced them that they should concentrate on human rights issues, mainly because it's a very noble cause that is viewed very kindly throughout the world. They have done that, and you can see the good results: all over Europe, there is talk of Cuban dissidents for human rights. We must keep on insisting on that, so that those groups and other kinds of dissidents, such as the independent journalists, play the key role that those in the Soviet Union and Poland had in overthrowing the regime. That is basic.

"La Voz de la Fundación and Radio Martí have done an excellent job in helping to organize them and in telling them about our goals and helping them to find the path of freedom.

"The dissidents know that we are with them and that the Europeans have begun to support them. They know that, in Holland, Germany and Spain, there are NGOs that uphold their human rights work and that, in Spain and Paris, Reporters Without Frontiers (Reporters Sans Frontières, RSF) has decided to help the independent journalists.

"Therefore, the dissident movement in Cuba is ever more encouraged and is challenging the regime."

7

Ramón Cernuda

Art collector and overseas representative of the Coordinating Body of Human Rights Organizations in Cuba (CODHC)

"I believe that there isn't an official policy of torture in Cuba."

The 1980s "will be remembered in the annals of the anti-Castro opposition as the era of struggle for human rights and the effective use of telecommunications to confront the regime."[1] That's right. But the story seems to be more complex.

Going back a bit, although we don't have any references which state whether it was acting on its own initiative or on the instructions of the CIA, it was the terrorist group Abdala that began to beat the human rights drum as an ideological element of war. By the end of the 1970s and early 1980s, even though it had been a "vital part of the Cuban American National Foundation's armed struggle," it was "the members of Abdala who represented the exile community in international forums, creating human rights committees."[2]

However, it was the Reagan Administration that initiated the detailed, calculated campaign. All possibilities were made feasible and concentrated so that the Cuban Government would be questioned in large international forums for supposed human rights violations. This may have been contained in Executive Directive 77. The Directive allowed the National Security Council to coordinate interagency efforts, overtly or covertly supporting groups anywhere on earth, which were viewed favorably by Washington or whose goals coincided with Washington's — in this case, of destroying the Cuban system.

Although this was a U.S. Government plan, it was the Christian Democratic International, whose headquarters are in Brussels, which pioneered in having its Miami group engage in lobbying. For that purpose, it got José Ignacio Rasco, the former leader of the Revolutionary Cuban Council, former member of Alpha 66 and former CIA agent, to resurrect the Christian Democratic Movement and for it to participate in international organizations. The campaign for the freeing

---

[1] Encinosa, *Cuba en guerra.*
[2] Ibid.

of former Batista policeman Armando Valladares was a dry run. Very soon, other counterrevolutionary organizations, such as Democratic and Independent Cuba, the Cuban American National Foundation and the Cuban Democratic Platform — this last in Madrid — joined it.

As apparent proof of how effective its strategy was, the Eastern bloc collapsed at the end of the 1980s. Everyone expected that Cuba, isolated in the Caribbean, would follow suit in a matter of weeks or months once its privileged partners had gone under, but nothing happened. Even though egging on the creation of all kinds of organizations that opposed the government was already a basic part of the destabilizing plan, it was stepped up threefold at that moment, directing those who had first raised the banner of human rights. The U.S. strategists and their allies had already proved its effectiveness: "The success scored by human rights movements in communist countries had been based on their single emphasis on human rights, so they couldn't be accused of being belligerent elements of the opposition."[3]

In the introduction to our interview with Mr. Hernández, we described the political ins and outs of the National Endowment for Democracy (NED). Now, let's look at a few examples of its financial support for counterrevolutionary organizations that began to raise the flag of human rights and democracy in Cuba in the specific situation that was created in 1990-93. We base our comments on the National Endowment for Democracy's own reports.

As has already been said, NED's main recipient was CANF.

Freedom House received $30,000 to publish four books with runs of 5,000 each. They were to be given to seditious elements in Cuba, to be distributed among the people.

The Cuban Committee for Human Rights, represented in Miami by Ricardo Bofill and headed in Cuba by the brothers Gustavo and Sebastián Arcos, received $30,000 in 1990, through the Foundation. The next year, it got $44,000 directly. That money was used for distributing counterrevolutionary information and paying for its members' trips to Spain, Italy, France and Russia.

The Republican Party's International Affairs Institute received $80,000 for a conference sponsored by CANF. Government officials and professors from the former Soviet Union, Czechoslovakia, Hungary and the United States attended, as well as exponents of the most reactionary sector of the exile community. The main topic was how to bring about changes in Cuba and how to channel systematic support to the "dissident" groups. Part of the conference was broadcast to Cuba over Radio Martí.

---

[3] Ibid.

At the end of 1992, Carl Gershman, director of the National Endowment for Democracy, reported an increase in funds for this kind of activity. Above all, he announced that there was more support for the internal counterrevolution. Making no bones about it, he said that tourism would be used as a means for sending money and counterrevolutionary propaganda into the country, as had been done in the Soviet Union and Poland.

Ratifying what the director of NED had proposed, President Clinton adopted the recommendations of Donald E. Schulz, of the Institute of Strategic Studies of the War College of the U.S. Army, linked to the contents of the Torricelli Act. This included promoting interpersonal contacts between Cuban and American citizens by means of correspondence, telephone, transportation services and tourism; promoting cultural and scientific exchanges; and setting up press offices. It also included helping dissident elements to communicate openly.[4]

Under the Helms-Burton Act, governmental and private sources began supplying the counterrevolution with abundant political and economic support. For example, in early December 1997, Helms himself used his power as Chairman of the Senate Foreign Relations Committee to demand that an allocation of nearly $2 million be turned over as quickly as possible to several "human rights" organizations which sought to "foment democracy" in Cuba. Thus, the ultraconservative Association of Former Cuban Landowners (Asociación de Ex-Hacendados Cubanos, AEHC) received $800,000 to enable its recently created Institute for Cuba's Democracy (Instituto por la Democracia de Cuba, IDC) to send materials and grant "aid" to the internal counterrevolution.

Frank Calzón was given $500,000 through the Free Cuba Center to continue promoting civil society in Cuba.

The International Foundation of Electoral Systems was given $136,000 so it would make an analysis of the technical challenges of "free elections in Cuba."

Ernesto Betancourt, the former head of Radio Martí, received $110,000 to finance a poll of Cuban travelers when they arrived in the United States.

The extent of the illogic of all this is shown by the fact that Section 109 of the Helms-Burton Act recognizes the "right" of the United States to contribute morally, financially and materially to counterrevolutionary

---

4 Donald E. Schultz, *EEUU y Cuba: De la estrategia de conflicto al compromiso constructivo* (The United States and Cuba: From the Strategy of Conflict to Constructive Compromise), (Institute of Strategic Studies of the War College of the U.S. Army, 1993).

actions in Cuba, but, because of the embargo — and this is the irrational part — the Treasury Department has established harsh punishments, consisting of up to 10 years' imprisonment and a fine of up to $250,000, for U.S. citizens who receive money from Cuba (from the government, an organization or a Cuban citizen).

There are other important links in the chain, as certain documents clearly show.

Nearly all of the world's mass media and several international human rights and political organizations frequently comment on "the heroic struggle of a handful of dissident, independent men and women" who, alone and without resources, are confronting the Cuban system.

Meanwhile, in March 1994, the Cuban authorities made public a top secret document signed by Joseph Sullivan, head of the U.S. Interests Section in Havana. The document — which, the Cuban Government said, had been given to it by friends — was addressed to the State Department, the Immigration and Naturalization Service and the CIA. Classified under reference H 18422 693-4, it concerned the current situation of the Cuban refugee program. Cuba presented it to the United Nations and the mass media, but there was no reaction, even though it flatly contradicted the report that UN special reporter Carl-Johan Groth had just presented on supposed human rights violations in Cuba.

We believe that Sullivan's report is revealing and, therefore, may lead to serious questioning of the reality and honesty of the dissident movement. In view of its importance, we include most of its text:

> Cases that aren't very solid continue to arise in the processing of visa requests from refugees. Most of the people are presenting requests because of the deterioration in the economic situation rather than because of any real fear of persecution. The cases presented by the human rights activists are particularly difficult for the officials of the U.S. Interests Section and National Security. Even though we have done everything possible to work with the human rights organizations, over which we exercise greater control in the identification of activists who are really persecuted by the government, the human rights cases constitute the least solid category in the refugee program.
>
> The requests presented by the members of the human rights groups are characterized by being general, imprecise descriptions of supposed human rights activities, because of the lack of convincing proof of persecution and because the basic processing parameters established by the program are not met. During the last few months, accusations of fraudulent requests by activists and of the sale of affidavits recommending the granting of visas have persisted. Due to

the lack of verifiable documentary proof, as a norm, the officials of the U.S. Interests Section and the members of National Security have considered the human rights cases as those most susceptible to fraud... Even though the officials of the U.S. Interests Section have tried to handle the cases that fall within the processing criteria, they have continued to be flexible with cases that don't meet any of the aspects but which are of interest to the United States.

Some of the former political prisoners have openly acknowledged that they have made use of the status of refugees as a means for escaping the ever more deteriorated economy, and not because of any real fear of persecution or harassment... Unfortunately, the quality of many of the requests is, generally speaking, bad. Few of the former political prisoners are now accepted as refugees, compared with those accepted as such in past years. As a rule, they have served sentences that are much shorter than those served by the first ones who were accepted in the program. Most of them played minor roles in the counterrevolutionary groups; took advantage of the system of political reeducation so their sentences would be reduced; and, later on, abandoned political activities and rejoined Cuban society...

An increase in the number of human rights cases has been noted since 1992. In spite of that, this increase is not based on a higher level in human rights activities, on an increase in their composition or on an increase in government repression. Most of the cases rarely present convincing evidence of persecution and frequently offer only minimal, unreliable proof of participation in human rights activities.

The testimony of the human rights leaders generally contains vague descriptions of human rights activities, such as moral support for the families of political prisoners. These descriptions show precisely that most of the human rights groups have a low level of activities and an attitude of nonconfrontation with the Cuban Government.

The general tendency has been the lack of evidence that the person is really an activist, which leave this category practically open to anyone who requests it. The young people who have been caught trying to leave the country illegally since the 1989 economic collapse have begun to present requests as human rights activists. The human rights leaders have told officials of the U.S. Interests Section that they are aware that most of their members joined the groups only to get the advantages offered under the refugee program...

In those cases in which the activists' evidence is poor but their level of commitment to the United States is well defined, the officials in charge of the preliminary evaluation give the person requesting the visa the benefit of the doubt.

The leader of one of the groups said that some people left his organization when they saw that it didn't give its members recommendations. He complained of the pressures brought by members who demand convincing recommendations concerning their human rights activities.

During their last visits, members of National Security have witnessed reiterated incidents of fraud and presumed fraud committed by human rights activists... They also met with the heads of human rights organization to determine their aims, the number of members and other aspects of the main groups. The U.S. Interests Section limited the acceptance of group recommendations to those of the leaders we trust...

Unfortunately, these measures haven't even prevented presumed fraud and bitter recriminations among the high-ranking leaders of human rights organizations. Shortly before the National Security personnel's visit in December, Gustavo Arcos and Jesús Yanes, of the Cuban Committee for Human Rights (Comité Cubano Pro-Derechos Humanos, CCPDH), accused Aída Valdés of selling fraudulent recommendations. In turn, she accused Arcos and Yanez of engaging in similar money-making practices.

This situation exacerbates the general concern regarding the danger of trusting in the presentation of affidavits. The profound rivalry and internal struggles among human rights groups make it inevitable that repeated accusations of fraud will be made.

During a meeting with the U.S. Interests Section and National Security, Félix Bonne, head of the Civic Current (Corriente Cívica, CC) group, described the program for refugees as "the primary objective of many leaders of human rights organizations."

Even though we have done our utmost to work with the human rights groups so they would present the most solid cases, most of the interviews have yielded nonconclusive cases... Most of the activists merely give a vague description of their participation in human rights groups...

The problems found in processing most of the human rights cases show that it is necessary for the U.S. Interests Section to keep working in close coordination with National Security to select solid cases.

Even so, the U.S. Interests Section will continue to be flexible, presenting cases which, even though they don't meet all of the criteria, may, because of their nature, still prove useful to the interests of the United States.

In view of the CIA's clear interest in the topic of human rights and its growing participation with and greater knowledge of the various human rights groups, we suggest closer cooperation with the U.S. Interests Section, in consonance with our common objectives.[5]

Even with a very low profile, it isn't just the U.S. Government that wants to destabilize the system, using individuals or small groups inside the country. Europeans are involved in this, too. "Most of the Foreign Offices in Western Europe have a counselor or secretary whose duties include listening to human rights militants... The group of diplomatic missions has offered this discreet attention for a long time."[6]

To be a little more precise, let's see what William Claes said in 1994, when he was Minister of Foreign Affairs of Belgium, before becoming Secretary General of NATO. Replying to a question that Van Nieuwenhuysen, a member of Parliament, asked about why Belgium had an embassy in Cuba, Claes said, "The presence of a Belgian Embassy in Cuba allows us to try to contribute, together with our allies in the European Union, to a peaceful transition toward democracy... This was also the reason for Belgium's presence in the various Eastern European countries, where our diplomatic missions were able to react rapidly to political and economic changes."[7]

And now, for Ramón Cernuda. He is a wealthy man who buys and sells works of art — which became popular in Miami rather suddenly. It all began in 1989, when customs agents swarmed through his house, accusing him of trafficking in Cuban works of art after the embargo had been imposed. A few days later, Mas Canosa boasted over the radio that he had pressured District Attorney Dexter Lethinen (Congresswoman Ileana Ros-Lethinen's husband) into doing this. Cernuda had made the big mistake of questioning the procedures of the former chairman of CANF in carrying out his counterrevolutionary activities. In the end, the federal courts dropped the case.

The mass media in Miami zeroed in on Ramón Cernuda when it was learned that he was the agent of Elizardo Sánchez — who headed the small group called the Human Rights and National Reconciliation Commission in Havana — abroad.

Cernuda became the center of an uproar when Sánchez proposed dialogue as a means for undermining the system. We already know that dialogue is a very touchy subject in Miami. In the many conferences he

---

[5] Translated from the Spanish.
[6] Jean-François Fogel and Bertrand Rosenthal, *Fin de siècle à La Havane: Les secrets du pouvoir cubain* (End of the Century in Havana: The Secrets of Cuban Power), (Paris: Editions du Seuil, 1993).
[7] Belgian House of Representatives, *Questions et Réponses (GZ 1993-1994)*, (Questions and Answers [GZ 1993-94]); question 314; November 23, 1993; DO 939400311.

has given abroad — in spite of repeating that he is an apolitical fighter for human rights — Sánchez proposed pressuring Fidel Castro to make him begin the political and economic changes required to bring about the dissolution of the socialist system, since he was the only one with enough power to do so. Then he went on to say that Castro was the main obstacle to those changes. When advised of that contradiction, he replied, "That is one of Cuba's paradoxes."[8]

As his representative, Cernuda actively promoted Sánchez internationally — so successfully that, on December 10, 1996, the French Government bestowed on Sánchez the highest award it gives to individuals engaging in human rights activities. The plaque and close to $20,000 were awarded to him for having "given legal and humanitarian assistance to the victims of government repression." It was not stated publicly just what kind of assistance he had given, nor to which victims, nor what "repression" was involved.

Exactly one year earlier, Amnesty International had reported in one of its bulletins that several people, including the relatives of Cuban prisoners, had gone to Sánchez's home to demand money which, presumably, the Puebla Catholic Institute,[9] a U.S. nongovernmental organization financed by the National Endowment for Democracy, had sent to them through him.

The French Government awarded him that distinction without even questioning the fact that the award-winner had been one of the promoters in Cuba of the so-called Cuban Democratic Arrangement (Concertación Democrática Cubana, CDC).[10] That federate group was organized by the Cuban Democratic Platform, whose leaders — including José Ignacio Rasco and Carlos Alberto Montaner — were just as reactionary and in favor of annexation. Hubert Matos was close to the

---

[8] *Trazos de Cuba* magazine, no. 15, Paris, February 1997.
[9] *Cuba, ofensiva del gobierno contra la disidencia* (Cuba, the Government's Offensive against the Dissident Movement), (Amnesty International, April 1996), Spanish version.
[10] Carlos Alberto Montaner, *Cuba hoy: La lenta muerte del castrismo* (Cuba Today: The Slow Death of Castroism), (Madrid: Fundación para el Análisis y los Estudios Sociales, Partido Popular español, 1995), no. 27. See also "Lista de organizaciones disidentes, opositoras y de derechos humanos" (List of Dissident, Opposition and Human Rights Organizations) on The Internet October 15, 1997, and verified in January 1998. On that list, Elizardo Sánchez's group was part of the governing body of the Cuban Democratic Arrangement. At that time, the Arrangement was number 106 on the list. Those who drew up the list in Miami say that the "sources" they relied on included "the reports of various international human rights organizations, such as Americas Watch and Amnesty International... "

Platform.[11] The award was given a few months after Sánchez had been made a member of the board of the Hispanic Cuban Foundation. Other board members included Jorge Mas Canosa, four other Cuban American National Foundation leaders, Carlos Alberto Montaner and several hard-line Spanish conservatives.

Eloy Gutiérrez Menoyo, a former political prisoner and leader of a group supporting dialogue with the Cuban Government, said that Sánchez "had joined the extreme right wing, which wants to cut off Fidel Castro's head."[12]

The fact is that Sánchez goes in and out of Cuba regularly. Abroad, he says what he wants against the Cuban Government, constantly contradicting what Cernuda says, and keeps himself looking very elegant and in the best of health. That is, contrary to what the communiqués of some international human rights organizations say, he is far from being a martyr.

* * *

"Mr. Cernuda, internationally, people have the idea that the Miami exile community plays an important role in the Cuban political situation and that the exile community is basically for changing the present system. Is that correct?"

"One of the big problems the exile community has is that it has wanted to be a protagonist in the processes of change in Cuba. It has always demanded a main role, which it shouldn't have, because it cannot fulfill that role either historically or politically.

"Even in Cuba, those who are opposed to the government often view those of us who are abroad with distrust, because they know that our social, economic, political and cultural reality is different from theirs. This situation is aggravated by the fact that we live in the United States, because, historically, the Cuban nation has had to fight against an annex-ationistic current of political thought. Starting at the end of the 18th century and throughout the 19th century, some of the Cubans in Cuba said that our destiny should be linked to the Americans, and there are still some people who say so. They have been in the minority, but, because they've had a lot of power, they've endangered the project of an independent nation. This was seen in 1898, when the United States occupied the country, and those Cubans created a republican structure making the island something like a protectorate of the North Americans.

"In the 1960s, a lot of people came to Miami who had actively

---

[11] Montaner, *Cuba hoy*. Regarding Matos's relations with the Platform, see Carlos Alberto Montaner, *Víspera del final: Fidel Castro y la revolución cubana* (Eve of the End: Fidel Castro and the Cuban Revolution), (Madrid: Ed. Globus, 1994).

[12] The authors' interview with Gutiérrez Menoyo in Miami in November 1996.

opposed Batista during the revolutionary war. But a lot of Batista's followers and members of the upper bourgeoisie came, too. Most of both groups became extreme right wingers, championing U.S. hegemony and interference — but not formal annexation, just the view that the United States should have a guiding role in the future of the Cuban nation. So far, that has been the prevailing view in the exile community.

"Therefore, you can see that the people here applaud the Helms-Burton Act, which seeks to impose a policy of extraterritoriality and which, in its most offensive paragraphs, tells the Cuban nation what its economy, its multiparty system, its freedom of the press and even its Constitution should be like. It is a sociopolitical-economic recipe that must be accepted, or the United States won't end the embargo. The exile community wants the Cuban nation to enter the 21st century as it entered the 20th.

"We had a president — Tomás Estrada Palma, our first president — who was a U.S. citizen, elected in 1902 without even being in Cuba. Here, some people have presented themselves as candidates to the Presidency of Cuba with American passports in their hands and having the support of the North Americans.

"So, it's natural that people have reservations about an exile who is obviously disconnected from the internal social processes of a nation and is in another nation which retains its hegemonistic pretensions. The exile community has a role to play, but it isn't that of the main protagonist. Its role should be to stimulate the internal autochthonous processes, not determine any processes from outside. It should be a supporting role."

"In view of those statements, Mr. Cernuda, it's easy to see why you are a controversial figure in the Miami exile community. Now, tell us what you think of the political situation in Cuba."

"I think that Cuban society should have an opening process in which the government finally understands that its political model doesn't correspond to present Cuban — and world — realities. The purpose of the Cuban Government is totalitarian; when we are in government, we will organize and solve everything in society.

"Somebody once said that communism never got as far anywhere else as in Cuba, where everything is organized by the government. But that government began to confront economic crises that didn't allow it to solve all of the nation's problems, which resulted in gaps and needs. At bottom, the Cuban problem is the government's eagerness to control all the political power."

"Mr. Cernuda, it cannot be denied that the Cuban Government's political system has had very positive results in terms of its development of society, culture, health..."

"I don't deny that Cuba had excellent results in health, education and sports, but neither the teachers nor the doctors nor the athletes were responsible for that. It was the government, with its totalitarian purpose. But what existed in the past has gone to the devil, and that model no longer meets the need. That's why the government should initiate an agreed-upon transition now."

"A transition agreed upon with whom?"

"Agreed upon by the government and all the population. I'll tell you frankly: the opposition in Cuba has little say. There isn't any opposition that endangers that government."

"Mr. Cernuda, how is it that there isn't any strong internal opposition to the Cuban system? Isn't what everybody's always saying true?"

"There is a chaotic — or potentially chaotic — situation in Cuban society, but I never spoke to you about real forces that endanger the government, because there aren't any. What there is is a handful of people who, using human rights activism, have created an opposition."

"How should the transformations which you say are so needed be promoted?"

"I'm not asking for immediate transformations. It can be a slow process. It may take 10 years or more, but it should be step by step."

"We read somewhere that you think that the Communist Party of Cuba should learn from Mexico's Institutional Revolutionary Party (PRI). Please explain this to us, because we know that, in addition to being utterly corrupt, the PRI hasn't even respected Mexican nationalism but has been handing the country over to U.S. citizens."

"Correct. But the Mexican PRI has turned from the only party into the prevailing party and has been in power for 50 years. The Communist Party of Cuba and the Cuban Government have enough resources and influence among the people to make that transition without repeating the PRI's mistakes."

"Mr. Cernuda, what will happen if the Cuban Government doesn't make those transformations you want?"

"There is a danger that the extreme right in Washington and Miami may come to power at a time of anarchy when Fidel Castro dies. And I say Washington because, even though you may not believe me, that's where the decisions are made — where the dog's head is. Washington isn't the tail. Don't be mistaken. Throughout history, Washington has wanted to control Cuba, and it's never renounced that aim."

"But we believe that the 'tail' in Miami isn't anything to be sneered at — at least, that's what they're trying to prove."

"Look, you know that the tail always follows the dog's head. Those in the tail have a lot of economic clout, because they're multimillionaires, which make them a political power — a sociopolitical power, because there are people here who, when they knock on the White House door, it's opened to them. Or they walk through the halls of Congress as if they owned it. Just imagine: they control nearly all of Florida, and they go around with the dog's head, because that's what will give them power in Cuba."

"Mr. Cernuda, at the beginning, you said that the people in Cuba viewed the Miami exile community with distrust. In that case, do you think they will allow that pro-U.S. minority to take power?"

"In Cuba, the people aren't about to tolerate that dominant exile minority. But if, by insisting on an out-of-date model, the Cuban Government uses up their reserves of patriotism and drives them up the wall, I think that, at some point, they may accept anything else."

"What does most of the Cuban community here in Miami think?"

"Most of the exile community has turned off the political debate. There are close to 1.2 million Cubans in Miami. How many are active in politics? Fifty thousand? The rest are living their own lives, trying to survive from one day to the next. The ones who have relatives in Cuba are going crazy trying to send them some money."

"Mr. Cernuda, let's talk about another burning issue. At the international level, quite a few governments and institutions treat the Cuban Government as if it were one of the most repressive in the world. What are the facts?"

"Look, the most visible violation of human rights in Cuba is a prison with 3,000 to 5,000 inmates. Fifty percent of them are there because of their opinions.[13] But I believe that there isn't an official policy of torture in Cuba. The Cuban Government doesn't apply torture. It has a policy of mistreatment, because the prisoners don't get appropriate food and medical attention. In the past, there used to be psychological torture — but that was in the past. Moreover, the number of prisoners has decreased."

"Why do you say that the number of prisoners has decreased, when people all over — in Miami, Washington, Madrid and London — are saying that the number is growing?"

"I'm honest. Look, the government realizes that it doesn't need that weapon to control the few political dangers there are inside the country. There are three main reasons.

"One: The Torricelli and Helms-Burton Acts have been an important gift to the regime. Why? If I live in Cuba and read what they contain, I am horrified. And, when it comes to choosing between an evil that I

---

[13] These are the figures that most of the counterrevolutionary organizations and several international human rights organizations quote. Curiously, since the Pope's visit to Cuba, even Elizardo Sánchez has begun to quote other, rather incoherent figures: "Over 500 Cubans are in prison on the island for political reasons, and at least 110,000 people for common law crimes," *Le Monde*, Paris, January 27, 1998.

know, which is Castro, and the one that is presented to me as something good from the United States, I'll choose the evil that I know and won't be in the opposition.

"Two: An important sector of Cuban society is placing priority on seeking an economic solution rather than getting involved in problems of a political nature. Moreover, you can't deny that the economic situation has improved a little bit.

"The third important reason is the migratory agreement that the U.S. and Cuban Governments signed in 1995. Every week, 80 people win the 'raffle' in Havana. That is, the Interests Section grants that many visas. Then people very wisely say that, instead of becoming members of the opposition, they'd rather wait for their number to come up so they can leave the country. Moreover, it isn't the Cuban Government that won't let them leave, but the embassies that don't give them visas.

"I assure you, those three things have neutralized the internal opposition."

8

Ricardo Bofill
Cuban Committee for Human Rights, Miami

"Now, get this: the exiles and the American Government must react more strongly against those communists!"

"A confused personality capable of sudden fits of rage… of manifesting an unquenchable yen for power and personal publicity…"[1] That was the first description we had of Ricardo Bofill while we were preparing this work. In any case, we had our reservations, because he had a very positive image in the reports that important international human rights organizations published in the mid-1980s. In brief, for them, Bofill had been both the first brilliant leader and the most charismatic and daring one in the nascent internal dissident movement with the sole ideal of freedom.

After 10 minutes in his house listening to him, we looked at each other incredulously. Was this the figure that Amnesty International had sent through Europe giving talks, the person to whom the press had dedicated entire pages?

In 1968, Bofill was sentenced to four years in prison for participating in a counterrevolutionary organization called the microfaction. He was accused of engaging in espionage and of plotting against the revolution. According to the charges, Bofill produced and sent documents abroad stating that the Cuban leaders were unreliable because they were "of bourgeois extraction" and weren't "faithful enough to the Soviet Union." At the same time, he asked the Soviet and East German governments "to bring political-economic pressure to bear to force Castro to structure a different Marxist system."[2]

When Ronald Reagan moved into the White House and stepped up the aggression against Cuba, he implemented the strategy of isolating the Cuban Government on the basis of supposed human rights violations. At the same time, Bofill, who had already been released, renewed ties with old colleagues of the microfaction and with diplomats, this time mainly those of the Western countries, and

---

[1] Fogel and Rosenthal, *Fin de siècle*.
[2] Encinosa, *Cuba en guerra*.

organized a small "human rights" group. The reports which that group smuggled out of the country wound up being used against the Cuban Government by the U.S. delegation to the United Nations. Bofill himself said that the initial contacts for channeling the reports "were with Amnesty International and the UNESCO Human Rights Commission."[3] At that time, Cuba's Ambassador to UNESCO was Martha Frayde — who was later imprisoned in Cuba for having maintained contacts with CIA agents while at UNESCO. It is only fair to say that not only Ms. Frayde but also "human rights" dissidents joined Bofill in those first activities abroad. They included Gustavo Arcos, Cuba's former Ambassador to Belgium, and Elizardo Sánchez, a former official in the Ministry of Foreign Relations.

In August 1986, Bofill sought refuge in the French Embassy, where he stayed until January 1987. When he left it voluntarily, he walked back home; nobody took any notice of him. A few months later, the group split up when Sánchez challenged Bofill in a power struggle. And, since splitting up splinter groups has, historically, been the norm of the Cuban counterrevolutionaries, Tania Díaz, who had been with Sánchez, decided to set up her own group in June 1988. Four months later, Ms. Díaz informed Miami that she had an organization with 10,582 members — an "extravagant number."[4] Some time later, Ms. Díaz "made a public statement repenting of her anti-Castro activities and accusing the leaders of the committees in Cuba of working for the CIA."[5]

A few months earlier, in March 1988, the Cuban mass media had published an article proving that Bofill maintained relations with diplomats of the U.S. Interests Section. Television showed him receiving money from them and even betraying other counterrevolutionaries. The authorities didn't prosecute him, but he was ostracized and left Cuba in October. Whereas, in Cuba, Bofill had been simply somebody who was leaving, he was given a great welcome abroad, with Amnesty International and other organizations providing him with a lot of publicity in Europe.[6] But, as the months went by, he stopped being

[3] Ibid.

[4] Fogel and Rosenthal, *Fin de siècle*.

[5] Encinosa, *Cuba en guerra*.

[6] Even though Amnesty International's intervention concerning supposed violations of human rights in Cuba had begun years earlier — more specifically, with the fraudulent case of Armando Valladares — Jorge Mas Canosa stated the following in the book *Indomitable Exile*: "In the autumn of 1989, a delegation of exiles met with members of Amnesty International in London... Cuba at that time had virtual impunity as regards human rights, and Amnesty International, whose well-deserved prestige in such areas of the geography of oppression hadn't been confirmed in the case of Cuba, opted for indulgence toward the comrades from Havana... The meeting must have had some effect, because the approach changed in the following months

news. Thus, he was left on the sidelines in Miami as just one more counterrevolutionary.

According to lists kept abroad, there are groups in Cuba consisting of just one person but with very pompous names, such as the Abraham Lincoln International Committee of Support for Democracy (Comité internacional de apoyo a la democracia "Abraham Lincoln," CIADAL) and the Fraternity of Businessmen of the Forbidden Gospels (Fraternidad de hombres de negocios de evangelio negado, FHNEN). In 1992, it was said that there were 65 of them; by January 1998, the last time we checked, the number had risen to 360.[7] That is, 295 apparently appeared in a period of five years, or around one new group every six days.

In 1961, two years after the triumph of the revolution, when Washington was giving priority to stimulating the internal counter-revolution, Allen Dulles, who was head of the CIA at the time, told Kennedy that there were 184 little groups — which meant that one had been created approximately every four days.

Now, as in 1961, those little ghostlike groups keep popping up and disappearing again. Thus, the people who have put the list on the Internet cautiously warn, "It may also be that some of the ones listed here have disappeared... Since the situation in Cuba is very changeable, we recommend that those who use this list check it and bring it up-to-date every so often."[8]

Some U.S. Government agencies' reports — such as the top secret document from the U.S. Interests Section — and other, independent studies, give you the feeling that the people who appear at the international level as leaders of the dissident movement are a kind of fiction inside Cuba. In spite of the widespread interest in eroding the Cuban political system and the immense resources sent to them from the United States and Europe, no counterrevolutionary leaders "inspired by

---

and years. Several exile groups began to feed information to the organization and guide its sensitivity in its watchfulness concerning the Antilles, and greater concern for the regime's victims began to be noted." Where did most of the information that those pro-human rights exiles gave to Amnesty International and other international organizations come from? In *Indomitable Exile*, Mas Canosa didn't hide those sources: "The exiles had good information about what was happening inside the country, not only from Bill Casey, the head of the CIA, with whom they had very friendly relations, but also from the Representatives and Senators on the intelligence committees of the House and Senate."

[7] "Lista de organizaciones disidentes." Those who drew up the list in Miami say that the "sources" they relied on included "the reports of various human rights organizations, such as Americas Watch and Amnesty International..."

[8] Ibid.

the Solidarity model in Poland"[9] have appeared.

As journalists who cannot be described as friends of Cuba have put it: "After having searched for 'dissidents,' representatives of foreign governments, the international press and humanitarian organizations have found nothing but members of human rights groups that are almost anonymous in Cuban society... Those same leaders have never spoken out publicly in Cuba, even in front of a few dozen people. In the street, outside their own neighborhoods, nobody recognizes them... Their existence is, above all, an argument for bringing international pressures to bear on Cuba, a subject of interest to foreign reporters. Since nobody pays any attention to them in Cuba, they work for the foreign market."[10]

Several cases have been manufactured for that market, the best known one being that of Armando Valladares, a veritable white elephant who left many important European intellectuals with red faces. Too late, they learned that the U.S. Government, its counter-revolutionary apparatus and some European organizations had used them as tools.

Valladares, a former policeman under Batista, was arrested in Havana on December 30, 1960, while setting explosives in public places. In the late 1970s, an international campaign was launched to free him; Carlos Alberto Montaner headed it in Europe. *Desde mi silla de ruedas* (From My Wheelchair), a book of poems supposedly by Valladares, was published to coincide with the launching of the campaign. Later, it was discovered to have been plagiarized, but "the paralyzed poet imprisoned for his opinions" had already been launched on the international scene. Pressures were brought to bear against the Cuban Government in a campaign in which even French President François Mitterrand participated.

"Régis Debray came here on a visit and told us that the situation of the French Government was untenable; he almost said that the French Government would fall. It was all a great drama,"[11] Fidel Castro commented. Organizations of intellectuals and of political prisoners and the Social Democratic and Christian Democratic Parties in Europe were mobilized, calling for Valladares's release. The International Pen Society gave him its Liberty Award, and Amnesty International called him a "prisoner of conscience." The Amnesty International branch in Sweden sent him a wheelchair.

He was released in 1982 and left for Madrid. The French Government

---

[9] Fogel and Rosenthal, *Fin de siècle*.
[10] Ibid.
[11] Gianni Minà, *Habla Fidel* (Fidel Speaks), (Madrid: Ed. Mondadori España, 1988).

sent a special plane to pick him up, but Mitterrand and Debray already knew that it was all a plot by the United States and its apparatus in the Cuban exile community. Therefore, no government officials were waiting to greet the famous former prisoner. Then Valladares practically skyjacked the plane, forcing Debray to show up. The crowd of journalists and representatives of nongovernmental organizations were left with their mouths open, seeing the poet-martyr skip down the boarding ramp while his wheelchair was discreetly removed. The next day, Valladares was strolling through the streets of Paris in perfect health.[12]

The proof presented by Cuban doctors had been suppressed or ignored by the well-oiled campaign. Nobody believed the video showing Valladares in jail doing strenuous daily physical exercises. Valladares gave talks throughout Europe, and the mass media spread his words. The National Endowment for Democracy office in Spain spent thousands of dollars on propaganda in Europe and published the book *Contra toda esperanza* (Against All Hope).

The United States Information Agency distributed that "biography" in over 30 countries. Wanting to get full value for money, the U.S. Government gave him U.S. citizenship, even though he hadn't met the requisites established by law. After that, Reagan immediately named him the U.S. Ambassador to the United Nations in Geneva. For two years, he showed his face and told his story, while somebody else did all the work. After 1993, all that remained of the famous Valladares was a foundation that bears his name, though it might be more accurate to say it is an old-buddy club. The U.S. Government and his champions tossed him away, much as you would throw away a piece of chewing gum after you have extracted all the flavor.

Many — though not all — European politicians and intellectuals must feel ashamed of having supported him. As Régis Debray, who was one of them, wrote in his book *Les Masques* (The Masks), "The man wasn't a poet, the poet wasn't paralyzed, and the Cuban is now a U.S. citizen."

The international efforts to create "leaders" didn't halt, even though most of Europe's organizations and VIPs didn't give them the same support as before — which made things more difficult. One of the last unsuccessful attempts was the one launched to build up Elizardo Sánchez, whom we have already mentioned.

Another such effort centered around Gustavo Arcos, who was joined by his brother Sebastián in founding the so-called Cuban Committee for Human Rights. Their thesis was to force the government to engage in a

---

[12] Pillas, *Nos agents à Havane*.

dialogue with the internal dissident movement and all the groups in the exile community, outside Cuba. That possible dialogue "was a way to make the Castro system look bad at the international level if it refused to negotiate. If it agreed to negotiate, a bloodless solution for the national problem might be worked out."[13] The same source said that Arcos was opposed to the lifting of the embargo and that his position was influenced by Carlos Alberto Montaner and José Ignacio Rasco, with whom he unified his group.[14]

Freedom House, an ultraconservative nongovernmental organization, gave Sebastián Arcos the floor in the United Nations. His address was so vitriolic that Elliot Abrams, Reagan's Assistant Secretary of State for Inter-American Affairs, described him as not only a courageous man but also a potential president of Cuba if a democratic transition should take place on the island.[15]

In November 1996, Gustavo Arcos was featured in several newspapers and magazines, mainly in Spain and Miami, as a member of the board of the conservative Hispanic Cuban Foundation.

Beginning in 1997, a text entitled "The Arcos Principles" was published in the Hispanic Cuban Foundation's bulletin and those of a few other European NGOs. In addition to laying down a kind of code of conduct that foreign businesses should abide by if they invested or thought of investing in Cuba, it proved that Gustavo Arcos still had relations with the pro-annexationist extreme right. Of Human Rights and Freedom House were its main sponsors, along with Elizardo Sánchez.

The text wound up by saying, "The companies signing the Arcos Principles should a) submit all of the sections referred to above to inspection by an internationally accredited group of auditors, and every signatory company with more than 25 Cuban employees should provide a written report; b) present such a report annually to one or more human rights organizations in Cuba, preferably the Cuban Committee for Human Rights (Comité Cubano Pro-Derechos Humanos, CCPDH), with a copy to Freedom House, through the Special Unit on Special Investments, at Of Human Rights, 1319 18th Street, NW, Washington, D.C., 20036, USA."[16]

This so-called code of conduct is the one that Pax Christi Netherlands has adopted in its campaign against Cuba — which is hardly surprising.

---

[13] Encinosa, *Cuba en guerra.*
[14] Ibid.
[15] Fogel and Rosenthal, *Fin de siècle.*
[16] Reproduced in *Boletín informativo,* Hispanic Cuban Foundation, no. 1, Madrid, February 1997.

This nongovernmental organization has been working with Freedom House publicly since the end of 1997, as is confirmed in the documents of the second meeting of the Platform for Human Rights and Freedom in Cuba, which was held in Rome a semi-clandestine way.

In 1990 — and this is no exaggeration — the leaders of the counterrevolution abroad began packing their bags, because they were sure that the Cuban regime was about to fall and they would have government posts. All of them did everything imaginable to arm at least one group inside Cuba so they would have more influence among the people. The Cuban American National Foundation and the Cuban Democratic Platform, each with its associates, were in the vanguard. When there were around 10 of those associates, they formed a kind of federation. The Foundation called its group the Cuban Democratic Coalition (Coalición Democrática Cubana, CDC), while the Platform called its group the Cuban Democratic Arrangement (Concertación Democrática Cubana, CDC).

A bulletin of the Foundation's stated, "The opposition inside Cuba is linked to two large organizational coalitions: the Cuban Democratic Coalition and the Cuban Democratic Arrangement... All told, they have thousands of members throughout national territory... "[17]

The Foundation made no bones about its objectives: "Pressure by the various dissidents on Castro to make him leave power. The Cuban Democratic Coalition will oppose any effort to begin talks with Castro aimed at bringing about a peaceful change. The new Coalition will get in touch with other dissident groups that agree to its ban on contacts with Castro. The Foundation will back up this Coalition."[18] The Arrangement had the same aim of overthrowing the socialist government, but without ruling out dialogue as a hidden weapon of struggle.[19] As we have already said, Elizardo Sánchez was the number-one man in the Arrangement, and Gustavo Arcos joined him later on.[20]

The Cuban American National Foundation installed Jorge Castañeda, a former TV actor, as the first chairman of the coalition. The former head of the Foundation wrote him, in a letter dated October 24, 1991: "And, finally, under no circumstances lose contact with us, so we can guide you in the best way possible in this final phase of the struggle for our homeland's freedom. I reiterate my absolute faith in the coming victory

---

[17] Fundación. Organo oficial de la FNCA, year 2, no. 9, Miami, 1993.

[18] "Lista de organizaciones disidentes." At that time, the Coalition was number 81 on the list.

[19] Ibid. At that time, the Arrangement was number 106 on the list. Also see Encinosa, *Cuba en guerra*.

[20] Concerning Sánchez's and Arcos's relations with the Arrangement and with the Platform, see Montaner, *Cuba hoy*.

and my complete confidence in you... " Unfortunately for the Coalition, Castañeda was a Cuban counterintelligence agent.

At the end of 1995, the Hispanic media in Miami announced that a meeting of all dissidents would be held in February 1996 and that an umbrella organization called the Cuban Council (Concilio Cubano, CC) was being formed for that purpose. In January 1996, the meeting was a burning issue in the relevant circles at the international level. According to an Amnesty International report, the Council "included around 140 nonofficial groups" of all kinds. The counterrevolution abroad cited the same number. The Cuban Government responded by imprisoning several of the ringleaders.

In response, Amnesty International deduced "that the reason for the new offensive against some activities that, up until now, have been entirely peaceful lies in the fact that, for the first time since the government of President Fidel Castro came to power with the Cuban revolution in 1959, it has to confront some degree of serious opposition of an organized and peaceful nature."[21]

Neither Amnesty International nor any other international non-governmental organization nor any of the large-circulation newspapers and magazines in Europe commented on the fact that the supposed leaders of the Council in Cuba would be working under the orders of and would be financed by CANF, the Cuban Democratic Platform, Brothers to the Rescue, Independent and Democratic Cuba and other groups of the extreme right wing of the exile community.

It is incomprehensible that such important information, which would make it possible to assess the Council objectively, should be omitted. And it cannot be said that it was due to lack of data, because the communiqués put out by the counterrevolutionary groups in Miami, Madrid, London and Paris were public knowledge. Moreover, *El Nuevo Herald* and *The Miami Herald* provided extensive details about the true origins of the Council.

Journalist Luis Ortega described the episode of the Cuban Council as follows:

If there is any possibility that [the leaders of the Council] were deliberately smeared to make them fail, why haven't they protested? Why haven't they denounced Miami's maneuver? Why haven't they confronted Miami's apparatus of corruption and set the limits? The fact that Sebastián Arcos Bergnes, in Miami, has accepted the check from Brothers to the Rescue indicates that they feel comfortable and untroubled by being associated with the people in Miami. That, in

---

[21] *Cuba, ofensiva.*

itself, is the Council's death certificate... It is a branch of the Miami businesses...

No serious opposition movement can arise against Castro's government in Cuba until the people there understand that the most important, key thing in fighting against a revolution that has been going on for 37 years, in a permanent state of siege against the United States, is to have political morale. Everything that is thrown into battle against the government in Cuba that is done in complicity with Miami's apparatus of corruption and receives help from the Americans is dead on arrival — DOA, as they say in English. Right now, the government is fully authorized to close all doors to it.[22]

For his part, Eloy Gutiérrez Menoyo said that his group, Cuban Change (Cambio Cubano, CC), had turned down the invitation to take part in the Council "because we knew it was a manipulated opposition that served U.S. interests and those of the extreme right in the exile community."

The former political prisoner went on to say, "We know that there are political and human rights organizations in Europe and the United States that have given and continue to give credibility to the Council. They have protested because the Cuban Government curbed the Council's leaders. Nobody can set himself up as an honest, independent dissident while receiving checks and instructions from the enemies of his nation. Nobody can be so naïve as to believe that the Cuban Government would sit by without doing anything when it knew that the powerful enemies who wanted an explosion on the island were behind the Council. Gentlemen, if you aren't really independent, you can't challenge a government such as the Cuban one, which, historically, has been harassed by the Americans."[23]

Finally, we present a few communiqués that some of those little groups have made public. They are easy to get hold of, in the news bulletins of the counterrevolution abroad or through the Internet. Certainly, they offer more traces, we think, for continuing to reflect on the political independence of the so-called dissident movement in Cuba.

The Nationalist Action Party (Partido Acción Nacionalista, PAN), the Máximo Gómez Democratic Nationalist Movement (Movimiento Nacionalista Democrático "Máximo Gómez," MNDMG) and the Patriotic United Front (Frente Unido Patriótico, FUP) all have the following objective: "Support the United States and the European

---

[22] Luis Ortega, "El Concilio perdió la virginidad" (The Council Loses its Virginity), *La Prensa*, New York, February 1996.
[23] The authors' interview with Eloy Gutiérrez Menoyo in Miami in November 1996.

Union's policy toward Cuba on maintaining the sanctions against Cuba in order to bring about the democratic changes that our country needs."

The supposed leader of the Cuban Human Rights Party (Partido Pro-Derechos Humanos de Cuba, PPDHC) said, "I have always admired Mr. Jorge Mas Canosa. Personally, I would like to thank him for everything he is doing for our people... He is the man we need most in this country so he may advance the freedom and democracy we need so much."

In a letter to Mas Canosa, the Cuban Committee for Denied Rights (Comité Cubano Pro-Derechos Negados, CCPDN) said, "Brother, we want to express our sincere gratitude to you today. We send you the sentiments of the members of this Committee, who feel very grateful to you for your noble contribution to the cause of Cuba's freedom."

Even though it was linked to Hubert Matos, the Democratic Solidarity Party (Partido Solidaridad Democrática, PSD) wrote, "We hope that, in the not too distant future, we may welcome you with open arms here in Havana... When we, who are forged in the struggle, hear the words of our beloved leader Jorge Mas, the tears run down our cheeks."

Angela Herrera, who replaced the former actor Jorge Castañeda as Chairman of the Coalition, wrote, "We have the support of our brothers and sisters in the exile community. They are like a light that God has placed in our path to help us recover the true freedom that has been wrested from us." When she arrived in Miami in July 1994, she said that CANF was "the most sincere and the greatest thing that God has created."

The Central Organization of Christian Trade Unions of Cuba (Central Sindical Cristiana de Cuba, CSCC) sent an "inspiring message of congratulations to the United States of America and to all of its citizens on this commemoration of their Independence Day as a demonstration of the respect and affection which the people of Cuba feel for the North American nation, sentiments which couldn't be eliminated in spite of 38 years of a systematic hate and slander campaign by the communist regime."

Now, let's go on to the interview with Ricardo Bofill, a disquieting and distressing testimony of the character of the dissident movement — and especially the "human rights" part of it.

* * *

"Mr. Bofill, you were one of the first to organize a human rights, dissident, opposition — whatever you want to call it — group. Would you tell us why there are so many of them in Cuba? It seems that they are splinter groups of splinter groups."

"There hasn't been any splintering in the Cuban dissident movement. There has been a multiplication of groups. Why should there be only one or two groups?"

"But there aren't just five or 10. For example, we have a document that mentions more than 360 supposed dissident groups!"

"Why not? Everybody gets together with whoever he likes, with his friends. Each group arises in accord with the characteristics of the people. In a group, we're all friends — or we aren't a group."

"But, Mr. Bofill, is this political, organizational work, or just a meeting of good friends?"

"No, sir! The Declaration of Human Rights lets me work with whoever I want. Anybody I want can come to this house!"

"All right. We won't argue. But, well, tell us: how many people has an opposition organization in Cuba managed to unite?"

"In the Human Rights Committee — the one I founded, which was the most important one — there were five of us. And the membership — nobody knows... But I never knew of any that had more than... I've already told you, it's a matter of friends!"

"But the leaders in the exile community, the world press, the nongovernmental organizations and quite a few governments keep saying that there's a growing feeling of repudiation of the system of government in Cuba. Why aren't those groups full of real political opponents?"

"No communist government has had to contend with a considerable internal opposition. We hope that that phenomenon will happen one of these days in world history. The thing is that, under a communist government, the government is the employer. In those systems, being in the party, with the government, is a great asset. If you aren't, you're a nobody, barely hanging on. In the Soviet Union, the Communist Party collapsed because of the contradictions that arose in the leadership, in the struggle for power. And who won? The reformists, the ones who wanted to be representatives of big U.S. or European companies. The system didn't fall because of any struggle by the majority of the people."

"Going back to Cuba, has Cuban Security infiltrated those groups?"

"Infiltrated? What are they going to infiltrate? ... What do you want, to hear a speech on infiltration? There must be... In Cuba, what there is is a few men and women who come to my house and throw a fit because they defend the government! Yes, sir! There are millions of them, young and old, in Cuba. That's the truth! Millions agree with the system, because they're idiots who believe in communism!"

"Mr. Bofill, it's hard for us to believe what you're saying. We don't understand how so many governments and so many NGOs have maintained that those groups constitute a valid opposition to the Cuban Government. What, then, do such people as Gustavo Arcos, Leonel Morejón, Osvaldo Payá

and Mr. Elizardo Sánchez — who was given the French Government's highest award in December 1996 for his supposed human rights work — really head?"

"What do they represent? ... I repeat: this is a minimal, voluntary thing that doesn't work. Their situation is the same as always. Those organizations exist only in the hearts of their members. Politically, they don't represent shit! No, sir! There isn't any Human Rights Committee, which I created, anywhere in Cuba! Elizardo has worked with us, and... No, sir! That is an action of the spirit!"

"It's hard for us to understand..."

"Understand what? There isn't much to understand."

"Keeping in mind the reality that you are describing, it's hard to understand, for example, how they have been presented as being so meaningful in such important international forums as the UN Human Rights Commission."

"Look, I was a special guest of Amnesty International. Yes, sir, I was in its office in London. Amnesty International gave me a grand tour, and I said what I had to say... But, if Cuba has been denounced in Geneva, it's because of the Castro government's lack of political savvy. There are thousands — I mean, hundreds — of governments that violate human rights much more than Cuba. But the thing is, the Cuban delegation goes there with great arrogance. The other governments, the worst violators, go there and negotiate. They save themselves by taking a diplomatic position. With their intransigence, Castro's people offend the other governments. With their political intransigence, they even offended the Swedish Government. Imagine that!"

"Doesn't it seem absurd to you that a country should be denounced for its political intransigence to other nations, rather than for what it is supposedly being denounced for? Is this why the reports that the U.S. Government, some European governments and NGOs present continue to be believed and used? Do you remember any of the UN sessions in which it was said that several people had been murdered or made to disappear by the Cuban Government? Do you remember that, several days later, those same people who had been 'murdered or made to disappear' held press conferences in the United Nations? And, if we aren't mistaken, their organization was one of the ones that helped prepare those reports."

"No... That story... Don't believe that..."

"But it's in official documents..."

"No, no... I don't know about them."

"Mr. Bofill, tell us about the activities which organizations such as yours carry out in the United States and Europe."

"Well, sometimes we wage campaigns for political prisoners. We send letters all over... This is voluntary, romantic work. Everyone does what it occurs to him to do. Everybody is independent... That is, my human rights program is what I decide in each case. The other people who work on this may do the same. This isn't a formal job. It's a very tiny thing, by a small minority. Here in Miami, with more than a million exiles, there are only 20 of us who work for human rights.

"We've achieved almost nothing in Europe, just a minimal thing in Spain. Who gives a damn about Cuba in Europe? I don't want to start talking about that here... It's a waste of time. I defend whatever I want, and I do what I can..."

"Mr. Bofill, what kind of a reception were you given in Miami, since you have always said that you were a leftist, which is almost a deadly sin here?"

"Even though I come from the real left, from before Fidel Castro, I was given a warm welcome by part of a large sector of the city's population here. Almost at once, I began taking part in several projects. For example, we met in Madrid in 1990 to found the Cuban Democratic Platform, which is headed by such anticommunist exiles as José Ignacio Rasco, a Catholic educated by the Jesuits, and Carlos Alberto Montaner, who has been against the revolution since 1960.

"I also took part in other projects, such as the one headed by Major Hubert Matos. I still have a program, called 'Your Human Rights,' on Radio Martí, which is a U.S. Government station. It is broadcast to Cuba twice a week. In Miami, nothing hinders my political project, which is on human rights..."

"Excuse us for interrupting, but we understand that human rights work as it is understood nowadays is supposed to be neutral and apolitical, yet you speak of it as a 'political project.'"

"Understand it any way you want, but it's my project.

"I was going to say that, of course, there are sectors of exile society that don't invite me to their meetings, but I don't care. Here, there are other people who attack me. They're the ones who ought to be supporting the embargo and not calling for dialogue with communism or making charter flights to Cuba."

"Mr. Bofill, do all those organizations outside Cuba — in the United States, Latin America and Europe — really offer a valid alternative for the Cuban people?"

"Each one has a speech... I don't have a lot of information. You probably know more than I do, because you're journalists. I'm not interested in that. I live my own life, with my own people. Just like the others who have human rights projects, both here and in Cuba. I don't care what they say about Cuba's future..."

"But we think that Cuba's future is their concern."

"Well, maybe so... This is their stamping ground... I've already told you, it's romanticism."

"That 'romanticism' seems to have brought many self-styled anti-Castro figures a lot of money..."

"I don't believe that. That's just Castro propaganda."

"What will happen if the military carries out a coup d'état on Fidel Castro or he dies?"

"Nobody knows. Everything I say here is useless. I don't even know what's going to happen in Cuba next year! There may be an improvement in Cuba or a regression... Not even with a crystal ball... It may be that everything will go on as usual. What may happen? I don't know."

"Mr. Bofill, we don't want to bother you with many more questions, so this is the last one. If the present Cuban system falls and the exile community goes back, will there be a possibility of civil war? We say this because many of the people here talk about vengeance..."

"It's very possible! That's because the communists have hurt the exile community and the Americans in many ways. Didn't Castro declare war when he took away the big companies' and landowners' property? Now, get this: before that, the exiles and the American Government must react more strongly against those communists! Then, what do you think will happen if they go back?"

"Yes? What will happen?"

"You act as if you didn't know that politics isn't for dreamers!"

9

Guillermo Gortázar

**Deputy and member of the Executive Committee of the
Spanish People's Party, in charge of Cuban affairs, and General
Secretary of the Hispanic Cuban Foundation (FHC)**

*"The Hispanic Cuban Foundation is becoming a complement to the action of the
People's Party government. The dictator should be given as little oxygen as
possible, so he'll waste away alone."*

Logically, we looked for Deputy Guillermo Gortázar at the national
headquarters of the People's Party in Madrid. When we said why we
wanted to see him, we were told that the Hispanic Cuban Foundation
(Fundación Hispano Cubana, FHC) had its own headquarters around
200 meters down the street, and we should go there. They gave us its
address and telephone numbers.

At the time agreed upon, we met with Deputy Gortázar, General
Secretary of the FHC, an association which held its first official meeting
on November 14, 1996 — a meeting that was rather troubled, since
around 300 members of nongovernmental and solidarity organizations
with Cuba demonstrated at the entrance and met the very select guests
with a hail of eggs and tomatoes. The demonstrators shouted at the
members of the Spanish Government and Spaniards who were going to
the meeting, calling them accomplices of terrorists and collaborators
with the Mafia, and at the Cuban-U.S. citizens and Cuban-Spaniards,
calling them fascists, Mafia members and murderers. The police had to
intervene to push the demonstrators — who had also managed to
obstruct traffic in the area — back some meters from the main entrance.

Inside, after they had recovered from their fright and were cleaning
themselves off, the main stars of the day were seated: Alberto Recarte, a
Spaniard and president of the FHC; Guillermo Gortázar; and the three
main members of the board (called the *patronato*): Spanish-Peruvian
writer Mario Vargas Llosa, Carlos Alberto Montaner and Jorge Mas
Canosa. During the speeches, Montaner said that the kind of reception
they had been given outside was unfair, since, "when all is said and
done, we're just a group of peaceful citizens." Vargas Llosa also
protested against the demonstrators' attitude, recalling that Cubans

"have been the most slandered and defamed exiles I can call to mind, and the ones most depicted as devils... One of the goals of the FHC is to confront those smear campaigns."

The Hispanic Cuban Foundation was created in response to a proposal of the most reactionary sector of the Cuban counterrevolution and was supported by the Spanish right wing, headed by the People's Party. Its principles are a strange mixture of those guiding the Cuban American National Foundation in Miami and those of the Cuban Democratic Platform of Madrid, adapted to the specific conditions of Spain.

Its main tasks are to carry out propaganda work in Spain; interfere with the Cuban Government's political and economic relations; poison the relations between Spain and Cuba; and consolidate a lobby, not only in Spain but also in other European countries. Its opposition to establishing any kind of relations or dialogue with the Cuban Government is set forth in a paragraph in the introduction to its statutes: "Cubans must carry out the task of effecting a political transition to democracy in Cuba, but there is a broad current of opinion in Spain and America that wants to support initiatives that help to defend human rights and reestablish freedom and democracy on the island."

The FHC, therefore, "convokes the most diverse sectors and leaders of the exile community and of the internal dissident movement in Cuba, together with outstanding Spaniards from the spheres of culture, business and politics, to support these objectives."

The most clearly defined aspects of the amalgam forming the FHC's *patronato* had been apparent since late 1995.

José María Aznar, who was running for president of the Spanish Government, visited Miami in November of that year. Rumor has it that the main purpose of his visit was to seek financial contributions for his campaign. On that occasion, he met with leaders of CANF, Democratic and Independent Cuba and the Cuban Democratic Platform and with Monsignor Román. During a public luncheon that the Foundation gave him — a luncheon at which diners had to pay a hefty sum to get in — he said, "Sooner rather than later... there will be a transition, freedom and democracy in Cuba."[1] From Miami, Aznar left on a tour of El Salvador and Costa Rica, returning a week later "aboard a plane owned by CANF and accompanied by Jorge Mas, Jr."[2]

A few days before the election, showing that he was aware of the candidate's intentions, Mas Canosa said, "We don't expect Aznar to break off relations with Cuba or to prohibit Spanish investments in

---

[1] *El Nuevo Herald*, Miami, November 28, 1995.
[2] Ibid.

Cuba," but added that he was sure Aznar would "introduce a moral element in Spain's policy toward Castro"[3] and that "Aznar's policy is the most consistent with promoting a democratic government in Cuba."

Aznar won the election. As soon as he was in power, he received Jorge Mas Canosa before receiving any official representative of the Cuban Government. Abel Matutes, his minister of foreign relations, did the same. It was an unusual act of diplomatic discourtesy that showed the new slant of Spain's relations with the Cuban Government. More seriously, it gave the counterrevolution a kind of status as a government in exile. Many began to think that, because of his considerable investments in tourism in the Dominican Republic, Matutes would not be averse to muddying Spain's relations with Cuba.

In view of the criticism that was voiced and after having officially received the head of CANF, Secretary of State for Cooperation Fernando Villalonga cried, "Enough with painting the Cuban exile community as devils! ... Mas Canosa isn't the gangster he's been accused of being."

The day after that incredible official defense, the White House, availing itself of the Helms-Burton Act, threatened the Sol-Meliá Company of Spain with sanctions because of its investments in Cuba. As already shown, Mas Canosa had been one of the great champions of the law. Instead of coming to the defense of the company, the new Spanish Government acted almost with indifference. Its policy toward Cuba was already set. Deputy Gortázar summed it up quite well: "Companies that decide to collaborate with Castro should face the risks alone." That was what the extreme right wing of the exile community, headed by CANF, Montaner's Cuban Liberal Union (Unión Liberal Cubana, ULC), Independent and Democratic Cuba and other groups had been seeking since 1992.[4]

According to the statutes, the founding group of the FHC would have almost absolute power concerning essential decisions. Only its members could decide on their replacements. Since most of its Spanish citizens, including José Ignacio Salafranca, who is deputy to the European Union, are members of the People's Party, it isn't difficult to imagine what kind of a line they will impose.

In the *patronato*, the majority are members of the Cuban extreme right wing abroad. Three of them — José Hernández, José Llama and Lombardo Pérez — are also members of the board of CANF. There was a fourth — Jorge Mas Canosa, who died in November 1997. Other members include Juan Suárez Rivas, who was a member of the board of

---

[3] *El País*, Madrid, March 2, 1996.
[4] "Carta abierta a los inversionistas extranjeros" (Open Letter to Foreign Investors), May 1992.

the Foundation up to 1992 and who is close to Carlos Alberto Montaner, also a member of the *patronato,* and Ms. Martha Frayde.

Deputy Gortázar came very close to acknowledging that the recruiting of Elizardo Sánchez, who had an international image as a leftist dissident, was a tactical move. The other counterrevolutionary on the *patronato* is Gustavo Arcos, represented in Spain by Ms. Frayde, as Deputy Gortázar himself told us. Osvaldo Payá, another so-called dissident, withdrew from the board immediately after he got on it.

As the deputy had told us, two more people joined in 1997: Félix Bonne Carcassés, a member of the Cuban Democratic Coalition[5] (which is directed from Miami by CANF) who lives in Cuba, and journalist Raúl Rivero, who also lives in Cuba and is linked politically to Independent and Democratic Cuba.[6]

So far, the Hispanic Cuban Foundation has led a series of attempts to build an apparatus that might achieve some space on the Spanish scene. Armando Valladares had tried to do this without achieving anything in particular — simply going through thousands of dollars provided by the National Endowment for Democracy. Later, Montaner and José Ignacio Rasco, with the support of the U.S. Government and the Liberal and Christian Democratic Internationals set up the Cuban Democratic Platform, which has had minimal results to date.

Some conferences and seminars were held as preparatory activities for the launching of the FHC. The "Working Group on Cuba" met in Madrid on February 9, 1996. The meeting, which was held in the midst of the electoral campaign, was promoted by the Christian Democratic International and sponsored by José María Aznar himself, heading the People's Party. According to the communiqués, its aim was "to coordinate initiatives of support for the forces that are struggling to democratize the island." Richard Nuccio, President Clinton's adviser on Cuban affairs at the time, attended the meeting. So did various members of CANF and of the Platform.

Later, the "Friedrich Hayeck Latin American Freedom University," of Miami, organized a seminar called "The Role of the Government and Society in Latin America," which was held in Madrid on October 8, 1996.

---

[5] It is in the "Lista de organizaciones disidentes, opositoras y de derechos humanos" on the Internet, October 15, 1997, and verified in January 1998. At that time, Bonne Carcassés was listed as leader of Civic Current, number 124 on the list. On page 15 of the Cuban American National Foundation's *Informativo* (news bulletin) no. 9 of 1993, Civic Current is also listed as one of the groups in the Cuban Democratic Coalition.

[6] As shown in the interview, Hubert Matos himself told the authors that Independent and Democratic Cuba had organized the Democratic Solidarity Party inside Cuba. Raúl Rivero appears as a member of it in the "Lista de organizaciones disidentes, opositoras y de derechos humanos." The group is number 276 on the list.

Spanish Minister of Education and Culture Esperanza Aguirre attended the inaugural ceremony. One of its sessions was on "The transition to an open, democratic society: The role of the Cubans in exile and Cuba's future." The speakers included Gortázar and Montaner. José Basulto and Congressman Lincoln Díaz-Balart had wanted to attend but were kept from doing so.

Something should be said about this "university." Its aims appear to to be ultrarightist and even racist. Judge for yourself: "Reeducate the Cuban and other Latin American people in the modern international concepts of freedom as the intellectual foundation of a new society based on the three great pillars of contemporary civilization of democratic capitalism: the market economy, political democracy and the Judeo-Christian moral and cultural system, all linked to the principles of international trade."

Its directors included José Sorzano; José "Pepe" Hernández; five other directors of CANF; Mario Vargas Llosa; and, as its number-one man, Jorge Mas Canosa. The VIPs supporting the activities of this "university" include Margaret Thatcher, former Prime Minister of Great Britain, and Jean-François Revel of France.

Why, as a tool of U.S. policy, has the Cuban extreme right wing put so much effort and poured so many resources into the Hispanic Cuban Foundation? The answer, as shown in practice, is simple: the European Union's policy on Cuba goes through Madrid. Ironically enough, whereas, nearly 100 years ago, Spain and the United States were fighting over who was to control Cuba, now, the ruling People's Party is lending itself to helping the United States recover the control over Cuba that it lost in 1959.

When President Clinton signed the Helms-Burton Bill in March 1996, the Canadian and European governments protested, saying they couldn't allow U.S. laws to dictate what they could and couldn't do in their international trade relations. Clinton was caught in the middle between his own Congress and his allies. To solve this conflict with the European Union, the president appointed Stuart Eizenstat his Special Ambassador for Cuban Affairs. In spite of the title, this was no capricious choice: Eizenstat was also serving as Under-Secretary of Commerce for International Trade.

Eizenstat began a tour in September of that year, meeting with government figures in Belgium, Italy, Spain and Ireland. He had the same message and proposal for all: that they coordinate their stands with that of Washington, taking a harder line with Havana. If the four countries agreed to do so and took it upon themselves to convince the other members of the European Union, the tension between the allies would be eased. In payment, he promised that the closely coordinated joint action would make it possible to temporarily suspend and possibly review the application of the Helms-Burton Act.

A few days later, as if it had already been working on it, Spain presented a document to the European Union. The text contained points that were almost identical to the ones Washington demanded of Cuba for lifting the embargo and normalizing relations: all or nothing. It had to be readapted and softened to make it palatable enough for the members of the European Union to swallow. Most of the European countries didn't believe that it was necessary to "order" Cuba to make an immediate global change in its political system in order to qualify for any kind of economic assistance. The final draft that Aznar presented — and which the European Union accepted — sought to "join efforts to bring political pressure to bear on Cuba to promote its democratization." That is, get the Cuban Government to pledge to leave socialism behind and to adopt capitalism — gradually but effectively.

The Clinton Administration and the U.S. Congress were appeased by the European Union's written pledge to "join efforts." It was the reciprocity and understanding that Washington expected, as State Department spokesman Nicholas Burns said. Shortly before the European Union approved the document, an important Madrid newspaper commented, "The Spanish proposal to the 15 on Cuba is a carbon copy of what the United States has demanded of the European Union."[7]

Let's look at the most important points that the Aznar Administration drew up in cahoots with Eizenstat and forced the European Union to accept in this regard.

The embassies were to take a more aggressive stand, with each one naming someone specifically to promote human rights.

They were to give more determined support to the dissident movement, establishing flexible channels of cooperation and assistance.

They were to demand that the Cuban Government allow all kinds of nongovernmental organizations and associations to function within Cuba, to channel humanitarian assistance. The European Union was to exercise strict control over all aid.

The European Union stipulated the conditions that Fidel Castro should meet if cooperation was to be increased. They concerned human rights, a reform of the penal code, an independent judiciary power, freedom for political prisoners and allowing the national NGOs and dissidents to do whatever they wanted.

Unquestionably, if this were implemented, the member countries of the European Union and the nongovernmental organizations would become a kind of Trojan horse in Washington's plans.

---

[7] *El País*, Madrid, November 17, 1996.

Once he had the European Union's pledge in his hands, Eizenstat reported to Congress on the positive results of his work. Application of the Helms-Burton Act was temporarily suspended. Whether or not it would be reinstituted would depend on how much the European Union pressured the Cuban Government and on the boost to "independent civil society" — which, in the case of Cuba, is simply the so-called dissident movement.

In June 1997, the Hispanic Cuban Foundation faced its first great difficulty. In a public communiqué, Gortázar announced that Carlos Alberto Montaner and Jorge Mas Canosa, two of the most outstanding counterrevolutionary leaders, had resigned. Montaner, the first to do so, said that he was leaving because of differences with Mas Canosa over how to promote the struggle against Fidel Castro's government. Mas Canosa immediately followed suit, saying that he didn't want his presence on the FHC to transfer to it his differences with other members of the exile community: "It is time to close ranks against the Castro dictatorship, not open breaches in the ranks of the opposition." For his part, Gortázar pointed out that the resignations considerably reduced the FHC's political tone.

In November of that same year, the United Left (Izquierda Unida, IU) Party presented a proposal in the Spanish Congress of Deputies asking the government to outlaw the FHC. The petition was based on the fact that José Antonio Llama — a member of the FHC who was also on the board of CANF — had been involved in a plan to assassinate President Fidel Castro at the Ibero-American Summit Conference held in Venezuela in the latter part of 1997.

The United Left Party added that the FBI had confirmed Llama's links to the attempt, which was broken up in Puerto Rico on October 28, and requested that "the foreigners living in Spain who are members of the said Foundation and who have taken part in terrorist activities be expelled and that they be denied entry to our country in the future." The text of the proposal also linked CANF to "the recent terrorist attacks that have taken place in Havana."

Abel Matutes, Spanish Minister of Foreign Relations, stated that, although the federal police in the United States knew that CANF was a party to those acts, he himself could only say that they were "mere assumptions." As was only to be expected, the majority in Parliament did nothing about the United Left's proposal.

However, as we have already pointed out, in the case of the assassination attempt against President Fidel Castro during the Ibero-American Summit Conference in Venezuela, the FBI has arrested six counterrevolutionaries of Cuban origin, including José Antonio Llama, a member of the boards of CANF and of the Hispanic Cuban Foundation.

"Pepe" Hernández, current president of CANF and also on the board of the FHC, is also accused, though he hasn't been arrested.

The terrorist Luis Posada Carriles told *The New York Times* that CANF, headed by its top-ranking executives, was involved with the bombs that went off in several Cuban hotels, wounding several people and killing an Italian tourist. Posada Carriles, who had been in charge of hiring Central American mercenaries to set the bombs, described the plans that were drawn up in Miami in considerable detail.

A few days later, the newspaper had to print a clarification, stating that Posada Carriles had never said that CANF had paid anyone to carry out the acts of terrorism. But all of his original statements, filled with very precise data, leave a lot of room for doubt and the conviction that the members of CANF were in agreement with the criminal acts. The FBI hasn't ruled out the possibility of complicity by the Foundation.

Now, a brief description of Gortázar. When he joined the People's Party, he came from the most radical wing of the Communist Party. After he had become an outstanding leader of the most conservative sector of the People's Party, an international wire service reported that he had met with "important figures in CANF." Gortázar himself said that the purpose of those meetings was "to deepen our relations."[8] A little over a year later, in July 1996, Gortázar represented the People's Party in CANF's annual congress, in which he was given the opportunity to deliver a fiery anti-Castro, counterrevolutionary speech. On returning to Madrid, he set about creating the FHC. Among other things, this included depositing a million pesetas in the Banco de Vitoria so the FHC could be officially registered.

In the FHC's founding ceremony, he said, "President Aznar has repeated that we Spaniards share the same values of democracy and freedom as other Europeans and the people of the United States and that the problem of Cuba is in Cuba itself and is called Castro. It isn't true that Castro is a David against Goliath."[9] And, concerning the FHC, which presumably didn't want to meddle in Cuba's problems, "This foundation is an instrument for preparing us for before, during and after the imminent transition to democracy" in Cuba.

While the first public steps were being taken toward reestablishing diplomatic relations between the Spanish and Cuban governments, Gortázar made some alarming statements to the *Diario de las Américas,* one of the most reactionary newspapers in Miami. In its June 12, 1998, edition, President Aznar's new visit to Miami was described as follows:

---

[8] EFE cable, April 21, 1995.
[9] Hispanic Cuban Foundation. *Boletín informativo* (News Bulletin), no. 1, Madrid, February 1997.

"Spanish President José María Aznar's gesture of coming to Florida rather than going to the island [Cuba] is a gesture of understanding and support for the Cuban people, in contrast to the actions of other rulers who prefer to visit Cuba." Even though Gortázar calls the shots regarding Cuba at both the governmental and People's Party levels, his outdated position of confrontation with the Cuban Government is apparently not being used at the highest levels. This is shown by the statements and actions of both President Aznar and the King of Spain.

* * *

"Mr. Gortázar, how did the idea of creating the Hispanic Cuban Foundation arise?"

"The idea arose among two or three of us in Madrid. It was the result of our noting that there were lines of convergence in the opposition to Fidel Castro both inside and outside the country that weren't being expressed either in Florida or in Cuba. They weren't noted because of personality clashes.

"I think that, except for the Cuban Council — which was a very general movement inside Cuba — it has been very difficult to unite all the people, all of us, who seek Cuba's freedom. This is so even though there are others who are calling for the same thing. Carlos Alberto Montaner is calling for freedom, democracy and elections in Cuba; Jorge Mas Canosa is calling for freedom, democracy and elections; Elizardo Sánchez is calling for the same. As a result, it seemed easy for a group of us Deputies and businessmen in Madrid to call a group of Cubans — some of whom live in Cuba and others who live abroad — together to establish the Hispanic Cuban Foundation. We united a wide spectrum of opponents to Castro's system."

"That is, it's a foundation to influence Cuba's internal politics?"

"No. As Spaniards, we can't say anything about Cuba's internal political problems. But we do want to concern ourselves with Hispanic Cuban relations. We know that those relations leave a lot to be desired, because there's a dictatorship in Cuba. Because it's a dictatorship, we want to help the people who are suffering, especially the dissidents, and inform public opinion about what is going on inside Cuba."

"What you've just said automatically means that the FHC is meddling in Cuba's internal politics."

"No. We don't participate in Cuban politics; we are concerned about those relations. It seemed to us that Spain's policy toward Fidel Castro wasn't correct. We needed a principled policy of unequivocal gestures in favor of freedom — which *is* Spain's business."

"Mr. Gortázar, do the FHC's statements influence the Spanish Government?"

"The FHC is a cultural organization that has political implications because our subject, Cuba, is under a dictatorship.

"As an organization, the FHC can't influence the Spanish Government or its parliament. Before the People's Party came to power, there was a climate of opinion in Liberal, Conservative and Social-Christian sectors which we didn't agree with: the policy of embraces between Fidel Castro and Felipe González. So, first from the opposition and then from the government, we have appreciated the Aznar Administration's positive policy of firmness toward the Cuban Government.

"Just like the People's Party, we believe that giving resources to Castro in exchange for nothing isn't correct. We believe that those resources should be given to the civic organizations in Cuba; that they should reach the independent sectors of the population, independent mass media, etc.; and that this should be done perfectly freely, without the Cuban Government's channeling them. In this, the Hispanic Cuban Foundation agrees with the Spanish Government's present policy on Cuba. Therefore, the Hispanic Cuban Foundation is a complement to the action of the People's Party government. The dictator should be given as little oxygen as possible, so he will waste away alone."

"Has there been much criticism in Spain because the Hispanic Cuban Foundation has members who are acknowledged members of the extreme right wing of the Cuban exile community?"

"Yes. But what you don't see is that we have the honor of having people such as Elizardo Sánchez and Gustavo Arcos among our members. Mr. Payá was a member of ours at the beginning but then withdrew — not out of any disagreement with the FHC but because it was very difficult for him to attend its meetings.

"I had trouble in Florida explaining why it was necessary to have a leftist in the *patronato* of the FHC. It wasn't easy for Mr. Elizardo Sánchez to be accepted. I explained several times that, in a project such as the FHC, a leftist would give it a broader image. And finally they understood. Here in Spain, Mas Canosa and the other Cuban exiles were attacked.

"The Hispanic Cuban Foundation has a project of freedom and democracy, where the members of the right can sit down at the same table with the members of the left. These individuals build up respect for the FHC, because we don't have a defined party affiliation. In Spain, the FHC is viewed as anti-Castro, when, in fact, it only wants Cuba's freedom. We want people to see that we're promoting leftists such as Mr. Elizardo Sánchez inside Cuba."

"Mr. Gortázar, Mr. Elizardo Sánchez's political actions make us doubt that he is a leftist. Moreover, he is a part of Mr. Montaner's Platform. Even though it is said that Montaner is a liberal, his writings show that he wants Cuba to

return to the U.S. orbit. And, looking at the rest of the members, in addition to Mr. Mas Canosa, there are four other directors and a former director of the Cuban American National Foundation of Miami. Mr. Arcos receives economic contributions from the extreme right wing in Miami and is also a member of the Platform. Vargas Llosa has become a champion of capitalism. And, as far as we know, you and the other members of the patronato *are members of the Spanish right. Where, then, is the political breadth?"*

"I see that you've done your homework for this interview...

"We invited members of the Spanish Socialist Party, but they didn't accept. The United Left attacks us; it must be because we don't pay any attention to Castro. But the FHC is open to anybody who wants to fight for freedom and democracy in Cuba. I tell you, in the coming months, we'll be able to report on new members in the FHC — people living in Cuba. More Spaniards will join, too, as advisers and in operations. The FHC is growing rapidly. The truth is, people like it. In Cuba, our news bulletin is snapped up. We know we have a lot of prestige there."

"To what do you owe that prestige? And what kind of support do you give to the so-called dissident movement?"

"We have prestige because they know we uphold a line of political support for the human rights organizations, and we do this because they are our point of reference. We try to send those organizations material support through tourists. The FHC wants to send a lot of economic assistance to the Cuban people and also explain the new Spanish position to them. We support those organizations without worrying about what Cuban Security may think, because Cuban Security has been forced to be relatively tolerant toward those people. The government can't do anything against Elizardo Sánchez and Mr. Arcos, because they have great international prestige. Doing anything against them would be very costly."

"Excuse me, but, when you say 'Spanish position,' do you mean the position of the government?"

"Yes, that of the present administration. As members of the FHC, we support President Aznar's position, because it is very meritorious."

"Mr. Gortázar, what is the FHC's position on the embargo?"

"I think that I should answer that as a People's Party deputy. Like the European Union, the People's Party feels that the Helms-Burton Act is not acceptable. It seems to us that it is a law that serves Castro's propaganda purposes. Even so, we have very good relations with the Cuban American National Foundation of Miami, which supports the embargo. But the People's Party believes that the most important thing is unity of purpose, so we must rise above our differences."

"Mr. Gortázar, how much influence has the present Spanish Government's position on Cuba had in the European Union?"

"I couldn't say that the Spanish Government has managed to influence the European Union completely, but the European Union's present position is largely due to Spain's leadership. Now, the European Union is saying the same thing as Spain: if Cuba wants cooperation, it should improve its human rights record and respect the internal dissident movement and the independent nongovernmental organizations."

"But that attitude is equivalent to supporting the U.S. embargo. Moreover, the position that the Spanish Government presented to the European Union differs very little from the demands that the United States has made of Cuba as prerequisites for its lifting the embargo. And you just said that Spain and the European Union were opposed to the embargo..."

"You may be right, but experience shows that nobody knows what the contributions that have been given to the Cuban Government have been used for. That's why we want to promote specific projects that will directly benefit the people.

"President Aznar's administration is going to end the incentives that Felipe González gave to Spanish companies to get them to invest in Cuba. The message that the government has given is clear: those companies that decide to collaborate with Castro should face the risks alone."

"Lastly, Mr. Gortázar, does the FHC have contacts with nongovernmental organizations in Europe?"

"No, not yet. You have to remember that each European country has its own dynamics in its relations with Cuba. But Mr. José Ignacio Salafranca, one of the most outstanding members of the FHC's *patronato*, is deputy to the European Union. I imagine that he will keep the principles of freedom and democracy in mind in everything he does regarding Cuba. What the Cuban Democratic Platform — which Mr. Montaner heads here is Spain — has done in influencing other governments and organizations in Europe seems very intelligent to me. I think that it has had very good results in Holland. I don't know very much, but I understand that they have managed to combine in Europe with other organizations and groups to help establish a European Platform for Human Rights in Cuba.

"The FHC has that work pending, for it would be to our advantage to work together with important European NGOs. In Spain, we're beginning to work with Caritas, an organization of the Catholic Church, but that's just beginning. I'm in charge of drawing up a program of relations for working with the nongovernmental organizations in this same area, so we can coordinate our actions and support one another.

"And, when we begin, we'll do so in strength, throughout Europe."

10

Robert Ménard
General Secretary of
Reporters Without Frontiers (RSF)

Jacques Perrot
Head of the Americas Region,
Reporters Without Frontiers

"We give $50 a month each to around 20 journalists so they can survive and stay in the country, because, every time we meet them, the first thing they ask us is to help them leave Cuba, because of economic problems."

Three things led us to interview the General Secretary of Reporters Without Frontiers (Reporters Sans Frontières, RSF), whose headquarters is in France.

First, several leaders of counterrevolutionary organizations in Miami — such as Humberto Esteve, General Secretary of the Christian Democratic Party; Janiset Rivero, of the Cuban Democratic Revolutionary Directorate (Directorio Revolucionario Democrático Cubano); and "Pepe" Hernández, of the Cuban American National Foundation — praised his work in supporting so-called independent journalists in Cuba.

Second, two of the people who attended a meeting that Eizenstat, the Clinton Administration's Special Ambassador for Cuban Affairs, had called in Paris in late 1996 told us that the positions of the RSF's delegate had been the closest to those upheld by their host.

And, third, we learned that Reporters Without Frontiers had been one of the European organizations represented in a semi-closed-doors meeting that Pax Christi Netherlands had called at The Hague to create a pressure group against the Cuban Government and support the so-called dissident movement.

On interviewing Jacques Perrot, head of the Americas Region, as well as Robert Ménard, General Secretary of the RSF, we not only understood why the groups of the extreme right in Miami approved of their work but also confirmed the rest. It was rather disturbing, in view of the goals, image and respectability of this large international association.

Our concern wasn't unfounded. In the late 1980s, people in Miami discovered that there were independent journalists in Cuba. Even though this was viewed with optimism, it wasn't surprising. Far from it — it was expected. At that time, the Eastern bloc was crumbling, and so-called independent organizations played a key role in that process. Among them, the human rights groups and press agencies — which were featured in the international mass media — were in the lead. Now, when poverty is the lot of the vast majority and Mafias are in power in those countries, there is a large body of literature which shows how those organizations were advised and paid by the Western powers, especially the United States.

Therefore, the appearance of independent press agencies in Cuba — which joined the existing human rights groups — was taken as part of a chain reaction and an omen of the system's imminent collapse. However, a doubt may remain: in the case of the Eastern bloc countries, the presence of independent journalists was nearly always a facade; would a professional sense of ethics prevail in Cuba? Would the term "independent" fit the definition in María Moliner's *Diccionario del uso del español* (Dictionary of Spanish Usage): "Referring to one who has and maintains his own opinions and doesn't allow himself to be influenced by those of others. Applied to someone who doesn't belong to any particular party."

We have already shown how the various U.S. administrations, particularly starting with the Reagan Administration, have used the mass media to damage the Cuban revolutionary process socially, ideologically and politically. We believe that the diverse texts and examples given bring out the role that Radio Martí, La Voz del CID, La Voz de la Fundación and other media play in trying to split Cuban society and to create and nourish counterrevolutionary groups. It should be kept in mind that Radio Martí and, in general, the other stations that broadcast to Cuba were among the projects — most of which have already been implemented — to which the Santa Fe Document assigned priority.

Even though the attempt to create independent press agencies was announced during the Bush Administration, it wasn't until Clinton's presidency that they began to be promoted seriously. The implementation of the Torricelli Act was a key factor that cannot be ignored in that strategy. It ordered (and anyone who has taken the trouble to read that law in full will know that this is the exact term to be used here) that any organization that would help to discredit and attack the Cuban Government should be incited, created and financed, both directly and indirectly. It included independent press agencies as an essential ingredient.

This subtle tactic of sowing groups — a basic element in

destabilization — was called "Track Two." "Track One" is the nefarious blockade.

As if this weren't enough, almost at the same time, Clinton started doing what his strategist Donald E. Schulz had suggested in 1993, promoting the establishment of press offices that would help the dissident elements to communicate openly and lead to greater fragmentation.[1]

Naturally, you can say that promoting the collapse of the Cuban political system is an old project of Washington's, tacitly — we insist — supported by its allies, and that not everybody in Cuba who says they are a dissident or an independent necessarily agrees with this. Maybe. But we've already seen how several of those who are recognized as human rights leaders internationally support that strategy.

We said that we were disturbed by Reporters Without Frontiers' deep commitment to defending and supporting the so-called independent journalists. It seems to us that RSF undertook that commitment without making a cool, dispassionate analysis of the general context in which the Cuban political process is developing, both inside the country and abroad, and that this is why such insistence is placed on the term "independent," which we don't think corresponds to reality.

Aware of our interest in this topic, someone at the RSF sent us a copy of *L'autre voix cubaine* (The Other Cuban Voice).[2] In the preface to the French edition, written by a communications professional who has published several books on Cuba, we found what must be the RSF's view of the world of the "independent" journalists.

In one section, it says, "The work method of these men and women is the 'proximity poll.' What does this mean? It means tracking down information that may even be very vague, asking friends and more or less declared sympathizers of democratization. It goes without saying that they don't have access to official documents and contacts...

"This is hard to do. It also means searching for information outside the capital in a country where suspicion and betrayal have been set up as national virtues for nearly 40 years. It is necessary to be known and recognized to gather bits of information with which to make an article..."

Here, we should make a short but useful aside. We who have been in Cuba know that, if the Cuban people are characterized by anything, it is their passion for talking; they talk about everything, criticize everything, argue about everything, at the top of their lungs. If you want to find out

---

[1] Schulz, *EEUU y Cuba.*

[2] *L'autre voix cubaine: Des journalistes dissidents témoignent* (The Other Cuban Voice: Dissident Journalists Speak Out), (Paris: Ed. Reporters Sans Frontières, 1997), preface by Jean-Pierre Clerc.

if there was bread and milk at school that day, all you have to do is stand next to people who are patiently waiting for the bus. If you ask the waiters in a restaurant about the country's economic situation, you'll get a long answer which may well turn into an impassioned discussion if there's enough time. They'll talk in a perfectly natural way with foreigner or fellow countryman alike, if the person who asks does so naturally.

There's a place in the park in front of the Inglaterra Hotel in Havana that's known as "the discussion corner." It's a great experience to mix with the people who are discussing things there, keeping in mind that the shouting doesn't mean anything serious. There, you can learn about everything that's going on in the country, which measures that the government has taken aren't popular with some individuals and whether the national baseball team's poor showing is due to the trainer or to some bureaucrat. We know this very well, and there's no other Latin American country that has this characteristic. We suppose it's a result of the revolution.

The document continues: "Once written, the text is telephoned abroad, usually to Miami or Puerto Rico. From there, it is spread through news bulletins that are circulated among the exiles and are then sent to Cuba in private letters. The text is also read over Radio Martí.

"It should be stated that the texts of independent journalists aren't authorized on the island. But a kind of dialectic [sic] has been created: the reports of the independent agencies publicize abroad elements of the Cuban situation that are hidden by the regime, and Radio Martí offers a singular opening on the world not only to the dissidents but also to a broad sector of the population..."

Honestly, we had to read that expression "a singular opening on the world" several times. We would like to think that the person who wrote it was unintentionally mistaken, because, knowing what Radio Martí's purpose is and who runs it, it's easy to imagine what kind of "opening" it offers those who live in Cuba. We believe that it was a mistake, because, a few pages earlier, they had pointed out that that radio station and TV Martí "were set up and are maintained by funds from the American CIA."

We acknowledge that we didn't go to the homes of any of those who, internationally, are said to be independent journalists. And, since the headquarters of their agencies are in some of their homes, we can't know from firsthand observation what equipment they use in carrying out their work. The preface of the RSF book says about one of them, "Some old typewriters and antediluvian tape recorders, a partly organized apartment, two telephones and each person's bicycle, placed at the service of the cause: that is the entire dissuasive power of the BPCI!"

Here, we should point out that, in Cuba, bicycles aren't synonyms of poverty among the inhabitants. They are simply a resource offered by the government to compensate for the shortage in public transportation, because of the general economic crisis that has been in effect since the beginning of the decade.

Now, that description given in the preface contrasts with the following. Amnesty International charged that, on July 10, 1995, Cuban Security had taken a fax away from independent journalist Néstor Baguer. Yet, on August 18, Baguer already had another one. According to the same source, "a fax machine, a video camera and photographic materials"[3] were taken away from José Rivero on July 12. The tactical intentions and strategy of the U.S. Government, which the European Union agreed to support in January 1997, give credibility to Amnesty International. In previous chapters, we showed that a large amount of money is earmarked for supporting the internal dissident movement. That is no secret. "The press agencies have made mistakes. Some of them have accepted material assistance from the U.S. Interests Section in Havana..."[4]

Reporters Without Frontiers calls them "the other voice." That is true. They are in opposition to the monopoly that the government holds on the mass media. But, judging from what can be observed in practice, the act of obvious rebelliousness, of dissidence, of disobedience, was what justified turning those means over to others. The few excerpts from the preface that we quoted contain some important data showing the path they have chosen. Here are a few more examples.

Rafael Solano, an exile in Spain, has his own view of political neutrality: "Theory says that journalism should be impartial. Practice shows the opposite. Official journalism in Cuba supports the Central Committee."[5] This is unquestionably true, but it contrasts with what he says a few lines later: "Radio Martí is another option. The exile press, especially that of Miami, draws on Cuba's independent press."[6] Mr. Solano was imprisoned in his country for several days. RSF explained one of the reasons for his and a colleague's detention as follows: "They had spread abroad the contents of some leaflets that a tourist plane that had come from Florida on January 13 [1996] had dropped over Havana.

---

[3] Amnesty International, *Cuba, ofensiva del gobierno contra la disidencia* (Cuba, the Government's Offensive against the Dissident Movement), April 1996. Under Cuban law, those things were confiscated because they were being used to spread "enemy propaganda." Those laws were readjusted when the United States passed the Helms-Burton Act.

[4] *Le Figaro*, Paris, February 2, 1996.

[5] *Trazos de Cuba*, Paris, June 1996.

[6] Ibid.

The leaflets, calling for civil disobedience, had been dropped by the Brothers to the Rescue organization, of Miami, which was supporting the people leaving Cuba on rafts."[7]

One of the things that worries us every time we read reports issued by many nongovernmental organizations, such as Reporters Without Frontiers, is that they don't include data that are essential for really understanding events. It is useful to know that individuals read those leaflets to the Cuban people over Radio Martí and La Voz de la Fundación and that the leaflets had a truly seditious function, because the flow of people on rafts had been halted eight months earlier.

We found Raúl Rivero, director of Cuba Press, listed as a member of the Democratic Solidarity Party,[8] which is directed from Miami by the ultrareactionary Hubert Matos. For its part, that group is politically close to the Cuban Democratic Platform. Since mid-1997, he has been a member of the board of the conservative Hispanic Cuban Foundation. He reports to Radio Martí and La Cubanísima in Miami; Caracol, the most right-wing radio network in Colombia; Radio Jerusalem, known for its conservative positions; *El Nuevo Herald*, which is influenced by the extreme right wing in Miami; *El Nuevo Día*, a right-wing publication in Puerto Rico; and *Trazos de Cuba*, a bulletin published by extreme right-wing exiles in France. These are the main media he supplies,[9] in addition to his regular contributions to the ultrareactionary *Diario de las Américas*, in Miami.

In spite of his clear, very well-defined degree of political commitment, he has the nerve to say, "I am a journalist. I have shown this for many years, and I seek to do 'depoliticized' work as a professional journalist without any leanings, one who limits himself to simply describing events."[10] On December 10, 1997, International Human Rights Day, he was awarded the Reporters Without Frontiers Award, which is given to "journalists who, through their professional activities, have borne witness to their attachment to freedom of the press"[11] — a devotion to freedom of information which, curiously,

---

[7] Reporters Without Frontiers, *Rapport 1997* (1997 Report), Paris, 1997.

[8] As may be seen in our interview with Hubert Matos, he told us that his group in Cuba was called the Democratic Solidarity Party. The group is number 276 on the "Lista de organizaciones disidentes, opositoras y de derechos humanos" on the Internet on October 15, 1997, and verified in January 1998. Mr. Rivero is listed there as one of the members of the Democratic Solidarity Party. Concerning Hubert Matos's political move toward the Cuban Democratic Platform, see Montaner, *Víspera del final*.

[9] *La Libre Belgique*, Brussels, January 30, 1998. The authors have added the political leanings of these information media.

[10] *La Libre Belgique*, Brussels, December 10, 1998.

[11] *Le Monde*, "Supplément," Paris, January 17, 1998.

serves one of the participants in the conflict.

Though not a journalist, José Rivero is deputy director of the agency. The Reporters Without Frontiers report for 1997 says that he "began participating a short time ago in the program 'La semana en una hora' (The Week in an Hour), broadcast over Radio Martí." In a July 1996 report, Amnesty International attested to this, stating that the program was beamed at Cuba and that the station was "financed by the U.S. Government."

In mid-1997, Reporters Without Frontiers waged a campaign against the provisional detention of Héctor Peraza. Several outstanding French intellectuals supported the campaign. Peraza is a member of the Democratic Solidarity Party,[12] which Hubert Matos directs from Miami. He also collaborates with *Trazos de Cuba*, a bulletin whose September 1997 issue tacitly supported the acts of terrorism that were being committed in Cuban tourist centers.[13] As stated in the preface to *L'autre voix cubaine*, *Trazos de Cuba* is an important source of information for Reporters Without Frontiers.

Reporters Without Frontiers chose Néstor Baguer to be its correspondent in Cuba.[14] He is also a member of the Martí Human Rights Committee (Comité Martiano por los Derechos Humanos, CMDH) and the Democratic Socialist Current (Corriente Socialista Democrática, DSD), both of which are linked to the Cuban Democratic Arrangement and the Cuban Democratic Platform,[15] which are directed from abroad by Carlos Alberto Montaner and José Ignacio Rasco. In addition, his contributions appear regularly in the bulletins put out by the Cuban American National Foundation and the Cuban Delegation in Exile.[16]

Reporters Without Frontiers published a short book of poems by Restano, written during the months he was in prison. He was one of the first people who, in the late 1980s, tried to set up an independent press agency. Shortly afterwards, he organized and headed a group called the

---

[12] "Lista de organizaciones disidentes."

[13] "¡Así que ya saben, en Cuba también revientan aguacates!" (Just So You Know, Bombs Are Going Off in Cuba, Too), *Trazos de Cuba*, Paris, September 1997.

[14] *Rapport 1997*.

[15] In the "Lista de organizaciones disidentes." At that time, the so-called Martí Committee was number 101 and the Socialist Current, number 126, on the list. Both joined the Cuban Democratic Arrangement, number 106 on the list. For more information about the growing political similarity between the Arrangement and the Platform, see *Víspera del final*.

[16] *Periódico formativo e informativo*, Cuban Delegation in Exile, year XXXIV, no. 390, Miami, April 1997.

Harmony Movement (Movimiento Armonía, MA),[17] which toed the line of the Cuban Democratic Arrangement and the Cuban Democratic Platform. Restano was an assiduous informant of both Radio Martí and La Voz de la Fundación.[18] He went abroad and didn't return to Cuba, apparently because the authorities refused to let him in. By June 17, 1997, he was using the Internet line belonging to Brothers to the Rescue to spread information. He now lives in Miami.

Olance Nogueras lives in Cienfuegos and has an editorial post in an independent press agency. "On August 15 [1996], Robin Dayan Meyers, a U.S. diplomat [accredited to the U.S. Interests Section], visited the journalist."[19] Is it possible that we are the only ones to wonder what was so special about Mr. Nogueras that led such an important official to go to that city? On September 5, 1996, after a televised debate between Jorge Mas Canosa and Cuban leader Ricardo Alarcón, Nogueras phoned in the following comment to La Voz de la Fundación: "The Chairman of the Board of the Cuban American National Foundation once more showed that he is one of the great exile leaders and one of the most capable people for confronting the Cuban Government."[20]

On October 8, 1997, the day on which the Fifth Congress of the Communist Party of Cuba began, a short document asking the authorities of that country to free Lorenzo Páez Núñez and to stop arresting "independent" journalists was made public.[21] Reporters Without Frontiers said that Mr. Páez Núñez was a member of a press agency and also "President of the José de la Luz y Caballero Nongovernmental Center for Human Rights." The RSF's accusation stated that, when arrested, "The journalist [who is really a mathematician, according to the RSF] phoned the representative of an association of Cuban exiles in the United States..."

For an objective understanding of the context of the arrest, it is only

---

[17] His membership in that group is attested to by Reporters Without Frontiers in its *Rapport 1997*; Amnesty International in *Cuba, ofensiva;* and *Fundación: Organo oficial de la FNCA,* year 2, no. 9, Miami, 1993.

[18] His name and that of the group are on a list that the Cuban American National Foundation made public, with the following introduction: "The opposition inside Cuba is characterized by being linked to two large organizational coalitions: the Cuban Democratic Coalition and the Cuban Democratic Arrangement... Below, we provide a list of the opposition organizations in Cuba which broadcast over La Voz de la Fundación... " The said Harmony Movement appears as belonging to the Arrangement on page 16 of *Fundación: Organo oficial de la FNCA,* no. 9.

[19] *Rapport 1997.*

[20] "Desde Cuba: opiniones sobre el debate" (From Cuba: Opinions about the Debate), *Fundación. Organo oficial de la FNCA,* year 5, no. 16, Miami, 1996, 30.

[21] *Cuba. Hors du Parti, point de salut* (Cuba. Out of the Party, a Healthy Place), (Paris: Reporters Sans Frontières, October 1997).

necessary to know that the "Nongovernmental Center" is linked to the Cuban Democratic Coalition, which is directed from Miami by the ultrareactionary Cuban American National Foundation,[22] which was an accessory to the placing of bombs in Cuban tourist centers.[23] Therefore, Mr. Páez wasn't phoning just any old exile association. The police came "while the Cuban American National Foundation was taping Lorenzo Páez Núñez, the group's spokesman."[24]

We will wind up this series of examples with something that happened in early 1997, but, first, we should give a brief introduction.

President Clinton signed the Helms-Burton Bill in March 1996. It is even more arrogant, meddling and pro-annexationist than the Torricelli Act. It "institutionalizes" the U.S. "sovereign right" to create and to give moral and financial support to the dissident movement in Cuba, including "independent" journalists.

At that time, as the governments of France, England, Spain and the United States itself were to do — and did in the not-so-distant past in the face of foreign aggression — the Cuban Government stated in its legislation that any internal collaboration with the pretensions of the Helms-Burton Act would be considered a crime against the nation.

Almost a year later, on January 28, 1997, the White House announced a document on support for a democratic transition in Cuba. It had been "drafted within the framework of the Helms-Burton Act [and] was to be publicized extensively over Radio Martí."[25] It promised massive economic assistance to the Cubans as soon as the Castro brothers and some of the other current leaders left or lost power. While that was going on, the U.S. Government "felt obliged" to support the so-called dissident groups. In other words, more and more of the same old thing.

The U.S. Interests Section immediately began programming seminars in addition to providing its habitual material and financial support.

Now, let's take a look at some communiqués that two so-called independent journalists wrote on the same topic:

Havana, February 1997. BPIC. — At midday on February 5 [1997], a televised program on civic journalism in which a member of

---

[22] Number 77 on the "Lista de organizaciones disidentes," it is listed textually as the "José de la Luz y Caballero Nongovernmental Center for Human Rights and the Culture of Peace [Centro No Gubernamental para los Derechos Humanos y la Cultura de Pax 'José de la Luz y Caballero,' CNGDHCP]. It forms part of the Cuban Democratic Coalition... ." The names of two members are given, the second of which is that of Páez Núñez.

[23] *El Nuevo Herald*, Miami, November 10, 1997.

[24] *Noticias de Cuba*, Internet information bulletin of CANF, July 26, 1997.

[25] *Le Monde*, Paris, February 1, 1997.

Philadelphia Square [sic] and William Harrys [sic], of the Department of Political Science of the University of Pennsylvania, participated was shown direct from Washington in the residence of Mrs. Mary [sic] Blocker, First Secretary for Press and Cultural Affairs of the U.S. Interests Section in Cuba.

Representatives of the Independent Press Agency of Cuba (APIC), Havana Press, the Independent Press Bureau of Cuba (BPIC) and the North Press Center (Centro Norte Press) of Villa Clara were present... Of the foreign press, only the Spanish news agency EFE and *The Financial Times* and the BBC of London were represented.

The second text adds details to and complements the other:

Havana, February 5 (BPIC). — Journalists of five independent press agencies were angered on Wednesday [sic] by a film team of National Television News during the broadcast of a televised program on civic and public journalism in the residence of Merrie [sic] Blocker, First Secretary...

'The aim is to create panic among the members of the independent press,' Raúl Rivero, President of Cuba Press, said...

The meeting consisted of the presentation of a debate on the new trends of democratic journalism born in the United States and with broad participation by the common man.

The program 'Public and Civic Journalism' was broadcast over the U.S. Government's public service channel, Worldnet, with the participation in Washington of journalist Jan Schaffer, of *The Philadelphia Inquirer*, and Professor William Harris...

'I have been waiting for this clash between the main [sic] sources of information from Cuba,' said Lázaro Lazo, Director of the Independent Press Bureau of Cuba, who believes that the act of provocation has situational aspects related to the report on support for a democratic transition in Cuba which President Clinton issued last week. [26]

Olance Nogueras, who wrote the article, explained the document on democratic transition as follows: "Chapter II brings out the need [for the United States] to strengthen the independent mass media, providing assistance for training journalists in objective, responsible methods of keeping citizens informed." We believe that no comment on the lack of journalistic — to say nothing of political — independence is required.

---

[26] Taken from The Internet. Communiqué of the Independent Press Bureau of Cuba (Buró de Prensa Independiente de Cuba, BPIC), July 4, 1997.

Robert Ménard, General Secretary of Reporters Without Frontiers, states unequivocally that the Association's priority in Latin America is Cuba. This is expressed in support for the work of "independent" journalists. Why such importance? Because, in the view of the RSF, "It is dangerous to be a journalist in Colombia or Peru, but there is freedom of the press." In those countries, journalists are "murdered and imprisoned" — but their relatives and colleagues can "make accusations." This is disquieting, because it isn't just the isolated case of those two countries. In a continent where the illiteracy rate is very high and only a minimal section of the population have access to the mass media, we think that considering freedom of the press more important than the right to life and safety is a very serious thing.

It may be said that *The Economist* isn't a specialist on this topic, but in April 1997 it listed the 12 countries in the world that most attack freedom of the press and expression, and all except China are close allies of the United States and the European Union. In Latin America, Colombia and Mexico were the first listed.

Fine. According to the Inter-American Press Association (Sociedad Interamericana de Prensa, SIP), 179 journalists were murdered "with absolute impunity" in Latin America during the past nine years, most of them by government repressive forces. That's almost 20 a year, or more than one and a half a month. In Cuba, no journalists at all have been attacked, tortured, murdered or made to disappear. Without looking at whom they serve — and without wanting to do so — the Inter-American Press Association awarded a prize to the "independent" press agencies for their "courageous" contribution to the "democracy" of information.

Neither Paraguay nor Argentina is in conflict with any other country, as Cuba is, yet Raquel Rojas, of the daily *La Nación* of Paraguay, wrote that, "doing investigative journalism in my country nowadays means risking your life every day." And, in the same article, Oscar Cardoso, of *El Clarín*, of Buenos Aires, added that President Menem "has proposed to offset freedom of the press with the freedom to beat up journalists."[27]

Our interview was held in the Paris headquarters of the International Secretariat of Reporters Without Frontiers. It began with Jacques Perrot and wound up with Robert Ménard. The former is a friendly, quiet young man. The General Secretary seemed impulsive — to such an extent that he couldn't hold back expressions that showed his deep fury against the Cuban Government.

We repeat: the RSF's defense of those who call themselves independent journalists is disquieting, because the ones who are known

---

[27] Felipe Sahagún, "Información veraz" (The Truth), *El Mundo*, Madrid, November 9, 1997.

internationally don't have any professional independence. What is unquestionably true is that the independence they boast of has placed them in one of the camps, because their hearts and pens directly or indirectly serve the power that wants to see their nation become the 51st star in the flag of the United States — another Puerto Rico.

* * *

"In your 1997 report, you say that there are five independent press agencies in Cuba. You refer to them as if they consisted of a large number of media professionals. But, as far as we know, there aren't so many of them — fewer than 10."

"Yes, there are more journalists, but it is true that most of them are collaborators."

"I'd like to concentrate on the role that a journalist should play when their nation is engaged in a nonmilitary war, which is the case of Cuba. I'd like you to place yourself in the position of the Cuban Government: in the midst of that aggression which the United States has declared for nearly 40 years, would you allow some of your citizens, because they were journalists, to send whatever information they wanted to the enemy?"

"I don't think that all of the articles attack the Cuban Government. Nor do I think that they ask for Fidel Castro's head. But why can't anybody criticize the government and Fidel Castro? Why can't a Cuban ask for the dictator Castro to leave power?"

"But the newspapers Granma, Trabajadores *and* Juventud Rebelde *regularly contain criticism of institutions and government officials. For example, I've read several articles that name names of corrupt political cadres."*

"Several of those journalists have worked on official media. They were fired for indiscipline, disrespect or affronts to the authorities."

"Let's take a look. When the Cuban Council appeared, it was said internationally that it was a valid independent opposition group to the Cuban system. But there are plenty of documents showing that the Council was organized, financed and directed not only by the extreme right wing of the exile community but also by the U.S. Government. And it is known that the so-called independent journalists have participated very actively, especially by passing information to counterrevolutionary media abroad — Radio Martí, above all."

"You should know better than I that some of the groups in the Cuban Council must be financed by the CIA. Nobody doubts that. But some of them must also be financed by Cuban State Security. We in the RSF constantly support independent journalists. But why was Raúl Rivero threatened, and why is he picked up every so often? Because he wrote for *El Nuevo Herald*?"

"You ought to know that that newspaper is practically controlled by the

extreme right wing of the Cuban exile community, the same people who want to annex Cuba to the United States. Don't you think that's enough for taking sides in the conflict? Moreover, Mr. Raúl Rivero and his brother broadcast over Radio Martí and have regular programs on it. And you know that that radio station is controlled by the State Department. Do you think the French Government would stand for such a thing if it were in Cuba's shoes? What's important: your homeland or your profession?"

"I believe completely that a journalist cannot censor himself to defend his homeland at any cost."

"I want you to know that I don't believe in journalistic neutrality. For example, as soon as you called Fidel Castro a dictator, you took a political position. We're all human, and we all have hearts, but there are people — journalists — who, in Cuba, are serving, collaborating with, one of the parties to the conflict: the historical enemy of their homeland. I really don't understand that idea of independence and neutrality. It must be that they have a different concept of independence and neutrality than the one given in dictionaries and encyclopedias."

"Listen: in their articles, those journalists write about daily life in Cuba, the difficulties they're experiencing."

"That's so, though all of the ones we've read are very negative. They're nothing but attacks on the Cuban Government. Doesn't it seem strange to you that there isn't even a trace of a positive approach? Why do you think the extreme right wing in the exile community is so happy with them? But, going on to another thing, what is the RSF doing for those people?"

"First, we make contact with them. We try to get their texts published abroad, so they will become known...

"But I want to know where it says that they're all financed or supported by the CIA..."

"I didn't say that. But, if you read some of the documents of the U.S. Government and of the extreme right wing of the exile community, it's easy to confirm that at least the better known of them receive several kinds of support. Moreover, many recent U.S. Government reports say that they are financed or provided with the necessary equipment."

"Well, I think those are things that should be proved."

"We don't have concrete proof that they are given money for doing nothing. But you know that they are paid for the articles they write that are published in the media of the extreme right wing and are used over Radio Martí. Now, their actions clearly show that, whether voluntarily or involuntarily, they support the counterrevolutionary strategy politically. And it's hard for us to believe that such intelligent people don't know how their work is being used abroad. But, tell us: how do those journalists send their texts abroad?"

"They phone in their articles to somebody in Miami, and that person puts them on the Internet. But, for sure, there's a position in Europe that's favorable to Fidel Castro's regime. And, right now, those journalists don't have very much effect. A little in Spain; in France, almost none at all… Sometimes, the *Courier International*…"

"What kind of relations are there between the people in Cuba and those journalists?"

"Every so often, meetings are held to denounce them. According to the journalists, the participants are members of the Communist Party in their neighborhoods who go to their houses shouting that they are betraying their country, etc. The journalists are pointed out as enemies of the people. Their lives are made difficult. In addition, State Security picks them up and holds them for hours or days at a time."

"Have you spoken with members of the Cuban Government and asked them to explain why this is done?"

"No, not really. But we should do it."

Then we went to the office of Robert Ménard, General Secretary of the RSF. There, at his large circular table, we took up specific details of the topic that we were most interested in.

"Mr. Ménard, should a journalist place more importance on their homeland, his nation, than on their job?"

"This isn't a debate that affects only Cuba. It includes the democracies. Remember the Gulf War; that was the question: Are you a journalist or a French citizen? It was somewhat contrary to the Vietnam War. In Vietnam, a journalist exercised his profession in complete freedom. But, in the Gulf War, the Americans told the members of the press — not explicitly, but remembering the Vietnam War — 'You are American citizens; you can't separate yourselves from the interests of the government; you can't report as you like.' Then they selected some journalists and took them where they wanted them to go. And, even though there were some protests, the world press accepted that principle.

"So, are there any limits for a journalist when his country is at war? I understand limits when the lives of the soldiers are dependent on them.

"But, in Cuba, the government has gone a little farther, because you can't say one word that is in favor of the Americans, within that war that the authorities in Havana consider has existed for nearly 40 years. And that is inadmissible. Inadmissible! I think that journalists have a role, even if it is against their own country. Information may be counter to the interests of their own country.

"In the Gulf War, there was no freedom, but Cuba is another thing."

"Do you think that the Cuban Government should stand by and let its enemies finance those who, it seems, don't care about their nation's sovereignty?"

"That's the problem. Why do you think the RSF helps those independent journalists financially? For exactly that reason, because some of them should be enabled to exist without any money from the Cuban Government — because, since they are its critics, it doesn't give them money. And they should be enabled to survive without Miami and the CIA.

"If you hope that the future will offer an alternative to Castro that's different from the bloody ones dreamed of in Miami, it will come from the involvement of organizations such as ours in Europe. That is why, when the authorities of the European Union say that the embargo should be strengthened, we say that things must be done positively in Cuba, and those who constitute an alternative to Castro inside the country should be helped.

"When we help the independent journalists in Cuba, we remind them that that money doesn't come from the Americans or even from the European Union. We give $50 a month each to around 20 journalists so they can survive and stay in the country, because, every time we meet them, the first thing they ask us is to help them leave Cuba, because of economic problems, so they can withstand the pressure and not need Radio Martí."

"Reporters Without Frontiers was represented in the meeting that Eizenstat, the U.S. Government's Special Ambassador, called..."

"Yes. Yes."

"Well, then you know that he went through Europe meeting with some nongovernmental organizations whose work concerns Cuba. You know that he's proposing support for the so-called internal dissident movement. Let's suppose that the RSF knows that that is one of the most important tactics drawn up in Washington to destabilize the Cuban Government and that the European NGOs are very important in this, because they don't inspire the distrust that most of the ones in the United States do. What was the RSF's position in that meeting?"

[Mr. Perrot replies.] "We've told you that we have been giving that support since September 1995."

"We know that, in other countries, some nongovernmental organizations have agreed to that plan, and we're trying to find out, even though it will be very difficult, which NGOs accepted or would be willing to receive the thousands of dollars that the U.S. Government offered."

[Mr. Ménard replies.] "Reporters Without Frontiers wants to be precise about our money: it is super clean!"

"I have never said that Reporters Without Frontiers has received any money from the U.S. Government..."

"But it's important to make that clear!"

"It seems that, in France, Ambassador Eizenstat didn't offer money to the

NGOs that would support his plan. But, for him, the most important thing is that the dissident movement in Cuba be supported. The plan is that a group of European NGOs be consolidated to bring pressure to bear on the Cuban Government and to support the dissident movement. And it seems to us that, however unconsciously, Reporters Without Frontiers is following that line."

"Ah, but we were already giving them support, and we'll go on giving it to them!"

"It doesn't matter that doing so is a direct part of Washington's strategy of destabilizing Cuba?"

"Independently of the Americans' or the European Union's strategy, we will keep on doing it! For the RSF, Cuba is the priority in Latin America. There are three reasons for intervening in Cuba. First, to denounce what is going on in Cuba — because, in Europe, especially in France, people think that Castro isn't a dictator like the other ones, and that is absurd! Second, to give the journalists material assistance. Third, to make their work known."

"Why is it a priority, when there are other countries where being a journalist — an honest journalist — is very dangerous? I have never heard of any so-called independent journalists being tortured or murdered in Cuba."

"Why? Because it's the only country in Latin America where there isn't any freedom of the press! It is dangerous to be a journalist in Colombia or Peru, but there is freedom of the press!"

"Excuse me, but the freedom of the press that exists in Colombia or Peru is very debatable..."

"Yes, you can debate it! In Peru and in Colombia, there are limits to freedom of the press, and journalists have been murdered and imprisoned, but you can make accusations. But, in Cuba, no dissident voices are allowed! There aren't any independent radio stations or TV channels or newspapers. Everything is controlled by that government! The only exception is the bulletin put out by the Catholic Church!"

11

Lidwien Zumpolle
Coordinator of the Latin American Section
of Pax Christi Netherlands

"Of course, the Americans are happy about our movement — I mean, about what we have called the Platform for Human Rights and Democracy in Cuba."

When we called her to ask for an appointment, Ms. Lidwien Zumpolle asked us a lot of questions, most of them centered around how we knew that Pax Christi Netherlands was supporting the so-called Cuban dissident movement. When we had cleared everything up, she smiled readily, commenting that Europeans haven't learned to keep their mouths shut. To diversify our sources of information, we told her that we had an article from the U.S. press that said her institution was connected with the Clinton Administration's strategy.[1] She laughed again and was convinced that we were interested in what was public knowledge.

In December 1996, Pax Christi Netherlands issued a call to several European nongovernmental organizations that were working in the field of human rights or development. They were invited to create a "politically independent" European Platform for Democracy and Human Rights in Cuba (Plataforma Europea para la Democracia y los Derechos Humanos en Cuba, PEDDHC). The first meeting was held in The Hague, Holland, on February 21, 1997. Many of the organizations which had been sent invitations didn't send any representatives to the meeting, because its purpose didn't correspond to the criteria they held concerning the Cuban process. Since the meeting was of a "nonpublic" nature, we know only that representatives of Reporters Without Frontiers, Justice and Peace (of Italy and Spain) and H. Böll Stiftung (of Germany) attended. Nor have we managed to get a copy of its final resolutions.

Going back a little in very recent history, it has seemed to us that this Platform is a continuation of something that the U.S. Government had already attempted to create in 1995. Richard Nuccio, who was President Clinton's adviser on Central America at the time, was in charge of

---

[1] *The Miami Herald*, Miami, December 28, 1996.

promoting the project. The initiative was aimed at involving the nongovernmental organizations in the United States which maintained relations with their counterparts in Cuba, to get them to help destabilize the Cuban Government. The plan would adopt measures that would influence not only the population but also the "moderate" members of the government, the Communist Party and the armed forces, drawing gradually closer to them, to convince them that there was no alternative to a transition toward capitalism.

Almost all of the nongovernmental organizations in the United States turned down Mr. Nuccio's plan. Freedom House supported it, however, and a first half million dollars was turned over to that organization in October 1995. A large part of the money was immediately earmarked to pay for tickets for former officials or citizens of Western European countries or of the former Eastern bloc — who, preferably, had lived in Cuba — to go back there as tourists. Their main task was to recruit former friends and organize dissident groups.[2] In 1996, when the Helms-Burton Act went into effect, Nuccio resigned, and Mr. Eizenstat was named in his place. Like his predecessor, his work included meeting with representatives of nongovernmental organizations. This time, however, the operation was carried out in Canada and Europe.

Subsequent statements that Mr. Eizenstat made before the Foreign Relations Committee of the U.S. Senate in January 1997 showed that Pax Christi Netherlands wasn't the first organization in Holland, much less in the rest of Europe, to be invited to participate in the project — which had nothing to do with humanitarianism or human rights — but that it was the first to agree to do so.

Without any misgivings, Mr. Eizenstat publicly stated that several positive steps had been taken to promote an independent civil society in Cuba. He added that nongovernmental organizations led by the Dutch chapter of Pax Christi had joined efforts to strengthen the independent sector.[3] Therefore, it was hardly surprising that Janiset Rivero, of the Cuban Democratic Revolutionary Directorate, and Humberto Esteve, General Secretary of the Christian Democratic Party, both in Miami, praised that Catholic organization when they spoke with us.

Our interview with Ms. Zumpolle led us to conclude that one of the goals of Pax Christi Netherlands is to help destroy the present Cuban

---

[2] On August 15, 1997, apparently as a dry run, Cuban Security stopped David Norman Dorn, a U.S. citizen, while he was engaged on this kind of illegal activity at the behest of Frank Calzón and financed by Freedom House. Dorn is director of International Relations of the American Federation of Teachers, a labor union linked to the American Federation of Labor-Congress of Industrial Organizations.

[3] Stuart Eizenstat, "Enfoque multilateral a los derechos de propiedad" (Multilateral Approach to Property Rights), *Las Américas*, Miami, April 27, 1997.

system. Therefore, it is only logical that Holland is becoming a second beachhead (after Spain) through which extreme right-wing groups — such as those headed by the Cuban American National Foundation, Hubert Matos, Carlos Alberto Montaner and José Ignacio Rasco — may continue spreading throughout Europe.

The stubborn determination of Pax Christi Netherlands to become involved with the dissident movement in Cuba and with the destabilization of the Cuban Government was proved on November 28 and 29, 1997.

Those were the dates of the second meeting of the European Platform for Human Rights and Democracy in Cuba, which was held in Rome. There were only three items on the agenda: 1) urging the Vatican to get the Pope to put pressure on the Cuban Government concerning "human rights and democracy," 2) urging the companies that invest in Cuba to abide by the "code of conduct" proposed in the so-called Arcos Principles[4] and 3) "child prostitution and sex tourism in Cuba."

When Pax Christi Netherlands issued the invitation in early October, it found itself at loggerheads with other Pax Christi groups throughout the world. Those in Latin America, Italy and the United States — which is one of the strongest ones — categorically opposed the agenda and conspiratorial nature of the meeting. As Ms. Zumpolle told us by phone, around 15 European nongovernmental organizations were represented in the meeting. Their names? "I can't tell you. They aren't being made public. These NGOs don't want to have tense relations with the others."

Ms. Zumpolle confirmed that no organization that had been established to combat child prostitution had sent a representative and that only one document, from England — whose source she didn't want to divulge, either — was presented. Later, we learned that two English sociologists had written the paper in 1996 at the behest of ECPAT International. Even though the study is mainly aimed at showing the sexual behavior of certain men who travel to that country (which is identical to what they assume goes on in other Third World countries),

---

[4] The "Arcos Principles" are a series of demands that Gustavo Arcos believes should be applied to companies investing in Cuba. In the introduction to our interview with Mr. Bofill, we show that these "principles" are basically supported by the organizations that include Frank Calzón — a former CIA agent and former member of the Abdala terrorist organization — as one of their leaders. It should be recalled that those NGOs — Freedom House and Of Human Rights — receive a lot of funding from the U.S. Government, through the National Endowment for Democracy. Now, however, as acknowledged in an article that appeared in *El Nuevo Herald* on October 31, 1998, Calzón is receiving money from the U.S. Agency for International Development, through the Free Cuba Center, of which he is also a director. According to him, in 1999 he "should receive $400,000, mainly for sending books and videos to the island."

on reading the Pax Christi Netherlands reports, you get the feeling that child prostitution and sexual tourism are as widespread in Cuba as are wine in France and tequila in Mexico.

The only public meeting held by the Platform was a press conference given by Dariel Alarcón, "Benigno," and Father Miguel Loredo. The former had been with Che in Bolivia in 1967 and abandoned the revolution a few years ago. "Benigno" didn't say that, since September 1996, he had maintained a personal relationship with "Félix Rodríguez, an old CIA hand, who has made an impressive number of missions through all of the world's continents in the past 30 years." *Le Monde* contributed that information. On October 10, 1998, the important French daily stated that "Benigno" had even spent two weeks at Rodríguez's bunker in Miami. That is, he had eaten at the table of one of the most fearsome men ever created by the CIA.

It is hardly possible that Pax Christi Netherlands was ignorant of this, because, in late 1996, a Miami television station had filmed and broadcast what was apparently their first meeting. Later, many other media throughout the world picked up this and other meetings.

Loredo, a special guest of Pax Christi Netherlands, was presented as a symbol of "the Cuban Government's repression of the Church." It is true that the priest spent 10 years in prison — for having hidden Angel Betancourt in his monastery for two weeks and having tried to spirit him out of Cuba clandestinely. Betancourt had murdered two crew members and wounded a third when he tried to hijack a Cubana de Aviación plane in March 1966. When Loredo got out of prison, he moved to New York, where he became involved with extreme right-wing groups of exiles.

A year later, a book of the documents of the Platform's second meeting was published in Italian. On the cover of *Cuba, la realtà dietro il simbolo* (Cuba, the Reality within the Symbol), the author is given simply as Pax Christi — which, as we understand it, makes all of the other sections of Pax Christi throughout the world responsible for the book. It contains the document by the English sociologists, the paper presented by Ms. Lidwien Zumpolle, 13 papers by so-called Cuban dissidents and a paper by Frank Calzón. On page two, tribute is paid to his organization — Of Human Rights — "for its valuable collaboration."

Pax Christi Netherlands issued an invitation to a round-table discussion to be held on the afternoon of December 3, 1998, in facilities pertaining to the European Parliament in Brussels. The theme was "Foreign investments in Cuba and human and labor rights." Only four hours were assigned for studying, analyzing and debating that important and complex topic. Even though Amnesty International has been working on the subject at the world level for several years, only the

Dutch section supported that activity. As in the earlier cases, almost none of the names of the organizations represented in that round-table discussion are known.

Ernesto Díaz Rodríguez, of Cuba, was one of the speakers. But, before going any farther, we should point out that, a few months earlier, in September, he had gone on a tour of several European countries together with members of the Democratic Revolutionary Directorate (Directorio Revolucionario Democrático, DRD), a group which describes itself as pacifist and for civil resistance inside Cuba.

Janiset Rivero and Orlando Gutiérrez, of the Directorate, met "with activists from Pax Christi Netherlands, Glasnost for Cuba [also Dutch] and the International Society for Human Rights based in Germany."[5] They also met, though not for the first time, with the Italian "Olivier Dupuis, of the Transnational Radical Party and a deputy to the European Parliament."

We don't know whether or not those European organizations are aware that, during the 1980s, Gutiérrez was a member of the Organization for the Liberation of Cuba (Organización Para la Liberación de Cuba, OPLC), which the U.S. authorities have charged with being the legal branch of Omega 7, one of the bloodiest organizations during the worldwide campaign against Cuba.[6] The leaders of Omega 7 — which has also been accused of trafficking in drugs — include the Novo brothers, who were allegedly involved in the murder of Orlando Letelier a minister in the Chilean Government when Salvador Allende was president.

In addition, Omar López Montenegro, another leader of the Directorate, belonged to the Liberty and Peace Cuban Pacifist Movement (Movimiento Pacifista Cubano Libertad y Paz, MPCLP), a tiny group that belongs to the Cuban Democratic Coalition,[7] which was organized by the Cuban American National Foundation.

Now, let's get back to Díaz Rodríguez. Pax Christi Netherlands presented him as a representative of the independent labor unions in Cuba and as a researcher into cases of violations of labor rights in his country. It forgot to add one basic and alarming fact: Ernesto Díaz Rodríguez had been imprisoned in Cuba in 1967 for being a member of the Alpha 66 group, to which he had belonged for several years.[8]

On being released, he went to Miami, where he continues to

---

[5] *Caminos* (Pathways), Information bulletin of the Democratic Revolutionary Directorate, year 1, vol. 4, Miami, October 1998.

[6] Encinosa, *Cuba en guerra*.

[7] Ibid.

[8] Talleda, *Alpha 66*. See also Encinosa, *Cuba en guerra*.

participate in that organization. His photograph appears in the book that contains the "cleaner" part of the history of Alpha 66. From the flag that can be seen behind him, it is possible to conclude that the photo was taken when that group was supporting Solidarity in Poland. But the book had just come out in 1995. In view of the degree of faithfulness and dedication that a member of Alpha 66 had to give that organization for it to pay him recognition of this kind, it is nearly certain that Díaz Rodríguez was already a hard-core member by that time.

We knocked on the door at the time agreed upon for the interview. Ms. Zumpolle came and, after greeting us briefly, settled us on her tiny back terrace. We were there for nearly three hours. When we had finished discussing the topic of Cuba, we began to speak of Colombia. As a good Eurocentrist, she is sure to be a key figure in the efforts to achieve peace in that country. The worst thing she told us was that she greatly admired Carlos Castaño, the Colombian paramilitary chief and trafficker in drugs. Castaño, the right hand of the army in its strategy against the people's and guerrilla movement, is responsible for several massacres in Urabá, a banana-growing area bordering on Panama. With a pleased sparkle in her eyes, Ms. Zumpolle said, "I could tell you many good things that Castaño is doing to promote the farmers' return."

* * *

"Ms. Zumpolle, why did Pax Christi Netherlands begin to take an interest in Cuba?"

"As you know, the Soviet Union was already withdrawing by 1990. Then the economy began to get really bad, and Castro's government added more political repression to the increased poverty. And no opening. That's why, in around 1991, it was decided to send a small delegation. At first, we were denied visas. We knew that the government had said, 'To hell with them...'"

"That's how it was put?"

"No, no, no. We knew the authorities in Havana hadn't reacted positively when they learned we were going to talk with the members of the dissident movement. What they said on that occasion was that we should go to Miami, not hell. But then the Gulf War began, and we had to put off our trip for six months, just when Castro and his allies were meeting in the Fourth Congress of the Communist Party."

"Then we began to realize what a lie Cuba was."

"What was that lie?"

"That Cuba was a socialist paradise. We found that there wasn't any education or health care, that that society was a dictatorship. We talked with a lot of people, but always in their houses, with the windows shut so the neighbors wouldn't find out about it."

"I know a lot of people who go to Cuba regularly and have never had to experience that. And they are people who don't always agree with the Cuban system. Moreover, I have been in Cuba, too, and I spoke with a lot of people, and I never thought I was harassed. What's the problem — did you feel harassed because you were plotting?"

"No, no, our work was known."

"How did you make contact with the so-called dissident movement?"

"By contacting people who contacted others. And people that you meet there, ordinary, run-of-the-mill people. Of course, that time, the only dissident we found was Osvaldo Payá, of the Christian Movement. And everything he told us was horrifying! I know about the situation in Colombia, which is terrible; 30,000 people are murdered through political violence there every year. But, in Cuba — !"

"And how many political murders were there in Cuba?"

"There aren't any murders in Cuba, but there is a schizophrenic psychological dictatorship. And, I tell you, I would rather live in Colombia than Cuba."

"But there aren't any political murders in Cuba. In Colombia, there are 30,000 a year, not counting the thousands who are arrested and disappear..."

"Look, it's very hard to explain. In Cuba, there is very sophisticated repression. It's something that the neighborhood committees, the Communist Party and the labor unions — there aren't any independent ones — engage in. There are so many forms of public control over the individual that you go mad. I'm familiar with many Latin American societies, and you can see that Cuban society is very different."

"I agree completely with you on that; it's another political system."

"Of course, the system has made improvements in education and the rural areas and has done something in health care and sports. That's why I say that it's another system. But that isn't anything when weighed against the repression. I think that those social improvements are simply cosmetic, to present a good facade abroad."

"As someone who is familiar with the poverty in Latin America, you may know how many hundreds of millions of people would like to have access to those 'cosmetic' improvements. What there is in the rest of Latin America is a lot of repression, not 'cosmetic' improvements."

"But in Colombia, for example, the people can have initiatives. They can try to do things to pull themselves out of their poverty. It's true that they are killed suddenly, but at least they can make the attempt. In Cuba, everything is paralyzed. And it's a lie to say that Russia's to blame for that situation because it doesn't help them, just as it's a lie to blame it on the Americans' blockade. The situation has always been bad. I've talked with Cubans for thousands and thousands of hours — I mean, hundreds of hours. They felt so hemmed in, so repressed, that, once they started talking, they never stopped. They went on and on."

"But all Cubans like to talk. I think it's a characteristic of nearly all Latins, though the Cubans take the cake."

"Yes, yes. Colombians talk a lot, too. But here, in my house, we've given some of them therapy, and they've gone out to shout out the window, 'Down with Fidel!' There, the people can't say such things out loud, or they feel persecuted by Cuban Security. It's very sick. I've never seen any other country where the people's facial expressions had become deformed from their saying things under their breath, out of fear — their faces become sort of twisted to the side... "

"I've never seen a Cuban — man or woman — whose mouth or cheekbones were deformed, even from disease. Not even those who say they are dissidents have any such deformations. Moreover, I've never found that they make any special faces or grimaces when they speak.

"In Colombia, didn't you notice the expressions that millions of farmers and city dwellers assume when they see a military man? And in Peru? And Guatemala? And El Salvador? And the children who live in the streets in Brazil? Shall I continue? Excuse me for saying so, but you're talking to someone who is familiar with Latin America's political and social problems."

"But all Cubans suffer from neurosis because they can't say what they think...

"But, to get back to the subject, I'm sure that, when the Cuban regime blames all that internal chaos on the Americans, it's just an excuse. That charge is ridiculous. I'm sure that Castro isn't interested in having the embargo or the Helms-Burton Act lifted. The embargo doesn't exist, and the regime can buy from any country!"

"But I understand that the Cuban Government's problem isn't that it can't buy; it's that it doesn't have hard currency. Cuba's currency, the peso, isn't accepted on the international market."

"Yes, that may be so, since 1989. But the boycott already existed."

"Yes, but Cuba had equitable trade relations with the countries of the former Eastern bloc."

"When Castro had that assistance, he said that he was thumbing his nose at the boycott. Why doesn't he do that now?"

"How can a country survive without hard currency? We can't deny that obstacles are always placed in Cuba's path in the field of international trade. You can't deny that the United States pressures all of the countries and individuals who want to do business with Cuba."

"We have talked with the representatives of a lot of governments, including the U.S. Government, and we've suggested to the U.S. Government that it restrain the extremists in Miami and make them ease up the pressure on applying the Helms-Burton Act, because it helps

Castro. He uses the embargo as a pretext for not giving the people enough to eat."

"Ms. Zumpolle, what activities did you engage in when you got back from your first visit to Cuba?"

"We wrote a report in several languages and distributed it; we began working with the United Nations and the European Parliament; and we launched a campaign supporting the voiceless people, the members of the dissident movement in Cuba, such as Osvaldo Payá. It was diplomatic work. At first, people said we were a part of the Americans' policy, but we said we were working for human rights and that the Cuban Government was criminal. I tell you, as I said about the Colombian Government..."

"I am Colombian, and I repeat that your comparing the Colombian Government — which is recognized as a murdering, terrorist regime — with the Cuban Government is a gross exaggeration."

"I consider Castro to be a criminal, and I don't have any hang-ups about saying so. He has repressed an entire nation. Look at education in Cuba: it's military. He's crazy, and I'm not afraid to say so. Let him come to my house, if he wants! I'm not afraid of him!"

"Ms. Zumpolle, is human rights work nonpartisan, or is it part of the worldwide political game?"

"Of course, it's nonpartisan... ! Why do you ask me that? Because of what I say about Fidel Castro?"

"Maybe. It surprises me that a person who holds such an important post in this Catholic organization should express herself this way..."

"But Fidel Castro has had that nation all boxed in. When the Soviets were leaving Cuba, they had talks with us — secret talks. They wanted to know if the people were ready to rise up against Castro. Those Soviets wanted Cuba to have an opening like the one their country was getting.

"Cuba is a feudal, medieval country in terms of work relations. We want Cuba to have independent labor unions. That's why we're waging our 'code of conduct' campaign, aimed at the investors in Cuba. Those international companies should support the Cuban workers and help them organize independently of the government."

"Have other European nongovernmental organizations supported you in those campaigns?"

"It isn't easy to mobilize European international organizations against the Cuban Government, but at least we're struggling to make them know that there is a dissident movement in Cuba and to believe in it."

"If I'm not mistaken, representatives of Pax Christi Netherlands have gone back to Cuba three times. Did you find other dissident organizations? And did the Cuban Government try to hinder your work?"

"We've gone back, but with tourist visas. But how could the government hinder us? Can't everybody talk with the people?

"We haven't found many groups, but that isn't necessary. Anybody on the street will tell you everything. Moreover, it's hard to find people in organized groups, because there's no transportation and no telephones. And there's so much repression!"

"But, even though you say there is too much repression, you were able to talk with a lot of people. It seems to me that you could also have contacted the so-called dissidents, because it is said that there are many of them. Moreover, there are telephones and transportation, though not to the same extent as in Europe."

"The thing is, everybody there is watching everybody else!"

"Do you know that those so-called dissident groups have received money or some other kind of support from the U.S. Government and from the extreme right wing of the exile community?"

"Which ones?"

"Gustavo Arcos, who is praised so much internationally, for example. In addition, there are official U.S. Government documents which say which groups it has financed. They include the Cuban Council, which received instructions and money from the extreme right wing of the exile community."

"But there are other groups, such as Elizardo Sánchez's, which are supported, however modestly, by European governments. So what? That doesn't justify repressing them. I didn't know what you've told me, but I believe you. What's the problem? Those people use that money to live on. And, if somebody sends them another kind of support, so what?"

"Let's suppose that you are the Cuban Government and that I, as one of your dissidents, am financed by U.S. agencies. What would you do?"

"I think I'd put you in jail. I'd do what the Cuban Government is doing."

"Then what's the difference?"

"But there are people there who receive money from the French, Belgian and Dutch governments... So what? I'm very much in favor of an opening."

"And it doesn't matter if that kind of opening is used to destabilize your nation?"

"Wait a minute. The Cuban Council had something basic; it wasn't violent... Of course, the Cuban Government must have financed several of those groups... But I do think that the Americans haven't been intelligent."

"The documents and practice show that the U.S. Government changed its tactics a few years ago. Its warlike language has changed, even among the leaders of the extreme right wing of the exile community. Clinton has named

special ambassadors on Cuban affairs..."

"We spoke with Eizenstat. He proposes that the peaceful dissident movement be supported. And we do, too. I think that that is very good, very intelligent. Moreover, this is the first time they've listened to the European organizations. Clinton is doing this because he doesn't want any problems with the European businessmen. Clinton knows that the Helms-Burton Act isn't required to make Castro's government fall. I hope they continue that way."

"We have been told that Mr. Eizenstat has offered the European non-governmental organizations money if they support his project."

"What organizations? He didn't say anything to us. When he began to talk about financing, we told him that under no circumstances should the United States support human rights groups in Europe financially, because we would be compared to the Miami people. But Eizenstat did say that it could be obtained through European agencies in Brussels. I told him that money wasn't a problem, because, when you're convinced about what you're doing, the money always turns up. I've always come up with the money for my projects."

"And Europeans are convinced about helping the so-called dissidents?"

"The money turns up. It turns up. At the beginning of 1997, representatives of around 15 European nongovernmental organizations and agencies that were related to human rights in one way or another met to create the Platform..."

"Excuse me for interrupting, but why weren't more represented, if there are so many of them in Europe?"

"We sent out a lot of invitations, but those were the only ones that accepted. Others, such as Terre des Hommes-France and Oxfam-Belgium, didn't dare send representatives, because they have projects in Cuba that they didn't want to lose. Of course, Oxfam-Belgium... It supports the government... I don't know. It doesn't want to denounce the Cuban Government.

"We held the meeting to see what we could do together for Cuba. And we decided to look for support for the dissident movement — not so much financial assistance, because that's of secondary importance, but international recognition, so the dissidents would feel that they had political and moral support.

"The Miami people called me to protest because they hadn't been included and because they thought we were going to receive a lot of money — dollars that, of course, we would be handling without keeping them in mind. Here in Holland, the pro-Cuban groups also said that the Platform was planned, directed and financed by the Americans..."

"I think it was easy to say that the meeting was financed or supported by the U.S. Government, because Mr. Eizenstat had just visited you a few days earlier.

A bit of a coincidence, don't you think?"

"We saw Eizenstat in November, but some of us were already trying to get organized. But, yes, I do think that the meeting helped Clinton, also in January, to convince the U.S. Congress to hold back on applying the Helms-Burton Act. After Eizenstat's trip, Clinton could tell the Congress that a movement in favor of human rights and democratization in Cuba was beginning in Europe. He could say that we Europeans didn't want to give so much support to Fidel Castro. Our meeting was one of the things that influenced him. In addition, the declaration of the European Union, which the Spanish Government pushed through, was a tremendous help. Are you familiar with that declaration? It's very strong! Very good! All of that was related to Eizenstat's tour, but it wasn't a result of it. And I'm happy!"

"Then this new tactic of the White House, which you view as something intelligent, harmonizes with the support for the dissident movement in Cuba that Pax Christi Netherlands and other European nongovernmental organizations are promoting?"

"Of course, the Americans are happy about our movement — I mean, about what we have called the Platform for Human Rights and Democracy in Cuba — because they have seen that the NGOs are becoming aware of what is happening in Cuba. They see that many people who are known as progressives are also speaking out in favor of human rights and democratization in Cuba."

"Was Pax Christi Netherlands one of the organizers of the meeting that was held here in Holland in April 1997?"

"No. Three Dutch parties were involved, but it was the Liberal Party that promoted it. It must have been because Carlos Alberto Montaner, of Madrid, is a member of the Liberal International. The Dutch parties couldn't organize it; they have no idea of what is happening in Cuba.

"Four Cuban exile parties were represented in the meeting. Other politicians and several Dutch businessmen were in the hall. I asked for the floor and used it to criticize the businessmen for their investments in Cuba. I asked them to use their economic clout to demand that the Cuban Government make democratic changes. Montaner and the other Cubans were very pleased by my remarks."

"It is felt that, if the present regime falls, the new president of Cuba will be someone from Miami. If not, it will certainly be someone else of whom the U.S. Government approves. That is included in the Helms-Burton Act."

"Yes. Yes. I agree with that completely. That's why Europe should take a hand in Cuba.

"But I don't know... I think that the United States has changed a lot... It's not like before, when it could manipulate everything. Europe should take a hand in Cuba so there will be more people involved."

"*Do you think that Europe can serve as a counterweight to the United States in Latin America? Look how it's even being pushed out of Africa. Don't you think that the rulers of the European Union, Pax Christi Netherlands and the other nongovernmental organizations that are involved in the plan to support the so-called dissident movement are making a big contribution to the aggressive U.S. policy?*"

"I don't know… But we must try to get in Cuba.

"Do you know what we suggested to Eizenstat? That the United States pull out of its military base at Guantánamo and that the international community, the United Nations, take it over as a guarantee of peace."

"*But the United States runs the United Nations! That has been crystal clear ever since the election of the last Secretary General.*"

"Well, the United Nations wouldn't do it, anyway, because it doesn't have enough money. But then the international community should do it — those who want a democratic opening for Cuba…"

"*Ms. Zumpolle, did you know that Cuban-U.S. members of Congress such as Ileana Ros-Lethinen, Díaz-Balart and Bob Menéndez are in favor of drawing closer to Europe in order to destabilize Cuba? Did you know that they are working together with Eizenstat? That they are politicians of the extreme right wing, close to the Cuban American National Foundation? And do you know that that Foundation is thinking of opening a public relations office in Brussels?*"

"No. I had no idea. But it doesn't surprise me. I think it is very important for the exiles to draw closer together. I'm very much in favor of that. It's great! The exiles should speak here in Europe, too — not just in Miami. I'd love to go to the United States to speak with those congressmen and the exiles. I think that I'll do that soon."

"*Finally, Ms. Zumpolle, you told me that the U.S. Government was happy about the Platform of nongovernmental organizations which Pax Christi Netherlands heads, and that it was happy about the European Union, too. Have you ever known Washington to be happy about anything that wasn't in its interests?*"

"The fact is, it's happy about Aznar's position; about the European Union's declarations; and about having found European nongovernmental organizations, such as Pax Christi Netherlands, which support the dissident movement."

12

Francisco Aruca
Businessman and radio commentator

"Being a dissident has become a business."

Almost immediately after beginning his career as a counterrevolutionary, Francisco Aruca was arrested and sentenced to 30 years in prison. He began to serve his sentence but soon escaped and left Cuba in 1961. He returned to his homeland in 1978 as part of an initiative of the Cuban Government's known as the Dialogue. On returning to New York, where he was living and had put down roots, he got together with some friends and, with $6,000, created the Marazul Company, specializing in charter flights to Cuba. "The demand was so great that we were selling seats for three months ahead."

In 1986, Marazul moved to Miami but found that the Hispanic media wouldn't run its ads. Therefore, it decided to buy time on Radio Unión. And, in addition to being a businessman, Aruca became a political commentator. "It wasn't just for the company. It's that I saw the need to create public opinion, a need for the people to receive a message other than one of hatred."

All kinds of insults and threats poured in. "Unknown persons" attacked the station and beat up a technician. Attacks were made against Marazul's four offices. Aruca wasn't intimidated. To the contrary, he started another program, over Radio Progreso, and he has won the affection and respect of a segment of the immigrants — Cubans and others. At one point, he went around with bodyguards; now, he just packs a pistol. "I can't say that they've actually done anything to me. Oh, yes — once a man bumped heavily into me and spilled my beer. All I thought about was the fuss my wife was going to make when I got home stinking like that."

* * *

"Mr. Aruca, even though we feel like a broken record, we would like to ask you, too, what you think of the Cuban exile community."

"The Cuban exile community is fictitious and unpatriotic, because, as soon as we arrive here, we start waiting for the Americans to give us the solution. Though with different approaches, the history of the exile community is a refusal to let the Americans leave us alone.

"Look, what they intend to do with the embargo laws is to create a social explosion in Cuba, so that, when that has happened or is about to happen, an army officer will appear and pull off a coup. But that military man will find himself holding a hot potato — or, worse, a pressure cooker with a blocked valve. He won't have a clue as to what to do to solve the problem. That's when those powerful Miami people will come on the scene, with the full backing of the American Government. Not having any alternative, the general will ask them what he must do so the United States will suspend its laws and things can go back to normal, with aid and trade — because the military man knows that he won't last long in power without it. And the reply he'll get is, 'Practice democracy. You should hold an election in which we'll win.'

"That's the outline, at the cost of the Cuban people and their sovereignty. Real pretty, isn't it?"

"Mr. Aruca, the so-called internal opposition in Cuba has had some publicity in Europe. Amnesty International has even described the Cuban Council as a 'serious opposition of an organized nature'."

"I don't know how familiar Amnesty is with Cuban reality, but those of us who do know it have said that the Cuban Council was going to end up as one enormous nothing. Unfortunately, those of the Council — and the so-called dissident movement as a whole — very quickly came to the conclusion that they couldn't survive without Miami, especially financially.

"The Council is nothing but history now. It was eaten up by its members' personal greed... Look, being a dissident has become a business. Many people call in to the radio stations every day saying they've organized human rights groups. What for? They're paving the way for getting help in leaving the country and then being welcomed as heroes in Miami or Spain. That is, being a dissident has also become a way of leaving the country without getting on a raft. There may be honest members of the opposition; the problem is finding them. What there has been so far is people who want to solve their personal problems or play ball with the enemies of their nation. I don't know if Amnesty International knows about all these things."

"Mr. Aruca, why do you think the United States and its allies haven't managed to bring the Cuban revolution to its knees?"

"Because they have ignored — haven't wanted to see — that, even with all its defects, the Cuban revolution has been a home-grown process that was carried out in Cuba in response to the desires of Cubans. It is a revolution that has, in fact, worked hard to improve society and that has created loyalty in a large segment of the population. The system has given the Cubans in Cuba a real feeling that they are the ones who control their country and its future. That has a lot of weight."

"OK, but it is said that Fidel and the Communist Party run everything in Cuba..."

"But it's the Cubans who are in charge. I'm talking about nationalism, not about running things. I am still to encounter a country where the people run things.

"Let's look at that system's other achievements. Education has been made available to all the people. They have the right to work, even though there's unemployment now, because of the economic situation. They have that right, and everybody had a job up until a short time ago.

"Even though there are always a few people who are racists, racism was ended as a social problem. In Cuba, an effort was made to be fair — sometimes, I think, *too* fair, because of a mistake in the system. A time came when egalitarianism was the most important goal, above everything else. I don't think that works very well. What did it result in? Cubans really feel themselves to be equals. Here in Miami, a few months after arriving on rafts, some of those people began complaining because they weren't treated as equals at work. In Cuba, if the administrator of a factory treats a worker any way he likes, he'll get in trouble."

"We think that it has been a revolution built by men and women, not gods, and that, therefore, it is bound to have made some mistakes. What do you think they are?"

"Well, I think that freedom of expression has been lost... Naturally, I understand that that freedom has to be measured in terms of the situation Cuba is going through, in which the enemy takes advantage of every opportunity to manipulate things, seeking a social explosion. People tend to forget that, when the United States and Europe were engaged in wars, their citizens weren't allowed to express their ideas as freely as they are in times of peace. The Gulf War was the latest example of this.

"Serious mistakes were also made in the economic sphere — mistakes which had political repercussions. One of them is that the government has centralized everything. I think that small private companies should be created so that an autonomous sector of the population may be generated to compete with the government. What I emphasize — and a lot of people don't like this — is that, even though mistakes have been made that should be corrected, you can't ask that the so-called dissidents be allowed to do whatever they want, because they're just waiting for the Cuban system to come a cropper, to finish it off."

"Let's talk about you. Yours is one of the very few dissident voices in the

Cuban community in Miami. What caused you to view Cuba differently?"

"In Cuba, I was a leftist counterrevolutionary. We believed that Cuba needed a revolution that would bring about profound transformations. It wasn't until I began studying economics in Washington that I realized that the Cuban revolution didn't have many alternatives during the first four years. It simply did what it had to do. At that time, Cuba was under siege by the Americans and the exile community. It had a revolution that had offered the people advances in all spheres, and it had to keep those promises. Therefore, if the Soviets hadn't helped, it would have perished. I came to the conclusion that I should never have conspired but should rather have stayed there. And, if I'd done that, I would surely be in the group of reformers now."

"Why were you imprisoned just after the revolution?"

"Because I conspired against communism. I was a leftist, but the product of a Catholic education. The Jesuits taught us that communism was inherently evil. That was the phrase. I'm going to tell you an anecdote to make this clearer. One day, when I was conspiring in Cuba, I was talking with a friend. This was more or less how the conversation went:

"I asked him, 'Hey, are we against the Agrarian Reform?'

"'No. Even though we don't like the details, the farmers have to have land.'

"'Are we against the nationalization of the American companies?'

"'No. The Americans had a lot of influence here, and that had to be stopped.'

"'Are we against the Urban Reform?'

"'No. There's no reason for people to pay rent.'

"'Well, then, why are we conspiring?'

"'Because this is communism, kid!'

"'Damn, you're right. If they weren't communists, we'd be with them!'

"Just imagine, and it almost cost us our lives!"

"Here's another question that we've asked everybody: What would happen in Cuba if Fidel Castro were to die today?"

"I don't know what might happen. He's someone whom it will be very difficult to replace. That's the problem with all great leaders. He has so much authority that, when he's spoken, there's nothing more to be said. It has resulted in an orderly system. Nobody wants the Americans or the Mafia to take over the country. Nobody wants what happened in the countries of the former Eastern bloc to happen in Cuba, too."

"But isn't there anybody to take up the reins of power? Aren't there any new, well-trained cadres?"

"Unlike what many people say, there is a whole generation of very well-trained young people who are making more and more of the decisions. Castro's generation hasn't made all of the decisions in Cuba for a long time now. In addition, the power structure isn't like the typical one that has existed in the rest of Latin America, in which there's a dictator — either military or civilian — politicians, generals and troops. The Cuban structure is more like the one in Europe, because it's very cohesive and developed.

"Moreover, the people have real participation in decision-making. In Cuba, everything is discussed at the block and neighborhood levels — sometimes exaggeratedly."

13

Willem C. van t'Wout
Director of Fondel,
a Dutch nickel-importing company

"The European countries are even afraid of being friendly with Cuba, fearing that their relations with the United States will be adversely affected."

The main U.S. strategy since 1959 has been to strangle Cuba economically. Most of the countries in the world have been accomplices in this. When the Eastern bloc collapsed and Cuba didn't fall with it, Washington tightened the screws. Many countries sadistically applauded or continued to remain spectators, which is much the same thing. However, there are some investors who, accepting the Cuban Government's conditions for establishing joint ventures, have risked being "punished" by the United States.

This has also meant leaving themselves vulnerable to having the "Open Letter to Foreign Investors," of May 1992, used against them. Among other things, it says, "We maintain the position that any investment made in Cuba in the present circumstances will not deserve the support of laws that a future Cuban Government may formulate for the protection of private property. We maintain that those investments should be considered part of the national heritage — and, as such, the future Cuban Government may do as it likes with them..."[1]

We contacted five European investors. Two said that they didn't want to talk about politics. Of the others, we present what was said by Willem C. van t'Wout, a Dutch importer of nickel and other Cuban products. Like the others, he and his company, Fondel, are on the U.S. Government's "black list."

---

[1] The organizations signing this threat include the Democratic Social Coordinating Body of Cuba (Coordinadora Social Demócrata de Cuba, CSDC), Independent and Democratic Cuba, the Cuban American National Foundation, the Cuban Liberal Union (Unión Liberal Cubana, ULC) and even the Cuban Human Rights Committee (Comité Cubano por los Derechos Humanos, CCDH) and the Cuban Human Rights Party.

* * *

"Your company has been investing in Cuba for many years. Hasn't this been very difficult, because of the U.S. embargo?"

"When we first started cooperating with Cuba, we very much felt the consequences of the U.S. embargo. But, as the years went by, we've found solutions for getting around it. I'm not going to tell you what they are, because I imagine the U.S. authorities would like to know how we're managing this. But the embargo has created a climate of fear in international trade, because of the repercussions and sanctions that may come from the Americans. And that hasn't improved; to the contrary, it has gotten worse. The Helms-Burton Act is the latest maneuver they've adopted to maintain that intransigent attitude toward Cuba."

"A few years ago, the Cuban Government began to implement changes in its foreign investment policy. What do you think of them?"

"After the Berlin Wall was torn down, changes began to be made in Cuba. I consider them positive, though they aren't being implemented quickly enough. The Cuban authorities have very good arguments for what they are doing, because they don't want to be forced into a situation similar to those in the former socialist countries, where the Mafia reigns supreme.

"The Cuban Government has its own view of things, which isn't the same as that which the Europeans want to impose. I think that the Cubans know perfectly well what they want and how to achieve it. In any case, no matter what is said, it is our experience that Cuba is one of the most honest countries with which to do business."

"What is your opinion of the European Union's attitude?"

"Really, the European Union isn't seeking a dialogue with Cuba; it's only interested in applying pressures and more conditions, because the European countries are even afraid of being friendly with Cuba, fearing that their relations with the United States will be adversely affected. That's why, unfortunately, they have treated that country in a very shameful way. They don't respect it."

"Cuba not only has to get around the trade embargo but must also withstand the pressures brought to bear against it for supposed human rights violations."

"Yes, that's so. In Holland — and in the European Union in general — the human rights argument is being used to impose conditions on relations with Cuba. There isn't any respect for Cuba. Since this is what is convenient to them, the European countries 'forget' that the United States has been waging war against Cuba for nearly 40 years. Cuba is threatened by the outside world. I'm not an expert on human relations, but I do believe — as the European governments must also know — that most of the political prisoners in Cuba are CIA spies.

"Some of the things that happen are simply absurd. For example, the four parties in the Dutch Government held a conference called 'Cooperation or Confrontation: How Can Democracy Be Promoted in Cuba?' in April 1997. There, most of the guests were against the Cuban Government. But the worst thing is that, after hearing the discussions, anybody who was even halfway familiar with the situation in Cuba could conclude that they were misinformed and that their sources were the typical ones of the exile community. That was absurd."

"Now that you've mentioned the exile community, doesn't it seem that the most reactionary sectors are trying to get a foothold in Europe?"

"There's no question about that. Using the human rights argument, people close to the Cuban American National Foundation are gaining acceptance in Europe. Carlos Alberto Montaner and other Miami Cubans were invited to the April conference, which means that several parties are welcoming them with open arms. They are trying to block all the relations that the Cuban Government has or may have, though I'm sure that those of us who do business with Cuba won't allow ourselves to be influenced.

"They and the U.S. Government are on the offensive in Europe. For example, U.S. Special Ambassador Eizenstat came to see me to try to get me to change my position on Cuba, and I know he visited other businessmen, as well. They've managed to influence some organizations, such as Pax Christi Netherlands. In mid-1996, Ms. Zumpolle sent me a letter proposing that I invite some Cuban dissidents who were on a tour to come visit me.

"It's very clear to me that human rights is the latest argument they have for attacking Cuba."

14

Xavier Declercq
**Head of mobilization and political action,
Oxfam-Solidarity, Belgium**

*"In the war that the United States is waging against Cuba, an important part of
its strategy is to involve the nongovernmental organizations to infiltrate and
divide Cuban society."*

The Third Conference on Nongovernmental Cooperation between
Europe and Cuba was held in Brussels on March 4 and 5, 1996. Forty-
seven NGOs from 12 European countries were represented. Represen-
tatives of nine Cuban NGOs participated, including the National
Assembly of People's Power and the Ministries of Investments and of
Foreign Relations.

The aims of the conference included "facilitating exchanges of
dynamics, methods and concepts of work among the participating
organizations and further promoting the Cuban nongovernmental
organizations' presence on the European scene." The conference was
held within the framework of the European Parliament, as part of the
work done by the Inter-Parliamentary group against the Blockade. Its
main purpose was to show the institutions and representatives of the
European Parliament "that the social reality of the movement of Cuban
NGOs is ever more dynamic" and to bring out the support that they
were receiving from their important European counterparts.

The conclusions of the conference included the following: "The
search for a new world view, based on the solidarity ethic, is the main
factor uniting the nongovernmental organizations of Europe and Cuba.
How to build societies with participative political systems and democratic, inclusive economies which develop liberated, universal cultures
and promote ecologically sustainable life-styles — that is the real
challenge that should unite us all, no matter in what geographic latitude
we carry out our activities.

"Together, we declare our rejection of the pretension of imposing on
Cuba or any other country models that have already been exhausted at
the end of the century, when all of us, in both North and South, are
exploring alternative paths."

In accord with that, it went on to say, "For the European nongovernmental organizations, the strengthening of the nongovernmental area does not mean the consolidation of a counter power within the Cuban Government which would seek to undermine it from within, as the present U.S. policy proclaims... We are convinced that this is not the way to support the economic, social and political changes promoted by the government itself, much less the way to support the initiatives of the social organizations that seek to improve structurally the Cuban people's living conditions..."

Oxfam-Belgium was one of the first European nongovernmental organizations that sent representatives to Cuba to participate in development projects. This brought problems, because it came into confrontation with the policy of the European Union, which refused to provide economic support for several projects that were presented for Cuba and elsewhere.

* * *

"Mr. Declercq, how do the European nongovernmental organizations view cooperation with Cuba?"

"Even though conditions started changing around eight years ago, the international nongovernmental organizations have, historically, done very little in Cuba. Some of them feel that it isn't possible to work there because there aren't any local counterparts. Others say that Cuba has such a high level of development that it doesn't need help. Some have spent years studying whether or not to support it.

"Many, that have forgotten the role corresponding to government, feel that everything should be organized by 'civil society.' They think that society should almost replace the government, forgetting that governments were created to guarantee the distribution and investment of wealth. They almost want everything to remain in the hands of private enterprise. For those nongovernmental organizations, of which there are many, civil society is the magic formula. And, using that concept, they enter into contradiction with the Cuban Government — which makes it difficult or impossible for them to work in Cuba."

"Then why did Oxfam-Belgium decide to work in that country?"

"Our view of cooperation with development is somewhat different from that of many other nongovernmental organizations. That is why, a short while ago, we changed our name to Oxfam-Solidarity. The accent should be placed on solidarity in order to emphasize justice, not half-measures for mitigating poverty, which is where many NGOs concentrate their efforts.

"Many NGOs have lost the overall view and no longer consider that the political structures which create poverty increase injustice. They have very easily forgotten to attack the origins of poverty. Too many NGOs cling fast to their little projects — which, though they may be very good and beneficial to the groups they're aimed at, don't help to change the roots of social and economic injustice.

"We see that there is a lot of justice in Cuba, with a very high level of health care, education, political participation, etc., for all the people. The government has organized and distributed that justice. Oxfam-Solidarity Belgium believes that this justice should be supported."

"But that means going a little against the current. The main criticism of the Cuban process is that the government has centralized everything."

"It's true that many NGOs aren't happy about the Cuban Government's having assumed full responsibility for taking care of society. They don't see that the Cuban Government has reacted to the crisis in a different way. The other countries are applying the formula of the neoliberal recommendations of the World Bank and International Monetary Fund. All of us have seen that the economic adjustments have adversely affected the majority, leaving them in greater poverty. The powerful minority isn't hurt, because, unlike the situation in Cuba, the political interests are dependent on their economic interests. In Cuba, the government is trying to spread the wealth equitably and is achieving this. It's a very egalitarian society, in which the government gives priority to meeting the people's basic needs."

"So it's worthwhile to help support that unique experiment?"

"Our intention, and that of a few other NGOs, is to support the Cubans' efforts to protect the achievements of their historic process. To do so, we are working with local NGOs and also with the mass organizations and with governmental agencies. Many people don't think it's logical to work with governmental agencies, but, if they serve the interests of the majority, why can't they be counter-parts?"

"But, according to what the representatives of some nongovernmental organizations have told us..."

"Many NGOs appear not to see the injustice that is committed against that country. The main instance of this is the U.S. effort to impose on the whole world the blockade it has maintained against Cuba. And it seems that the other countries in the world don't realize, or don't want to realize, that that blockade is directly threatening the living standard of all the Cuban people. Moreover, looking a little beyond Cuba, you can easily see that a very dangerous trend is gaining ground in current international relations: the United States is denying the existence of international law. That trend is being institutionalized. Cuba is an example showing how the superpower has decided to consolidate its interests: might makes right.

"I think that a more ethical international policy is required. That, too, should be a task for the nongovernmental organizations. And committing yourself to the Cuban process is a good beginning."

"Oxfam-Belgium has a lot of experience in cooperation with several countries in the world. Are your relations with Cuba any different?"

"To some extent, yes. International cooperation is something new for the Cubans. They have had little experience, and, occasionally, this proves a stumbling block. Working with them is also different because they're very proud — or, rather, they are more aware of their historic process, as a result of which both the government and the people have a great sense of dignity and won't allow anything to be imposed on them.

"For some of the international NGOs, respecting the priorities and terms of cooperation has been only a matter of words and papers. But, in Cuba, you have to respect the conditions they set — which is very valuable for learning about and assessing their political process. Relations with the Cubans must be honorable, aboveboard.

"It is important to mention that the community of international NGOs has, in three meetings,[1] arrived at a consensus with its Cuban counterparts on the principles of cooperation. The most important thing, in my opinion, is that the international NGOs should support the initiatives taken by their Cuban counterparts. We aren't the ones who should decide what projects the Cubans need."

"Excuse us for interrupting you. What is your view of the incident that arose between Doctors Without Borders (Médicos Sin Fronteras, MSF) and the Cuban Government in 1993?"

"There's a very big problem with the nongovernmental organizations of the developed countries. We think we can solve the Third World's problems and that our way of doing things is the best or the only way.

"Wasn't the Cuban Ministry of Public Health right when it refused to allow Doctors Without Borders to open its own office to distribute medicine? The Cubans have managed to create one of the best health systems in the world — even better than those in the United States and Europe. Why, then, should they try to change it?

"The Cubans are the ones who decide where the medical aid that we give them should go. I assure you, we can always check that it has gone for a good purpose. The point is, an institution there can't decide that kind of thing on its own. But I don't think that the Doctors Without Borders incident was all that serious.

"There was the case of a U.S. nongovernmental organization that offered $2 million to a Cuban NGO. The only condition it set was that Cuba should let its people in to hand out free Bibles. At first glance, that

---

[1] In Havana in 1993, in Madrid in 1995 and in the European Parliament in 1996.

may seem perfectly harmless, but it was far from it. Those are organizations that work very subtly, with hidden purposes. You can't forget that many nongovernmental organizations are used to further the political interests of the rich countries. And, in the case of Cuba, the United States wants them to serve its own purposes."

"That statement is a little ticklish. Could you go into it a little more for us? Don't you think that the Cuban Government is paranoid about infiltration?"

"In the war that the United States is waging against Cuba, an important part of its strategy is to get the nongovernmental organizations to infiltrate and divide Cuban society. The Cubans are only too familiar with infiltration, since they've had to confront all of the infiltration attempts that the Americans have made since 1959 — attempts in which, apparently, certain European nongovernmental organizations want to join.

"You must know that the U.S. Government is talking about two tracks. One is the blockade, and the other is infiltration by means of the nongovernmental organizations. I'm not making this up: it's contained in official documents, and many experts have analyzed this subject in depth.

"For several years, the U.S. Government has been urging the nongovernmental organizations in its country to cooperate with the dissident movement in Cuba, but now that policy is being extended to include the NGOs in Europe. Eizenstat, Clinton's Special Ambassador for Cuba, met with the representatives of several NGOs in Europe. In some cases, he offered to provide a multi-million-dollar fund for those that agreed to work with the dissident movement. So far, I don't know of any NGOs that have accepted the money; it would be very stupid for them to do so. However, this has created confusion in some cases."

"Do you know of any European nongovernmental organizations that are in agreement with following the strategy proposed by the White House?"

"Fortunately for the Clinton Administration, there may be a few European nongovernmental organizations that are willing to support the dissident movement in Cuba without getting any money for it.

"But, so far, there's only one that I know of that's working under U.S. instructions. That's Pax Christi Netherlands. It is doing so even though the Pax Christi chapters in other countries strongly oppose that action. That nongovernmental organization is just beginning to make its intentions toward Cuba known, and Cuba has to be very careful, because Pax Christi Netherlands has managed to flirt with other European NGOs. The incredible thing is that its documents contain many of the same phrases that the Clinton Administration is using — the demands made on European private businesses, for example. I also know of an official U.S. Government document that congratulates that

Dutch NGO for its initiative in giving support to the dissident movement in Cuba and a chance for it to be heard.

"I think that the European nongovernmental organizations should be aware of these things. If they don't have a clear understanding of the general picture, it's hard for them to evaluate the various initiatives — to see what the real intentions are. Human rights is a delicate subject that the U.S. authorities are using to convince the European NGOs.

"Who isn't in favor of respect for human rights? But, when that subject is used as a weapon of war, for a campaign against the Cuban system, I begin to smell a rat."

15

Wayne Smith
Former Head of the
U.S. Interests Section in Havana

"Those dissidents and human rights groups in Cuba — that are nothing but a few people — are only important to the extent that they serve [the United States] in a single cause: that of destabilizing Fidel Castro's regime."

Among the contradictions that arise within the U.S. establishment, two political figures are outstanding because they have taken stands against their country's strategy on Cuba and don't entirely agree with its political system. One of them is former U.S. Attorney General Ramsey Clark. In many different forums, he has repeated that for four decades, with its crushing economic and military clout, the United States has tried to overthrow the government of its neighbor, Cuba, a small and comparatively much poorer country.

Ramsey Clark argues that, confronting that impressive power and constant threats, Cuba — which had suffered from extreme poverty, illiteracy, sicknesses, violence, corruption and foreign exploitation just 40 years before — has emerged as a world leader in almost all the spheres of human development. Illiteracy has been virtually eliminated, an excellent system of higher education was established and an enormous number of highly trained technicians and professionals who offer their services in poor countries has been created. The Cuban public health system is unequalled elsewhere in the Third World in terms of disease prevention and treatment, health care and research, and it has become a model for all nations.

Clark also points out that, in 30 years, Cuba has reduced its infant mortality rate from around 90 for every 1,000 live births to a rate lower than that of the United States and most of the richest countries in the world. It has developed vaccines that meet international standards. Cuban doctors, nurses, other health workers and medicines have saved millions of lives, at the service of the poor in dozens of nations. There are no homeless in Cuba. There is proper work for all. Art, music, dance, cinematography, poetry and literature are developed throughout Cuba. The people's physical condition was demonstrated in Atlanta, where the

Cubans won gold medals in boxing and baseball, with a better showing that those achieved by nations with similar populations and economic conditions.

Clark considers that the U.S. blockade against Cuba is a crime against humanity. He points out that the United States intends to hurt the Cuban people, and, of course, the weakest and most vulnerable are the children, old people and chronically ill. The United States knows what may happen to the close to 200,000 diabetics in Cuba if they can't get insulin.[1]

The other political figure is Wayne Smith, a university professor and former head of the U.S. Interests Section in Havana. He has lost some battles — for example, when Congress, influenced by the extreme right wing in Miami and New Jersey, authorized TV Martí. Smith was diametrically opposed to it, both because it violated all kinds of international agreements and because it would be an extremely expensive project, requiring an investment of millions, that — as happened — the Cuban Government could block out completely with interference.

At the time, representatives of the two governments were engaged in a dialogue on immigration and other topics of common interest. Smith knew that the Cubans would withdraw from the conference table if TV Martí began broadcasting. This is what happened, and Smith resigned.

Smith is also opposed to the Helms-Burton Act. He is sure that it is inefficient as a method for achieving a rapid transition to capitalism. His writings and lectures show that he prefers the style that has been used in the countries of the former Eastern bloc, where, he says, there wasn't any need for more aggression to reinstate capitalism.

Unfortunately, he couldn't give us much time for the interview, but we believe that the statements he made in those few minutes he could spare are very important. Smith acknowledges things that it's hard for a U.S. political figure to say in public.

* * *

"Mr. Smith, why don't you agree with the Helms-Burton Act?"

"Because the United States is making a mistake by implementing it. When the pressure against Cuba is increased, the regime reacts by stepping up its internal discipline and rallying the people around their flag and sovereignty. At the international level, analyzed from the point

---

[1] From "A Crime against Humanity," a paper that Ramsey Clark presented in the Helms-Burton and Europe Seminar sponsored in Amsterdam in 1996 by the Global Reflection Foundation.

of view of our interests, the law makes little sense. As long as Cuba doesn't constitute any threat to us, we are undermining our trade relations with the Canadians and Europeans by violating international law.

"And, even though the Europeans and Canadians have reacted well to the law, letting the United States know that that policy comes with a price tag, their possibilities are limited. Europe is very strong on abiding by the law and thinks that, if it tells the United States that it ought to respect international agreements, the United States is going to change. Forget it! The United States won't even accept the jurisdiction of an international court. The Helms-Burton Act was promoted by a group of people who believe that, now that the United States is the only world power, it can't be limited by international law. The danger is that the Helms-Burton Act may be just a first step, not in the U.S. actions against Cuba, but in its imposing its interests on the international community and forcing a Pax Americana on the rest of the world."

"It seems to us that, basing itself on that law, the U.S. Government has forced the European Union into a position in which it will have to support the destabilization of the Cuban Government. Moreover, in a very tactical, subtle way, it has convinced some of the European NGOs to join in its design of supporting the so-called dissident movement."

"Yes, that's right. There's a special ambassador just for that, and it's being supported in certain exile organizations, as well — the exile community isn't autonomous; it functions as a tool of the U.S. Government.

"The Cuban American National Foundation; the Cuban Democratic Platform, which Montaner heads in Spain; and other exile pressure groups are already at work in Europe, and they're going to work as they do in the United States, to get Europe to take an intransigent line toward Cuba. They have a lot of money, and they're powerful and aggressive. I don't think there will be a lot of resistance to them in those countries. The Spanish Government is already influenced by the Cuban American National Foundation and the Democratic Platform. There, they've already achieved a large part of their goals. And they're going to continue in other countries.

"They are artists at infiltrating and understanding how political systems work. They study the situation, seeking out information that will tell them which politicians can be bought, and they go into the private lives of the ones who don't want to collaborate, digging up dirt for intimidating and blackmailing them.

"So far, this modus operandi has given them very good results in the United States."

"The Cuban-U.S. citizens..."

"Let me tell you something. The Cuban Americans have had and still have a lot of influence, but only when their interests can be coordinated with those of the various administrations. I worked in the State Department during the Carter Administration. The Cuban American National Foundation didn't exist yet, but there were still a lot of exile organizations. In that period, we managed all of them very easily. I went to Miami several times to explain to the leaders that we intended to normalize relations with Cuba. They understood that.

"But then Reagan and Bush became president, and they wanted a hard line on Cuba, and the Cuban American National Foundation was created. Clinton made friends with the Cuban Americans, had dinner with Mas Canosa and adopted a hard policy against Cuba. As a result, he got a lot of money for his electoral campaign. The same thing happened in 1996.

"Now, the most conservative sector of the Cuban Americans continues to support Clinton. The president's attitude toward them has nothing to do with U.S. foreign policy or human rights or democracy: it's all a matter of electoral interests and money."

"Mr. Smith, after nearly 40 years of war against the Cuban revolution, what is the goal your government seeks?"

"The U.S. goals have changed over the years. During the Cold War, the main thing was the change in its foreign policy. Since 1975, Cuba has been forced to withdraw its troops from Africa, to halt its aid to revolutionary movements in Latin America and to reduce its military ties with the Soviet Union. Apparently, during the Cold War, we weren't interested in the internal organization of its system: Cuba could have a socialist government if it behaved itself internationally.

"In 1988, Cuba withdrew its troops from Africa. And, since 1990, it has stopped helping the revolutionary movements. The Soviet Union collapsed in 1992, which ended the Cuban-Soviet military alliance. The U.S. foreign policy goals were achieved, but that didn't result in any improvement in its relations with Cuba, because, really, our main goal has been to topple the Castro regime. Why, since it is a small island without any great economic resources? Because Cuba has the same effect on the U.S. administrations as the full moon has on wolves: it's an obsession.

"First, Fidel Castro's personality challenged the biggest power in the world and won; he has survived nine of our presidents; and he is accepted and respected in all international forums. During the Cold War, we didn't believe it would be possible to get that stone out of our shoe. Now, we do. That's why we're taking up the policies of economic pressure, through the Helms-Burton Act, and of democracy and human rights."

"How is the political pressure on human rights being developed against Cuba?"

"We aren't really interested in democracy and human rights. We just use those words to hide our true reasons. If democracy and human rights really mattered to us, Indonesia, Turkey, Mexico, Peru and Colombia — for example — would be our enemies. Cuba is a paradise compared to those countries and most countries in the world.

"Since 1985, we have stated publicly that we will encourage and openly finance dissident and human rights groups in Cuba; this, too, is in our interests. The United States isn't financing all of those groups — only the ones that are best known internationally. Those dissidents and human rights groups in Cuba — that are nothing but a few people — are only important to the extent that they serve us in a single cause: that of destabilizing Fidel Castro's regime.

"Through those two policies — economic pressure and human rights — we want to force the overthrow of Fidel Castro and then install a transitional government that we like — to reinstate the people we want and, thus, control Cuba once again."

Some Final Comments

In today's world, what happened yesterday isn't news. Some historical events shouldn't be forgotten, however, because some people want them to be repeated.

The Sandinistas took power in Nicaragua in 1979. The U.S. Government immediately said it was a communist revolution, and the media started repeating that statement over and over until people began to believe it. The proof was concrete and impossible to refute. For example, illiteracy was being eliminated, the public health system was being extended to offer coverage to all the people, land ownership stopped being monopolized by a few families and was turned over to farmers' cooperatives, some companies were nationalized and the people began to take part in decision making.

Nicaragua, which didn't have a single submarine or even an ordinary-range missile, became the "great threat" to the security of the United States, the most powerful country in the world in economic and military terms. It was the "bad example" which that revolution of happy, affectionate dreamers was setting that made it an enemy. It showed other oppressed peoples that it was possible to fight, to win and to begin to live with dignity. That was extremely dangerous. Moreover, the empire knew that Latin America had had a distinguishing historical characteristic ever since the Spanish colonial era: no matter where they started, the flames of revolution would spread as if through dry grass, blown by the wind. The model of Sandinista behavior had to be wiped out — if possible, even expunged from the people's memory.

And, as had been the case with Cuba, it didn't send in the Marines. As in Cuba, it simply paid individuals to shoot, bomb, massacre, rape and terrorize. For a handful of dollars, some Nicaraguans — directed from Washington and supported by Cuban counterrevolutionaries — pledged to put out the most beautiful new light that the Latin American people had in the decade of the 1980s.

While some mercenaries wrought havoc with acts of terrorism, others made speeches and wrote articles — for this, too, was essential to bring down the Sandinista effort. The U.S. Government, in complicity with some European governments and under the cover of certain nongovernmental organizations, exhibited them in every known international human rights forum. They even read texts to which they hadn't contributed even a comma — texts which made them witnesses to Sandinista "monstrosities," claiming that the Sandinistas repressed the masses, imprisoned thousands, tortured, murdered, trafficked in drugs, exported terrorism and starved their people. Oh, no, they weren't lying! And how the major world press lapped it up!

And, when the Sandinista government tried to impose order on those who, living inside the country, were collaborating — without guns or bullets — in demolishing the revolution, the empire and its allies raised a hue and cry, saying it was attacking freedom of speech and of association. The Universal Declaration of Human Rights, arranged to fit their needs, was hauled out as proof, judge and executioner.

In addition to leaving Nicaragua utterly alone so the buzzards could keep on pecking away at it, the European governments pressured it to agree to hold the election Washington wanted. The Sandinistas agreed to that and even to allowing many parties to participate. The contras, who had plenty of money, divided into several parties to oppose the Sandinista government. Europe contributed to some groups and sat back to await the results. Even the dumbest politician knew that, if the Sandinistas won, the attacks would continue.

We all know that the "fighters for freedom and democracy," as Ronald Reagan called them, won. They had promised peace, wealth and heaven on earth. In fact, they made Nicaragua, once again, one of the countries with the most glaring social, economic and political inequalities in the world. Worse, it is no longer a sovereign country.

Once its "democratic" formula had been reestablished, the U.S. Government went back to an untroubled sleep.

Or almost untroubled. In its hemisphere, in its territory, in its back yard, a little cricket was still disturbing it. For almost 40 years, a small country without any great strategic resources had refused to yield, to be humiliated, to get on its knees. Almost alone, it was resisting. Its name was Cuba.

What plots hasn't the United States hatched to bring to its knees that hard-working, rum-drinking, dance-loving nation of men and women who express their solidarity in deeds, not words? The plots run from military invasions to chemical and economic attacks, waged daily both inside and outside the country, backed by the largest outpouring of propaganda known in the history of wars, whether declared or not, and, as in Nicaragua, with the overt and covert complicity of certain individuals.

Unfortunately, some of the rights of a nation that is besieged in that way must be limited and regulated if that nation is to preserve its independence and self-determination. The future of the majority cannot be placed at risk to allow a few who are willing to sell their souls to collaborate in destabilizing their country — all to benefit a power that wants to impose the same path that has made so many other countries regress. The Europeans did the same in Africa, which is now moribund.

Those who are familiar with Cuba's present electoral system know that all anybody who doesn't agree with the revolution — but is faithful to their homeland's sovereignty — and wants to form a real political opposition has to do is work at the grass-roots level. If they do that, they may be elected, because you don't have to be a member of the Communist Party to be elected to the National Assembly. In Cuba, you don't need money for electoral campaigning; all you have to do is convince the masses by demonstrating your ability and dedication to them — but that doesn't bring you applause outside the country, nor does it make you a dissident, so it doesn't bring in dollars, either.

As some international media noted, all of the conditions for a coup d'état existed during the Pope's visit to Cuba: the members of the police and security were forbidden to carry arms, the people were in the streets in a state of effervescence, and all kinds of speeches were broadcast over the radio and television.

In addition, more than 3,000 journalists from all over the world were there, most of them seeking out any discontent among the people that would put the rebellion they sought on a silver platter. For this purpose, they gave as much space as possible to the "dissidents" — who couldn't demonstrate even a minimal level of the consensus that, internationally, they are said to possess. As Giulio Girardi pointed out in *El País*, of Spain, on February 16, 1998, they didn't even make use of "the presence of 16 officials of the U.S. State Department, who had landed in Havana a week before the Pope and stayed until a week after he left, who were ready to ensure the 'democratic transition'."

Frei Betto, the prominent Brazilian Catholic theologian, sent us a letter, a part of which we include here:

A society is bad if it doesn't protect the lives of all its people. Thus, Cuban society is good in the light of Christian faith and of the criteria of the Gospels, because it is the only one in Latin America that protects the lives of its people. Cuba constitutes a great threat to the United States, because it has shown the way of life to all the exploited in the Third World. With Europe as acolyte, the United States continues to impose the policy of death all over the world.

Once a U.S. journalist asked me why Cuba didn't have democracy, and I replied, "Do you know of any democratic countries?" He said, "Yes: my country." And I asked him, "How many millionaires are there in the United States, and how many in Cuba? How many poor people lacking food, clothing and housing are there in the United States, and how many in Cuba? How many blacks are discriminated against or shot down by the police in the United States, and how many in Cuba? How many children don't receive medical care or education in the United States, and how many in Cuba? How many people are there in the United States whose human dignity is insulted, and how many in Cuba? "Then," I asked him, "in which of the two is there more democracy? For me, there's only one reply: in Cuba."

A claque of people is chorusing that human rights aren't respected in Cuba. I wonder if it isn't a luxury to talk about human rights in Latin America — to say nothing of the rest of the Third World. Animals in Europe, for example, have more rights guaranteed than do most of the 500 million of us. If she weren't an extreme right-winger, it might be a good idea to have former actress Brigitte Bardot as the president of Brazil, Honduras, Argentina, Chile and some other Latin American countries, because she might implement the law protecting animals for which she's fighting in France. And our lives would be much better.

We have to ask ourselves: what do we mean when we talk about democracy? What do we mean when we talk about human rights?

On October 30, 1996, Cuban-U.S. journalist Luis Ortega wrote in New York's *La Prensa*, "I respect the simple people who dislike Fidel Castro and the revolution. It's a very natural personal reaction. But it's serious when the individual becomes an accomplice to a bad policy aimed at destroying the Cuban people under the pretext of putting an end to Castro. It's bad when that feeling is turned into a business. It's bad when somebody deliberately collaborates in a campaign to crush Cuba."

Dissidents or mercenaries? Or mercenaries touted as dissidents?

Glossary

A

Abdala. Created in New York in the late 1960s as a student organization to confront the groups that supported the Cuban Government, it became the legal arm and logistical base of the National Liberation Front of Cuba (Frente de Liberación Nacional de Cuba), playing a key role in the terrorist strategy of the worldwide campaign against Cuba. Many of its members have been arrested and/or sentenced for having committed acts of terrorism and/or having engaged in the traffic in drugs. Even so, ironically, it was the first organization of the recalcitrant exile community that began to carry out campaigns supposedly promoting human rights in Cuba.

Its members have included individuals who now have great prestige in political, intellectual and human rights spheres in the United States. They include Congressman Lincoln Díaz-Balart; Ramón Mestre, the former director of Radio Martí's investigation service; and Frank Calzón, the head of Freedom House and Of Human Rights. Abdala was dissolved in the mid-1980s. [See also **National Liberation Front of Cuba**.]

Allende, Salvador (1908-73). Founder of the Chilean Socialist Party, he was elected president on October 24, 1970. On September 11, 1973, he was killed in combat against a military coup headed by General Augusto Pinochet.

Annexationism. A U.S. policy, one of whose first supporters was Thomas Jefferson — who in 1807 declared that it would be a good idea to annex Cuba. Ever since, the United States has considered Cuba to be a natural extension of its territory. The Helms-Burton Act is the latest expression of the U.S. annexationist ambitions, supported by the Cuban counter-revolutionary leaders, although with different nuances.

Aznar, José María. Head of Government of Spain since 1996, he is the leader of the rightist People's Party (Partido Popular). In November 1995, as presidential candidate, he visited Miami, where he met with the representatives of several extreme right-wing organizations of the Cuban exile community. Since becoming president, he has sponsored actions in the European Union that have favored U.S. policy against Cuba. His party and the extreme right wing of the Cuban exile community constitute the base of the Hispanic Cuban Foundation (Fundación Hispano Cubano).

B

Batista Zaldívar, Fulgencio (1901-73). In 1952, he headed a coup d'état approved by the U.S. Government. As president (1952-58), he was responsible for the murders of around 20,000 Cubans. At dawn on January 1, 1959, he fled to the Dominican Republic and then went to Spain, where he spent the rest of his life.

Bermúdez, Enrique. One of the most ruthless military officers during Anastasio Somoza's dictatorship in Nicaragua. When the Sandinistas came to power in 1979, the Carter Administration put Bermúdez in charge of creating the mercenary contras. In addition to all the war crimes he committed, he was also involved in the Iran-Contragate scandal.

Bonne, Félix Antonio. According to public documents of the Cuban American National Foundation, Bonne is one of its most important members inside Cuba, heading the Civic Current (Corriente Cívica) group. When the extreme right wing of the Cuban exile community — with Washington's endorsement — tried to organize the seditious group called the Cuban Council (Concilio Cubano), Bonne was made one of its leaders. He is still a member. Since 1997, he has been on the board — *patronato* — of the Hispanic Cuban Foundation (Fundación Hispano Cubana).

Bosch Avila, Orlando (1926-). In 1960, he moved to the United States, where he was recruited by the CIA and specialized in undercover operations. In 1968, he was sentenced to 12 years in prison for having sunk a Polish freighter in Miami, but served only four years of his term. He was a prominent activist during the upsurge in terrorism during the worldwide campaign against Cuba and served as adviser to General Pinochet's repressive services in Chile.

In October 1976, he and Luis Posada Carriles planned the blowing up of a Cubana de Aviación plane off Barbados — a crime for which he was imprisoned in Venezuela for 10 years. On being released, he went to the United States, where he was arrested by the FBI. The Cuban extreme right wing, headed by Congresswoman Ileana Ros-Lethinen and the Cuban American National Foundation, rallied to his defense and President Bush ordered that he be freed. The FBI has considered him one of the bloodiest terrorists in the Americas. He lives in Miami.

Brigade 2506. U.S.-supported mercenary force that invaded Cuba at the Bay of Pigs in April 1961.

Bush, George (1924-). President of the United States between 1989 and 1993. As a CIA official, he was one of those responsible for recruiting mercenaries for Brigade 2506. In 1976, he was named director of the CIA. As Ronald Reagan's vice-president, he was linked to Iran-Contragate. The investigations of the Senate's Kerry Commission showed that he knew of and agreed to the traffic in drugs to finance the contras, even though Bush was the man directly in charge of the task force responsible for waging the "war on drugs."

C

Calle Ocho (8th Street). It goes through the popular sector of Miami known as Little Havana and symbolizes the Cuban community in Miami.

Calzón, Frank. A former special agent of the CIA, he was a leader of the terrorist organizations Abdala and National Liberation Front of Cuba (Frente de Liberación Nacional de Cuba) until the late 1970s. One of the first directors of the Cuban American National Foundation, he is now on the boards of Freedom House and Of Human Rights, whose main financing comes from the U.S. Government, through the National Endowment for Democracy. He is an important source of financing for Gustavo Arcos and other counterrevolutionaries in Cuba. Calzón is also receiving large sums of money from the U.S. Agency for International Development, through the Free Cuba Center, of which Calzón is also a director. Calzón and his cohorts have become an important support for Pax Christi Netherlands.

CC. Concilio Cubano. See **Cuban Council.**

CDC. Coalición Democrática Cubana. See **Cuban Democratic Coalition.**

CDC. Concertación Democrática Cubana. See **Cuban Democratic Arrangement.**

Christian Democratic International. In October 1978, André Louis, a Belgian member of the Executive Committee of the Christian Democratic International, presented a document called "For a World Strategy of Christian Democracy." One of the most important points of the plan, which was approved, was to strengthen its presence in Latin America. Even though it unrealistically proposed to gradually replace U.S. with European interests in the area, it ended up by joining forces with the United States.

On May 14, 1984, *The International Herald Tribune* announced that the CIA had given $960,000 to the Salvadoran Christian Democratic Party (Partido Demócrato Cristiano) for the presidential campaign of Napoleón Duarte, a man in the pocket of the Christian Democratic International. The executives of the CDI, mainly in Belgium, also provided resources for the groups inside Nicaragua that were working with the contras. Since the early 1980s, they have given the Cuban Christian Democratic Movement (Movimiento Demócrato Cristiano, MDC) in Miami their full support so it would be reactivated and engage in human rights work at the international level. José Ignacio Rasco, Vice-President of the CDI, has been its main ally.

Cienfuegos, Camilo. A guerrilla leader in the Sierra Maestra Mountains and a major in the Rebel Army, he became one of the most popular figures in the struggle against Batista. He disappeared at sea in 1959 while flying a small plane to Havana.

Civil society. Several U.S. Government documents on Cuba (which various experts have cited and to whose authenticity they have attested) speak of the need to promote a policy for strengthening Cuban civil society. In the U.S. strategy, this is assumed to be a natural counterpart to the Cuban Government — one that should be represented by an extremely broad diversity of nongovernmental organizations and other kinds of associations. Antagonism to the government and civil disobedience are promoted, as is a complete separation between the government and society. In the case of Cuba, this version of civil society is simply the counterrevolution, better known as the dissident movement, which can be financed from abroad. The United States and its allies seek to base themselves on it in order to destroy Cuba's political system.

Clinton, William. U.S. President since 1993. After he promised to support the Cuban Democracy Act (better known as the Torricelli Act), the Cuban American National Foundation contributed around $400,000 to his war chest in his first presidential campaign. On being reelected, he signed the Helms-Burton Bill into law in 1996. At the beginning of 1997, Clinton offered a reward of up to $8 billion if the present Cuban political system disappeared. In October 1997, speaking in Argentina, he said that CANF was his principal guide on Cuba.

Commission on Human Rights. A UN agency with headquarters in Geneva, Switzerland. A branch of the Economic and Social Council of the United Nations, it is the most important human rights body in the UN system. In 1997, Cuba was once more reelected as a member of the Commission. (It was first elected to membership in 1976.)

Contras. Nicaraguan mercenaries whom the Carter Administration began organizing in the late 1970s to attack the popular Sandinista government. Consolidated when Ronald Reagan moved into the White House, it was placed under the National Security Council, which set up a structure directed by Colonel Oliver North in Washington and Félix Rodríguez in Central America. The Kerry Report shows that part of that mercenary war was financed by the traffic in drugs. Cuban counterrevolutionaries working for the CIA played a key role in all levels of this war.

Coordinator of Unified Revolutionary Organizations (Coordinadora de Organizaciones Revolucionarias Unidas, CORU). Created in the mid-1970s by the most reactionary exile leaders in Miami, it is headed by Orlando Bosch and the Novo brothers. During the first 10 months of its activities, CORU carried out more than 50 terrorist actions against Cuban entities abroad and against trade offices and diplomatic missions of countries that traded with Cuba. The organization also defended the blowing up of a Cubana de Aviación plane near Barbados in October 1976. The FBI has shown that CORU was financed by the traffic in drugs.

CORU. **Coordinadora de Organizaciones Revolucionarias Unidas**. See **Coordinator of Unified Revolutionary Organizations**.

Corvo, René. The FBI and the Kerry Commission accused this CIA special agent of having trafficked in weapons and drugs for the Nicaraguan contras; he admitted doing the former. His statement initiated an extensive investigation into the activities of the Cuban counterrevolutionary groups. The brothers Alberto and "Pepe" Hernández, directors of CANF, worked with Corvo in carrying out several activities for the contras from Miami, El Salvador and Honduras.

CRC. **Consejo Revolucionario Cubano**. See **Cuban Revolutionary Council**.

Cuban Council (Concilio Cubano, CC). A coalition of groups described as dissident or independent, it was created in Cuba in October 1995, guided and financed by the counterrevolutionary leaders abroad and supported by Washington. Seemingly unaware of its roots and purposes, some international organizations have called it "a serious and valid opposition to the Cuban Government." On the death of Jorge Mas Canosa, leader of the most reactionary sector of the Cuban exile community, those who are still officials of the Council issued a communiqué stating that his death was "a serious blow" because he had been "a man who dedicated his life to the cause of the Cuban people's freedom."

Cuban Delegation in Exile (Representación Cubana en el Exilio, RECE). A counterrevolutionary group created at the CIA's orders. The Cuban Delegation in Exile was the first organization to ask the exile community for money for a new invasion of Cuba, and it collected several million dollars. It launched only a few, small commando operations, all of which were neutralized by the Cuban army and militia, but its finances simply disappeared. The organization's leaders included Jorge Mas Canosa and José "Pepe" Hernández. Even now, its monthly news bulletins can be obtained at the reception desk of CANF.

Cuban Democratic Arrangement (Concertación Democrática Cubana, CDC). In September 1991, following in the footsteps of the Cuban American National Foundation, Carlos Alberto Montaner and José Ignacio Rasco, leaders of the Cuban Democratic Platform (Plataforma Democrática Cubana), decided to create another kind of federation inside Cuba, called the Cuban Democratic Arrangement. Hubert Matos and others later joined it, although maintaining a low profile. Elizardo Sánchez Santacrúz and poet María Elena Cruz Varela were among the first people in charge of organizing it in Cuba, and they were later joined by Gustavo Arcos.

Since the Platform was created to influence the European media, the Arrangement's language has had to use terms that are more acceptable to the media, such as "dialogue," "pacification," "reconciliation," "human rights" and "peaceful transition." Like the Platform, the Arrangement presents itself as the "moderate opposition" to the Cuban Government. Montaner, its main leader abroad, is one of those explicitly calling for Cuba's annexation by the United States.

Cuban Democratic Coalition (Coalición Democrática Cubana, CDC). In August 1991, CANF decided to create a federation inside Cuba that would join its counterrevolutionary groups together. That organization was called the Cuban Democratic Coalition. Through the National Endowment for Democracy, the U.S. Government has been one of the main sources of the Coalition's financing.

The aims of the apparatus include the following: "To increase the pressure on Castro by various dissidents to get him to leave power. The Coalition will oppose any effort to initiate talks with Castro for the purpose of bringing about a peaceful change. The new Coalition will communicate with other dissident groups as long as they accept its prohibition on contacts with Castro. This Coalition will be... supported by the Cuban American National Foundation." By 1995, it changed its tune, including the terms "reconciliation," "peaceful transition" and "dialogue among all dissidents."

Cuban Democratic Platform (Plataforma Democrática Cubana, PDC). Though basically the same as the other organizations of the extreme right wing in the exile community, the Platform differs from them in how it carries out its work, using language more appropriate to the present climate of world "détente." It is the "soft" opposition for overthrowing the Cuban system, drawing on the tactics used in the countries of the former socialist bloc. Therefore, it embodies the formula that Washington is presenting in Europe to obtain support more easily.

Carlos Alberto Montaner is in charge of creating this "moderate opposition" to the Cuban Government. He lives in Europe, where he has gathered together a few other counterrevolutionaries, José Ignacio Rasco among them. All have been members of or are close to the CIA and head groups — called parties — that claim to be related to such international ideological currents as Social Democracy, Christian Democracy and Liberalism.

The Platform was founded in August 1990. As the document announcing its founding meeting in Madrid stated, the Platform should force the Cuban Government to submit to an election "similar to those that wiped out the dictatorships in the Southern Cone, Nicaragua and Eastern Europe." It went on confidently to say that, if such an election were held, "communism will be swept out." The Platform would invite the Cuban Government to a dialogue with the "opposition" to avoid bloodshed and to organize a peaceful transition. The proposal made no mention of the aggression that the U.S. Government has maintained against Cuba for nearly 40 years.

As soon as the Platform was officially constituted, its members set about seeking allies inside Cuba. Elizardo Sánchez and writer María Elena Cruz Varela were among the first to take up its banner; Gustavo Arcos later joined them. Following the orders of the Platform, these three organized the Cuban Democratic Arrangement (Concertación Democrática Cubana), a federation that joined several groups together. The Platform presents itself in Cuba and at the international level as the representative of all the moderate opposition, thus covering up the fact that individuals such as Hubert Matos are also members.

At the international level, the Platform has lobbied to get governments to step up their political and economic pressures against Cuba and contribute to its isolation. The Platform has had some effect on political and governmental sectors in Spain, Russia, Poland and — most recently — Holland.

In practice, Carlos Alberto Montaner runs the Platform as a one-man business. This style of leadership — with Montaner making decisions without consulting anyone — plus the fact that its members don't agree on the U.S. blockade, has led to a drop in membership, and it has fewer members now than at its founding. Montaner is a fierce champion of the blockade, but the Christian Democratic Party [Partido Demócrato Cristiano] is opposed to it.

Cuban Liberal Union (Unión Liberal Cubana, ULC). Although it had fewer than 100 members, didn't have an organic structure and also lacked a political program, Carlos Alberto Montaner declared it a party in 1990. Immediately after that, he obtained recognition from the Liberal International and was named a vice-president of that organization. The ULC is a member of the Cuban Democratic Platform (Plataforma Democrática Cubana).

Cuban Revolutionary Council (Consejo Revolucionario Cubano, CRC). Created by the CIA shortly before the Bay of Pigs invasion, it was supposed to give international legitimacy to the mercenary operation. It consisted of several counterrevolutionary groups and was to present itself as an alternative to the revolutionary government and declare itself a provisional government if the invasion triumphed. It was dissolved in 1964.

D

Debray, Régis. French writer captured in Bolivia, where he had gone to write about Che Guevara's guerrilla group. He turned from being a great supporter of the Cuban revolution to being one of its fiercest critics. At the request of former French President François Mitterrand, he organized a campaign to free Armando Valladares, a former policeman under the Batista regime in Cuba. In 1996, one of Che's daughters accused Debray of having handed over — while not under torture — the information required for her father's capture. Andrés Nazario, the head of Alpha 66 and an enemy of Che Guevara, shared that view.

The dialogue. Seventy-five people representing the Cuban community abroad met with high-ranking Cuban leaders in Havana in November 1978, at the initiative of the Cuban Government. In addition to beginning a rapprochement, the dialogue resulted in the freeing of around 3,000 counterrevolutionaries and made it possible for many families to be reunited. This last point was insisted on, for the Cuban Government had been offering the possibility since 1967. The extreme right wing of the exile community took violent action against those people, but the "dialoguers" increased their activities, taking part in several meetings in Cuba promoting exchanges of ideas and experiences.

Díaz-Balart, Lincoln. A Cuban-U.S. Congressman (R.) and former member of the Abdala terrorist organization, he helped to draft and has been an ardent champion of the Helms-Burton Act. CANF has made substantial contributions to his electoral campaigns. Together with Congresswoman Ileana Ros-Lethinen, he appeared for the defense and urged the freeing of terrorist Orlando Bosch.

E

Eisenhower, Dwight David. U.S. President between 1953 and 1961. In 1959, his administration began helping the counterrevolutionary groups in Cuba. The Eisenhower Administration's original plan was to destabilize the nascent revolution — not engage in a conventional military invasion, but send in infiltration teams that would reinforce the counterrevolutionary armed groups.

Eizenstat, Stuart. Under-Secretary of Commerce for International Trade. In 1996, when the Helms-Burton Act was passed, President Clinton named him Special Ambassador for Cuban Affairs. In September 1996, he was sent to negotiate with representatives of the European Union, to smooth the sharp contradictions created by the new law. His tasks included meeting with representatives of nongovernmental organizations, trying to get them to pledge to support the so-called dissident movement in Cuba. In his report to the U.S. Congress and later, publicly, he said that Pax Christi Netherlands headed the group of NGOs in Europe that had agreed to the plan.

Escambray Second Front. One of the guerrilla fronts in the struggle against the dictator Batista, led by William Morgan (a U.S. citizen), Eloy Gutiérrez Menoyo and the Sargén brothers. After the triumph of the revolution, they disagreed with the line that most of the revolutionary leaders upheld. Nearly all of the Front's leaders left for the United States, where they joined counterrevolutionary groups controlled by the CIA.

Estefan, Gloria. Famous Cuban American singer opposed to the Cuban political system. As an expression of this opposition, she has financed Brothers to the Rescue (Hermanos al Rescate) and other counterrevolutionary organizations. Even so, she spoke out against letting the powerful extreme right-wing groups in Miami veto performances by musical groups from Cuba. This led to a boycott of her records and appearances in September 1997.

Executive Directive 77. Signed by President Reagan in January 1983, it is known in the United States as Project Democracy. Its legal branch, approved by Congress, is called the National Endowment for Democracy. It has largely replaced the CIA in financing union, press, human rights and religious organizations. The National Endowment for Democracy has given millions of dollars to Cuban counter-revolutionaries, both in Cuba and abroad. Clandestinely, it gave logistical support to the contras' mercenary force.

F

FLNC. Frente de Liberación Nacional de Cuba. See **National Liberation Front of Cuba.**

Fort Benning. This military base in Georgia is the headquarters of the U.S. Army Infantry School. It is also a special center for training in underground communications, propaganda, undercover operations, intelligence and counterintelligence. Only counterrevolutionaries who had the CIA's full confidence, such as Jorge Mas Canosa, Félix Rodríguez and Luis Posada Carriles, were trained there. The infamous School of the Americas — where many of the military chiefs responsible for the dirty war in Latin America were trained — was moved there.

Frayde, Martha. Former Cuban Ambassador to UNESCO in Paris. Cuban State Security discovered that she had been recruited by the CIA while holding that post, and she was sentenced to three years' imprisonment. Together with Elizardo Sánchez, Gustavo Arcos and Ricardo Bofill, she organized the first counterrevolutionary group that sent information on supposed human rights violations to the U.S. delegation to the United Nations. She represented Gustavo Arcos in the ceremony founding the Hispanic Cuban Foundation (Fundación Hispano Cubano).

Freedom House. A U.S. organization represented in Washington by Frank Calzón. Although CANF and Freedom House were rivals at one time, they now maintain good relations. Under its auspices, the National Endowment for Democracy has financed several counterrevolutionary groups both within Cuba and abroad, helping them to carry out "human rights" campaigns. In 1995, the U.S. Government gave it half a million dollars to be used to encourage the so-called dissident movement in Cuba. The government pledged to give it another half million for the same purpose in 1998. In mid-1997, Cuban State Security halted and expelled David Norman Dorn, a U.S. citizen and official of the American Federation of Teachers, who was carrying out that task on behalf of Calzón and Freedom House.

G

Grau San Martín, Ramón. President of Cuba between 1944 and 1948. His administration became infamous for its corruption and submission to

Washington and for its allowing the Mafia to extend its power in Cuba.

Guantánamo Naval Base. Under duress in 1903, the Cuban Government signed an agreement with the United States through which it leased the Bay of Guantánamo. The United States turned it into a military enclave. The revolutionary government has never wanted to collect payment for the leased land but has always demanded that it be returned. From that base, the United States has launched hundreds of attacks and acts of pro-vocation against Cuba.

Guevara, Ernesto (Che). Argentine doctor who joined the Cuban expeditionary force on the *Granma*. He was the first combatant whom Fidel Castro promoted to the rank of major during the revolutionary war. After the triumph of the revolution, he was assigned various responsibilities and was particularly outstanding for his contributions to economic policy. A convinced practitioner of internationalism, he fought for the liberation of several African peoples. Wounded and taken prisoner at La Higuera, Bolivia, on October 8, 1967, he was murdered the next day — an action ordered by the U.S. Government and overseen by Félix Rodríguez.

Gutiérrez Menoyo, Eloy. A former major of the Cuban revolution, he opposed the line supported by most of the other leaders. He acted as a double agent in the "Trujillo conspiracy." In 1961, he sought asylum in the United States and joined the Alpha 66 terrorist group. In January 1965, he was captured while trying to return clandestinely to Cuba to organize counterrevolutionary groups. The Spanish Government negotiated his release in 1986. Ever since his first address, he has expressed the need for holding a dialogue with the Cuban Government. For that purpose, he organized a group in Miami called Cuban Change (Cambio Cubano). He has returned to Cuba several times at the invitation of the government to take part in political discussions.

H

Helms, Jesse. A U.S. Senator (R.) known for his relations with the extreme right wing, he maintained good contacts with the dictatorial regimes in Latin America. CANF contributed to his war chest. He is the person mainly responsible for the Helms-Burton Act.

Helms-Burton Act. Officially called the Cuban Liberty and Democratic Solidarity Act, it was passed by Congress in 1996. This U.S. law beefs up the trade embargo against Cuba, threatening to apply a wide range of sanctions against countries, individuals and companies, whether of the United States or foreign, that have commercial relations with Cuba. With this law, the U.S. Government has established mechanisms for forcing the rest of the world to support its war against Cuba.

The law even includes the first steps that Cuba should take if it wants the embargo and other sanctions to be lifted: the present government should be replaced with a transition government; within a year, the army, the Ministry of the Interior, the Committees for the Defense of the Revolution and all the other institutions under government control should be disbanded; the public sector should be privatized and a market economy introduced; and an election should be held with the participation of Cubans living both inside and outside the country — except that present governmental leaders will be excluded. Moreover, concerning this last point, those who are elected must be approved by the U.S. president before they may begin negotiations for the possible suspension of the embargo.

Hernández, Alberto. One of the first directors of CANF, he was also a member of the Alpha 66 terrorist group. He testified in favor of the terrorist Orlando Bosch, raised funds for his defense and expenses while Bosch was in prison — and then pocketed them. He also gave moral and financial support to the terrorist Luis Posada Carriles. He was in Angola supporting the UNITA forces and in Central America with the contras.

I

Iran-Contragate. This is the name of the scandal that broke in late 1986 when the Reagan Administration's responsibility in providing logistical and military support for the Nicaraguan contras — which Congress had forbidden — was made public. After that, it was discovered that the administration had sold weapons to Iran via Israel and that the profits from those sales had been used to finance the contras. This was done while Reagan was publicly blasting the Iranian authorities as devils and calling on other nations to break off all relations with that government.

To a large extent, this distracted attention from the most delicate aspect of the situation, which was that millions of dollars were raised for the contras from the traffic in drugs. As the Kerry Commission's investigation brought out, people in high places in the U.S. Government had accepted that procedure, either directly or indirectly. This was done after President Reagan had declared an all-out war on the traffic in drugs. The proof was so conclusive that only a secret pact between the Democratic and Republican Parties can explain why Reagan — or, at least, Vice-President Bush — wasn't forced to resign.

K

Kennedy, John Fitzgerald (1917-63). President of the United States between 1961 and 1963. The Bay of Pigs mercenary invasion of Cuba was launched during his administration. He negotiated with Nikita Khrushchev to achieve the withdrawal of the missiles that the Soviet Union was installing in Cuba. Many counterrevolutionaries maintain that Kennedy refused to let them "liberate" Cuba, so he is the man they hate most — after Fidel Castro. Several investigations — including some conducted by the U.S. Government itself — don't rule out the possibility that Cuban counterrevolutionaries took part in Kennedy's assassination.

Kennedy, Robert (1925-68). Brother of President Kennedy and Attorney General in the Kennedy Administration. After the Bay of Pigs disaster, the president placed him in charge of the political ramifications of Operation Mongoose. He was assassinated in 1968 while campaigning for president. Cuban counterrevolutionaries may have participated in the assassination.

Kerry Commission. A special commission of the U.S. Senate so named because it was headed by Senator John Kerry. In 1989, after two years of investigating the Iran-Contragate scandal, it presented documentary evidence showing that the CIA had carried out secret operations, directed from the National Security Council, to provide the contras with logistical and financial support behind the backs of the majority in Congress. The investigation brought out the key role that many Cuban-U.S. citizens played in those operations.

Khrushchev, Nikita (1894-1971). Soviet leader. First Secretary of the Central Committee of the Communist Party of the Soviet Union in 1953. Chairman of the Council of Ministers in 1958. He resigned in 1964. He negotiated with Kennedy on the withdrawal of the Soviet missiles from Cuban territory.

L

Letelier, Orlando. Minister in Salvador Allende's government in Chile. He and his secretary were assassinated in Washington in 1976 when a bomb went off in his car. The Novo brothers, acting for the Coordinator of Unified Revolutionary Organizations (Coordinadora de Organizaciones Revolucionarias Unidas), were allegedly responsible for the crime.

Llama, Juan Antonio. A Cuban-U.S. citizen, he is one of the directors of CANF in Miami and a member of the *patronato* of the Hispanic Cuban Foundation (Fundación Hispano Cubano) in Madrid. The United Left (Izquierda Unida) Party of Spain has denounced him before the Congress of Deputies as a terrorist because he took part in a plot to assassinate Cuban President Fidel Castro. According to the FBI, the crime was to have been carried out during the Ibero-American meeting of Heads of State that was held in Venezuela in November 1997.

Loredo, Miguel. Franciscan priest who hid Angel Betancourt Cueto in a monastery in March 1966 and kept him hidden for two weeks. Betancourt had murdered two crew members of a Cubana de Aviación plane and wounded a third when he tried to skyjack the plane. After spending 10 years in prison, Loredo went to the United States. There, he joined in the activities of the Cuban extreme right wing in New York. Pax Christi Netherlands presented him in a meeting held in Rome on November 28, 1997, as proof of the "repression of the Church in Cuba."

M

Martí Pérez, José. National Hero of Cuba. Cuban 19th-century thinker, writer and political figure. He lived in the United States for a period but returned to Cuba to lead its 1895 War of Independence against Spanish colonialism. In 1892, he organized the first revolutionary party, uniting all sectors that wanted their country's freedom. He was killed in battle in 1985. His writings, together with Marxism-Leninism, are part of the Cuban Government's ideological guidelines. The counterrevolutionaries who support the U.S. policy seem to have forgotten that Martí said, "I have lived in the monster, and I know its entrails."

Mas Canosa, Jorge (1940-97). A member of Brigade 2506, although he didn't go ashore. He was given special training at Fort Benning. According to FBI documents, the CIA included him in the group leadership of the Cuban Delegation in Exile (Representación Cubana en el Exilio) in 1964. Together with "Pepe" Hernández and others, he raised money in the exile community for more invasions of Cuba. The only actions that were carried out were commando attacks on easy civilian objectives along the coast, but the millions that had been donated apparently disappeared. He claimed that the stake for his first business venture came from washing dishes and selling milk, but many others say that the money with which he bought a construction company in 1968 came from that fund-raising venture. By 1980, he had amassed a vast fortune in the telephone cable business.

His coincidence in views with the Republican Party, plus the close relations he maintained with U.S. intelligence agencies, gave him substantial room for business and political maneuvering, which was considerably increased when Ronald Reagan became president. That, together with his counterrevolutionary activism, led the National Security Council to back him as president of CANF. His staunch service to U.S. interests gave him their support for his counterrevolutionary plans. When he died in November 1997, both President Bill Clinton and State Department officials sent messages of condolence.

Migratory agreements. Representatives of Cuba and the United States signed the first migratory agreements to stop the so-called rafters crisis in May 1995. Among other things, they stated that illegal departures from Cuba and illegal entries in the United States would be hindered and that the United States would grant at least 20,000 visas a year to Cubans. However, the U.S. authorities have never granted more than 10,000, thus promoting an illegal migration of those who want to leave for economic reasons or because they want to join their relatives. Moreover, the United States continues to accept those Cubans who bring it political dividends.

Montaner, Carlos Alberto. In 1961, having been found guilty of participating in a CIA-sponsored terrorist organization that hid explosives in packs of cigarettes, he was sent to a center for juvenile delinquents — from which he escaped. He then sought political asylum and left Cuba. In 1962, during the October Missile Crisis, he joined the Cuban special forces in the U.S. Army. Later, when he was a university student, Cuban State Security reported that he had been recruited by the CIA.

In 1970, he moved to Spain, where he founded Editorial Playor, a publishing house specializing in counterrevolutionary books. He also created the Firmas Press agency, which sent anti-Cuban information to media in Europe and the Americas. It has never been clear where he got the financing for all this, although the Cuban Government has always said it came from the CIA. The same source says that Montaner was responsible for getting Juan Felipe de la Cruz — a terrorist who died when a bomb he was setting went off in his hands — into France.

During the 1980s, Montaner organized many congresses in Europe and Latin America, several of which were financed by the National Endowment for Democracy. His publishing house has printed a number of books whose author is given as Armando Valladares — although many people say that Montaner himself really wrote them. It also published a book by Ricardo Bofill that turned out to have been plagiarized, as its real author proved publicly.

Together with José Ignacio Rasco, Montaner was very active in the campaign to free Valladares, which helped him to broaden his contacts. He and some friends created the Cuban Liberal Union (Unión Liberal Cubana) in 1990 and then, bringing in other counterrevolutionaries from Miami, the Cuban Democratic Platform (Plataforma Democrática Cubana). The Platform's main aim has been to organize international pressure that will lead the Cuban Government to negotiate with its representatives. Inside Cuba, following the example of CANF, he got Elizardo Sánchez and other so-called dissidents to help him create the Cuban Democratic Arrangement (Concertación Democrática Cubana).

Montaner has always sought to present himself as a moderate in the exile community. While he insists that he favors a peaceful transition and dialogue, the core of his message is the elimination of the leaders of the Cuban Government, especially Fidel Castro. Along with other members of the extreme right wing, he has signed documents which state that, when the present Cuban system is toppled, reprisals will be taken against those who are presently investing in Cuba. They consider it absolutely necessary to isolate Cuba economically and politically.

His writings express admiration for neoliberalism. A founding member of the Hispanic Cuban Foundation (Fundación Hispano Cubana), he withdrew from it several months later after losing a power struggle against Jorge Mas Canosa. For several years, he has had the full support of the rightist People's Party (Partido Popular) of Spain, and José María Aznar, now President of Spain, wrote the preface to one of his books. Several members of the Socialist Party (Partido Socialista) have listened to his proposals, as well.

N

National Liberation Front of Cuba (Frente de Liberación Nacional de Cuba, FLNC). A terrorist group created in the 1970s by former members of the CIA and Brigade 2506 and by leaders of Abdala. The latter provided logistical and personnel support. [See also **Abdala**.]

National Security Council. A high-ranking team that is responsible for topics of national and international security and meets with the president of the United States once a week. Its permanent members are the Secretary of State, Secretary of Defense and Director of the CIA. Behind the backs of most of the U.S. Congress, working through Colonel Oliver North, it directed the Nicaraguan contras in the 1980s.

North, Oliver. A former Lieutenant Colonel in the U.S. Army and veteran of undercover operations in the wars in Southeast Asia. While on the National Security Council, he helped to organize and direct the Nicaraguan contras. Saving Reagan's and Bush's skins, he accepted responsibility for the most delicate aspect of the Iran-Contragate scandal — the traffic in drugs. His sentence was to do social service in poor neighborhoods in Washington — not for his drug dealing, but for having lied to and hidden information from Congress. At Christmas 1992, President Bush pardoned North and the others who were implicated, saying that the common denominator of their motivation — aside from whether they were right or wrong — was patriotism.

O

Of Human Rights. One of the first human rights groups created by Abdala and the National Liberation Front of Cuba (Frente de Liberación Nacional de Cuba), both terrorist organizations. Frank Calzón, a former CIA agent, has always been its director. It provides considerable financial support for Ricardo Bofill's subversive activities in Miami and those of Gustavo Arcos in Cuba. Monsignor Agustín Román is on its board.

P

PDC. Plataforma Democrática Cubana. See **Cuban Democratic Platform**.

Pérez Roura, Armando. Manager of and announcer on Radio Mambí in Miami. Up until a few years ago, he incited his listeners to attack people who opposed U.S. policy on Cuba. His usual line is that, when the present Cuban Government falls, "We will be there to see the people drag the bodies of the dictator and his miserable henchmen through the streets. I know that the blood will flow! Get ready!" He is a leader of Cuban Unity (Unidad Cubana), a paramilitary group.

Pinochet, Augusto. Chilean general who took power in 1973 by leading a CIA-supported coup against the Social-Democratic government of President

Salvador Allende. He supported the terrorist activities of the Cuban counter-revolutionaries, through the Novo brothers and Orlando Bosch. His dictatorship was one of the bloodiest in Latin America.

Platt Amendment. The United States imposed this appendix to the nascent Republic of Cuba's first constitution in 1901. It stipulated that the United States had the right to intervene in Cuban internal affairs, limited Cuba's right to sign compacts and treaties with other countries and gave the United States the right to acquire land and naval bases in Cuba — all "for the preservation of Cuban independence." It also gave the United States the right to establish a government "for the protection of life, property, and individual liberty." It was repealed in 1934.

Posada Carriles, Luis. The CIA recruited him in Havana in 1960. A veteran of the Bay of Pigs, he was trained at Fort Benning, along with Jorge Mas Canosa and Félix Rodríguez. There, he attained the rank of captain. In 1964, he joined the Cuban Delegation in Exile (Represent-ación Cubana en el Exilio). In 1969, he joined DISIP, the Venezuelan intelligence service, and was its liaison with the CIA. He and Orlando Bosch were responsible for blowing up a Cubana de Aviación plane, for which he was sent to prison in Venezuela. CANF helped him to escape and to join the CIA's apparatus in Central America during the war against the Sandinistas. He organized and received the financing for the attacks that were made on Cuban tourist centers between April and September 1997.

R

Raft people. [See also **Migratory agreements**.] The drastic limitation of visas by the United States, the increase in counterrevolutionary propaganda and the economic difficulties which have arisen since the beginning of the 1990s led hundreds of Cubans to leave Cuba for Miami by sea, illegally, aboard rafts and all kinds of other craft.

Rasco, José Ignacio. In 1959, he and the conservative sectors of the Cuban Catholic Church founded the Christian Democratic Movement (Movimiento Democrático Cristiano). Soon afterwards, he left Cuba and was recruited by the CIA. He joined the Cuban Revolutionary Council (Consejo Revolucionario Cubano), a front that tried to give the Bay of Pigs legal standing. After that, he disappeared from the political scene, though maintaining close links with Alpha 66, a terrorist group. He reappeared in the 1970s, calling for dialogue with the Cuban Government as a tactical means for toppling it.

In the early 1980s, backed by the Christian Democratic International, he challenged and ousted the old leaders of the nearly nonexistent Movement and set about lobbying in international human rights organizations. He turned the Movement into a party, which held a congress in 1991. Although the Christian Democratic Party's membership is extremely small, it was accepted as a member of the international body. Encouraged by the resounding collapse of the socialist bloc, he and Carlos Alberto Montaner founded the Cuban Democratic Platform (Plataforma Democrática Cubana) in Spain. Rasco is Vice-President of the Christian Democratic International.

Reagan, Ronald. President of the United States between 1981 and 1989, he described the contras as "freedom fighters." Although not stated in the Kerry Commission's conclusions, the investigation presented substantial proof that Reagan knew of the clandestine scheme for financing the contras in Nicaragua. Among his plans for destabilizing the Cuban Government, he gave the go-ahead for the creation of CANF, Radio Martí and TV-Martí and provided structured, systematic support for the so-called dissident groups in Cuba. Paradoxically, the Reagan Administration — which, in fact, was one of the most reactionary and corrupt in the history of the United States — championed the human rights cause to attack the Cuban and Sandinista governments.

RECE. Representación Cubana en el Exilio. See **Cuban Delegation in Exile**.

Rivero, Raúl. He worked for the media in Cuba until fired for indiscipline. In 1991, he began sending articles attacking the Cuban Government to Radio Martí and other extreme right-wing media in Miami and asking them to help the counterrevolutionary groups. He has been arrested several times for these activities. After splitting a group of dissidents, he set up his own press agency. He belongs to the Democratic Solidarity Party (Partido Solidaridad Democrática), a group linked to Hubert Matos — whose political viewpoint is similar to that of Carlos Alberto Montaner. In 1997, Rivero was made a member of the *patronato* of the Hispanic Cuban Foundation (Fundación Hispano Cubana). In spite of all this political activity linked to the right and extreme right, he was awarded the Reporters Without Frontiers (Reporters Sans Frontières) prize in December 1997.

Rodríguez, Félix. One of the first people in Miami to be recruited by the CIA. Before the members of Brigade 2506 reached Cuba's shore in the 1961 invasion at the Bay of Pigs, Rodríguez had already been infiltrated into the island; when the mercenary force was defeated, he sought asylum in the Venezuelan Embassy. Later, he was given training at Fort Benning. The CIA sent him to Bolivia to help in the capture of Che Guevara. He boasted of being the last Cuban and the last U.S. citizen to have seen Che alive. After that, he went to Southeast Asia as part of a special operations commando whose work was financed by the traffic in opium. On his return to the United States, he was given the highest decoration awarded by the CIA, which CIA Director George Bush presented to him personally. In the early 1980s, he was sent to El Salvador to advise and provide logistic support for the contras; he became one of the key figures in that mercenary war.

Roque, Juan Pablo. Early on the morning of February 23, 1992, Juan Pablo Roque swam to the Guantánamo Naval Base and asked for political asylum.

The extreme right wing in Miami welcomed him with great fanfare. He participated in activities with CANF but mainly worked with Brothers to the Rescue (Hermanos al Rescate). On February 20, 1996, he returned to Cuba; he had been a Cuban counterintelligence agent. Before leaving the United States, he turned a lot of information over to the FBI, which he had also infiltrated. The information showed that Brothers to the Rescue, CANF and other counterrevolutionary organizations were preparing terrorist actions against Cuba.

Ros-Lethinen, Ileana. Cuban-U.S. Congresswoman who went to the defense of the terrorist Orlando Bosch. She wants Cuba to be annexed by the United States and has worked devotedly to implement the Helms-Burton Act.

S

Savimbi, Jonas. Head of UNITA in Angola. His military group, seeking the military objectives outlined by the United States and South Africa, split the Angolan Patriotic Movement. Since the Cuban Government was giving the latter its support, the Cuban American National Foundation lobbied to get the U.S. Congress to appropriate an additional several million dollars for UNITA. In appreciation, Savimbi gave Mas Canosa a rifle carved out of ivory.

Shackley, Theodore. Former Deputy Director of Operations of the CIA, he was a key figure in the CIA's secret wars in Berlin, Vietnam and Laos. Shackley was the head of the CIA's secret station in Miami, known as JM/WAVE, which worked on preparations for a second invasion of Cuba after the Bay of Pigs fiasco.

Sorzano, José. A Cuban-U.S. citizen and one of the first directors of CANF. He has been both a member of the National Security Council of the United States and a U.S. diplomat. He is known for his conservative positions in favor of Cuba's annexation by the United States.

Special period. The name of an exceptionally critical period in the Cuban revolutionary process that began in 1990, with the collapse of the socialist bloc, when Cuba lost its main trading partners. This was complemented by the United States tightening of its trade embargo against Cuba. During this period, the Cuban Government has adopted a strategy of concentrating its resources and limiting its economic activities and level of consumption. In spite of the economic crisis, it has kept all of the schools, old people's homes and hospitals open. Social protection has also been maintained — although, logically, with some deficiencies.

T

Torricelli, Robert. A U.S. Congressman (D.). He opposed Washington's policy on Cuba at first, but following hefty financial contributions from the extreme right wing in the exile community, he turned into one of Cuba's worst enemies. He introduced the Cuban Democracy Act, better known as the Torricelli Bill, which beefed up the trade blockade and paved the way for overt and covert support for the so-called dissident movement in Cuba.

U

ULC. Unión Liberal Cubana. See **Cuban Liberal Union**.

United States Information Agency. The most powerful U.S. apparatus of ideological propaganda, it works directly under the State Department. One of the first important tasks it carried out against the Cuban revolution was Operation Peter Pan. It has financed and helped in the worldwide distribution of a large number of counterrevolutionary publications and is in charge of Radio Martí and TV Martí.

United States Information Service. It serves the United States Information Agency at the international level and also works directly under the State Department.

United States Interests Section. It was created through an agreement between the governments of Fidel Castro and Jimmy Carter to open a direct, permanent channel of communication. It should also facilitate trade, scientific, cultural and sports exchanges. At the beginning, it worked out of the Swiss Embassy in Havana. Although it now has an enormous building of its own, it still works under the "protection" of Switzerland. Officially, its work is eminently consular, but ever since it began operations in 1977, it has provided cover for a large number of intelligence agents. Its espionage work in Cuba has led the Cuban Government to expel 20 of its functionaries. Its work includes passing on payments and documents to so-called dissidents.

V

Vargas Llosa, Mario. Writer. Peruvian-born, he is a naturalized Spaniard. Originally a radical member of the left, he became a right-wing conservative. In Peru, while in charge of a special investigation into the massacre of several journalists, he covered up the fact that high-ranking military officers were responsible. He is a personal friend of several leaders of the extreme right wing in the Cuban exile community and a member of the *patronato* of the Hispanic Cuban Foundation (Fundación Hispano Cubana).

Also from Ocean Press

BAY OF PIGS AND THE CIA
Cuban Secret Files Reveal the Story Behind the Invasion
By Juan Carlos Rodríguez
Cuba's account of the mercenary invasion in 1961.
ISBN 1-875284-98-2

CIA TARGETS FIDEL
The Secret Assassination Report
The CIA's own report on plots to assassinate Castro. Introduced by
former head of Cuban counterintelligence General Fabián Escalante.
ISBN 1-875284-90-7

CUBA AND THE UNITED STATES
A Chronological History
By Jane Franklin
This chronology relates in detail the developments involving the
neighboring countries from the 1959 revolution through 1995.
ISBN 1-875284-92-3

DEADLY DECEITS
My 25 Years in the CIA
By Ralph W. McGehee
A new, updated edition of this classic account of the CIA's deeds and
deceptions by one of its formerly most prized recruits.
ISBN 1-876175-19-2

HAVANA MIAMI
The U.S.-Cuba Migration Conflict
By Jesús Arboleya
This book reviews how the migration issue has been used to heighten
political tensions between Cuba and the United States.
ISBN 1-875284-91-5

PSYWAR ON CUBA
The Declassified History of U.S. Anti-Castro Propaganda
Edited by Jon Elliston
Declassified CIA and U.S. Government documents are reproduced here,
with extensive commentary providing the history of Washington's 40-
year campaign to destabilize Cuba and undermine its revolution.
ISBN 1-876175-09-5